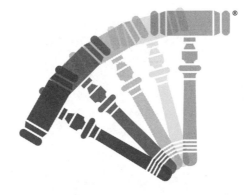

Casenote® Legal Briefs

INTELLECTUAL PROPERTY

Keyed to Courses Using

Merges, Menell, and Lemley's
Intellectual Property in the New Technological Age

Sixth Edition

Wolters Kluwer
Law & Business

This publication is designed to provide accurate and authoritative information
in regard to the subject matter covered. It is sold with the understanding that the
publisher is not engaged in rendering legal, accounting, or other professional
services. If legal advice or other expert assistance is required, the services of a
competent professional person should be sought.

> — From a Declaration of Principles adopted jointly
> by a Committee of the American Bar Association
> and a Committee of Publishers and Associates

About Wolters Kluwer Law & Business

Wolters Kluwer Law & Business is a leading global provider of intelligent information and digital solutions for legal and business professionals in key specialty areas, and respected educational resources for professors and law students. Wolters Kluwer Law & Business connects legal and business professionals as well as those in the education market with timely, specialized authoritative content and information-enabled solutions to support success through productivity, accuracy and mobility.

Serving customers worldwide, Wolters Kluwer Law & Business products include those under the Aspen Publishers, CCH, Kluwer Law International, Loislaw, Best Case, ftwilliam.com and MediRegs family of products.

CCH products have been a trusted resource since 1913, and are highly regarded resources for legal, securities, antitrust and trade regulation, government contracting, banking, pension, payroll, employment and labor, and healthcare reimbursement and compliance professionals.

Aspen Publishers products provide essential information to attorneys, business professionals and law students. Written by preeminent authorities, the product line offers analytical and practical information in a range of specialty practice areas from securities law and intellectual property to mergers and acquisitions and pension/benefits. Aspen's trusted legal education resources provide professors and students with high-quality, up-to-date and effective resources for successful instruction and study in all areas of the law.

Kluwer Law International products provide the global business community with reliable international legal information in English. Legal practitioners, corporate counsel and business executives around the world rely on Kluwer Law journals, looseleafs, books, and electronic products for comprehensive information in many areas of international legal practice.

Loislaw is a comprehensive online legal research product providing legal content to law firm practitioners of various specializations. Loislaw provides attorneys with the ability to quickly and efficiently find the necessary legal information they need, when and where they need it, by facilitating access to primary law as well as state-specific law, records, forms and treatises.

Best Case Solutions is the leading bankruptcy software product to the bankruptcy industry. It provides software and workflow tools to flawlessly streamline petition preparation and the electronic filing process, while timely incorporating ever-changing court requirements.

ftwilliam.com offers employee benefits professionals the highest quality plan documents (retirement, welfare and non-qualified) and government forms (5500/PBGC, 1099 and IRS) software at highly competitive prices.

MediRegs products provide integrated health care compliance content and software solutions for professionals in healthcare, higher education and life sciences, including professionals in accounting, law and consulting.

Wolters Kluwer Law & Business, a division of Wolters Kluwer, is head-quartered in New York. Wolters Kluwer is a market-leading global information services company focused on professionals.

Format for the Casenote® Legal Brief

Nature of Case: This section identifies the form of action (e.g., breach of contract, negligence, battery), the type of proceeding (e.g., demurrer, appeal from trial court's jury instructions), or the relief sought (e.g., damages, injunction, criminal sanctions).

Fact Summary: This is included to refresh your memory and can be used as a quick reminder of the facts.

Rule of Law: Summarizes the general principle of law that the case illustrates. It may be used for instant recall of the court's holding and for classroom discussion or home review.

Facts: This section contains all relevant facts of the case, including the contentions of the parties and the lower court holdings. It is written in a logical order to give the student a clear understanding of the case. The plaintiff and defendant are identified by their proper names throughout and are always labeled with a (P) or (D).

Party ID: Quick identification of the relationship between the parties.

Concurrence/Dissent: All concurrences and dissents are briefed whenever they are included by the casebook editor.

Analysis: This last paragraph gives you a broad understanding of where the case "fits in" with other cases in the section of the book and with the entire course. It is a hornbook-style discussion indicating whether the case is a majority or minority opinion and comparing the principal case with other cases in the casebook. It may also provide analysis from restatements, uniform codes, and law review articles. The analysis will prove to be invaluable to classroom discussion.

Palsgraf v. Long Island R.R. Co.

Injured bystander (P) v. Railroad company (D)

N.Y. Ct. App., 248 N.Y. 339, 162 N.E. 99 (1928).

NATURE OF CASE: Appeal from judgment affirming verdict for plaintiff seeking damages for personal injury.

FACT SUMMARY: Helen Palsgraf (P) was injured on R.R.'s (D) train platform when R.R.'s (D) guard helped a passenger aboard a moving train, causing his package to fall on the tracks. The package contained fireworks which exploded, creating a shock that tipped a scale onto Palsgraf (P).

🏛 RULE OF LAW
The risk reasonably to be perceived defines the duty to be obeyed.

FACTS: Helen Palsgraf (P) purchased a ticket to Rockaway Beach from R.R. (D) and was waiting on the train platform. As she waited, two men ran to catch a train that was pulling out from the platform. The first man jumped aboard, but the second man, who appeared as if he might fall, was helped aboard by the guard on the train who had kept the door open so they could jump aboard. A guard on the platform also helped by pushing him onto the train. The man was carrying a package wrapped in newspaper. In the process, the man dropped his package, which fell on the tracks. The package contained fireworks and exploded. The shock of the explosion was apparently of great enough strength to tip over some scales at the other end of the platform, which fell on Palsgraf (P) and injured her. A jury awarded her damages, and R.R. (D) appealed.

ISSUE: Does the risk reasonably to be perceived define the duty to be obeyed?

HOLDING AND DECISION: (Cardozo, C.J.) Yes. The risk reasonably to be perceived defines the duty to be obeyed. If there is no foreseeable hazard to the injured party as the result of a seemingly innocent act, the act does not become a tort because it happened to be a wrong as to another. If the wrong was not willful, the plaintiff must show that the act as to her had such great and apparent possibilities of danger as to entitle her to protection. Negligence in the abstract is not enough upon which to base liability. Negligence is a relative concept, evolving out of the common law doctrine of trespass on the case. To establish liability, the defendant must owe a legal duty of reasonable care to the injured party. A cause of action in tort will lie where harm, though unintended, could have been averted or avoided by observance of such a duty. The scope of the duty is limited by the range of danger that a reasonable person could foresee. In this case, there was nothing to suggest from the appearance of the parcel or otherwise that the parcel contained fireworks. The guard could not reasonably have had any warning of a threat to Palsgraf (P), and R.R. (D) therefore cannot be held liable. Judgment is reversed in favor of R.R. (D).

DISSENT: (Andrews, J.) The concept that there is no negligence unless R.R. (D) owes a legal duty to take care as to Palsgraf (P) herself is too narrow. Everyone owes to the world at large the duty of refraining from those acts that may unreasonably threaten the safety of others. If the guard's action was negligent as to those nearby, it was also negligent as to those outside what might be termed the "danger zone." For Palsgraf (P) to recover, R.R.'s (D) negligence must have been the proximate cause of her injury, a question of fact for the jury.

▶ ANALYSIS
The majority defined the limit of the defendant's liability in terms of the danger that a reasonable person in defendant's situation would have perceived. The dissent argued that the limitation should not be placed on liability, but rather on damages. Judge Andrews suggested that only injuries that would not have happened but for R.R.'s (D) negligence should be compensable. Both the majority and dissent recognized the policy-driven need to limit liability for negligent acts, seeking, in the words of Judge Andrews, to define a framework "that will be practical and in keeping with the general understanding of mankind." The Restatement (Second) of Torts has accepted Judge Cardozo's view.

Quicknotes

FORESEEABILITY A reasonable expectation that change is the probable result of certain acts or omissions.

NEGLIGENCE Conduct falling below the standard of care that a reasonable person would demonstrate under similar conditions.

PROXIMATE CAUSE The natural sequence of events without which an injury would not have been sustained.

Issue: The issue is a concise question that brings out the essence of the opinion as it relates to the section of the casebook in which the case appears. Both substantive and procedural issues are included if relevant to the decision.

Holding and Decision: This section offers a clear and in-depth discussion of the rule of the case and the court's rationale. It is written in easy-to-understand language and answers the issue presented by applying the law to the facts of the case. When relevant, it includes a thorough discussion of the exceptions to the case as listed by the court, any major cites to the other cases on point, and the names of the judges who wrote the decisions.

Quicknotes: Conveniently defines legal terms found in the case and summarizes the nature of any statutes, codes, or rules referred to in the text.

Wolters Kluwer Law & Business is proud to offer *Casenote® Legal Briefs*—continuing thirty years of publishing America's best-selling legal briefs.

Casenote® Legal Briefs are designed to help you save time when briefing assigned cases. Organized under convenient headings, they show you how to abstract the basic facts and holdings from the text of the actual opinions handed down by the courts. Used as part of a rigorous study regimen, they can help you spend more time analyzing and critiquing points of law than on copying bits and pieces of judicial opinions into your notebook or outline.

Casenote® Legal Briefs should never be used as a substitute for assigned casebook readings. They work best when read as a follow-up to reviewing the underlying opinions themselves. Students who try to avoid reading and digesting the judicial opinions in their casebooks or online sources will end up shortchanging themselves in the long run. The ability to absorb, critique, and restate the dynamic and complex elements of case law decisions is crucial to your success in law school and beyond. It cannot be developed vicariously.

Casenote® Legal Briefs represents but one of the many offerings in Legal Education's Study Aid Timeline, which includes:

- *Casenote® Legal Briefs*
- *Emanuel® Law Outlines*
- Emanuel® *Law in a Flash* Flash Cards
- Emanuel® *CrunchTime®* Series
- *Siegel's Essay and Multiple-Choice Questions and Answers Series*

Each of these series is designed to provide you with easy-to-understand explanations of complex points of law. Each volume offers guidance on the principles of legal analysis and, consulted regularly, will hone your ability to spot relevant issues. We have titles that will help you prepare for class, prepare for your exams, and enhance your general comprehension of the law along the way.

To find out more about Wolters Kluwer Law & Business' study aid publications, visit us online at *www.wolterskluwerlb.com* or email us at *legaledu@wolterskluwer.com*. We'll be happy to assist you.

A. Decide on a Format and Stick to It

Structure is essential to a good brief. It enables you to arrange systematically the related parts that are scattered throughout most cases, thus making manageable and understandable what might otherwise seem to be an endless and unfathomable sea of information. There are, of course, an unlimited number of formats that can be utilized. However, it is best to find one that suits your needs and stick to it. Consistency breeds both efficiency and the security that when called upon you will know where to look in your brief for the information you are asked to give.

Any format, as long as it presents the essential elements of a case in an organized fashion, can be used. Experience, however, has led *Casenote® Legal Briefs* to develop and utilize the following format because of its logical flow and universal applicability.

NATURE OF CASE: This is a brief statement of the legal character and procedural status of the case (e.g., "Appeal of a burglary conviction").

There are many different alternatives open to a litigant dissatisfied with a court ruling. The key to determining which one has been used is to discover *who is asking this court for what.*

This first entry in the brief should be kept as *short as possible.* Use the court's terminology if you understand it. But since jurisdictions vary as to the titles of pleadings, the best entry is the one that addresses who wants what in this proceeding, not the one that sounds most like the court's language.

RULE OF LAW: A statement of the general principle of law that the case illustrates (e.g., "An acceptance that varies any term of the offer is considered a rejection and counteroffer").

Determining the rule of law of a case is a procedure similar to determining the issue of the case. Avoid being fooled by red herrings; there may be a few rules of law mentioned in the case excerpt, but usually only one is *the* rule with which the casebook editor is concerned. The techniques used to locate the issue, described below, may also be utilized to find the rule of law. Generally, your best guide is simply the chapter heading. It is a clue to the point the casebook editor seeks to make and should be kept in mind when reading every case in the respective section.

FACTS: A synopsis of only the essential facts of the case, i.e., those bearing upon or leading up to the issue.

The facts entry should be a short statement of the events and transactions that led one party to initiate legal proceedings against another in the first place. While some cases conveniently state the salient facts at the beginning of the decision, in other instances they will have to be culled from hiding places throughout the text, even from concurring and dissenting opinions. Some of the "facts" will often be in dispute and should be so noted. Conflicting evidence may be briefly pointed up. "Hard" facts must be included. Both must be *relevant* in order to be listed in the facts entry. It is impossible to tell what is relevant until the entire case is read, as the ultimate determination of the rights and liabilities of the parties may turn on something buried deep in the opinion.

Generally, the facts entry should not be longer than three to five *short* sentences.

It is often helpful to identify the role played by a party in a given context. For example, in a construction contract case the identification of a party as the "contractor" or "builder" alleviates the need to tell that that party was the one who was supposed to have built the house.

It is always helpful, and a good general practice, to identify the "plaintiff" and the "defendant." This may seem elementary and uncomplicated, but, especially in view of the creative editing practiced by some casebook editors, it is sometimes a difficult or even impossible task. Bear in mind that the *party presently* seeking something from this court may not be the plaintiff, and that sometimes only the cross-claim of a defendant is treated in the excerpt. Confusing or misaligning the parties can ruin your analysis and understanding of the case.

ISSUE: A statement of the general legal question answered by or illustrated in the case. For clarity, the issue is best put in the form of a question capable of a "yes" or "no" answer. In reality, the issue is simply the Rule of Law put in the form of a question (e.g., "May an offer be accepted by performance?").

The major problem presented in discerning what is *the* issue in the case is that an opinion usually purports to raise and answer several questions. However, except for rare cases, only one such question is really the issue in the case. Collateral issues not necessary to the resolution of the matter in controversy are handled by the court by language known as *"obiter dictum"* or merely *"dictum."* While dicta may be included later in the brief, they have no place under the issue heading.

To find the issue, ask *who wants what* and then go on to ask *why did that party succeed or fail in getting it.* Once this is determined, the "why" should be turned into a question.

The complexity of the issues in the cases will vary, but in all cases a single-sentence question should sum up the issue. *In a few cases,* there will be two, or even more rarely, three issues of equal importance to the resolution of the case. Each should be expressed in a single-sentence question.

Since many issues are resolved by a court in coming to a final disposition of a case, the casebook editor will reproduce the portion of the opinion containing the issue or issues most relevant to the area of law under scrutiny. A noted law professor gave this advice: "Close the book; look at the title on the cover." Chances are, if it is Property, you need not concern yourself with whether, for example, the federal government's treatment of the plaintiff's land really raises a federal question sufficient to support jurisdiction on this ground in federal court.

The same rule applies to chapter headings designating sub-areas within the subjects. They tip you off as to what the text is designed to teach. The cases are arranged in a casebook to show a progression or development of the law, so that the preceding cases may also help.

It is also most important to remember to *read the notes and questions* at the end of a case to determine what the editors wanted you to have gleaned from it.

HOLDING AND DECISION: This section should succinctly explain the rationale of the court in arriving at its decision. In capsulizing the "reasoning" of the court, it should always include an application of the general rule or rules of law to the specific facts of the case. Hidden justifications come to light in this entry: the reasons for the state of the law, the public policies, the biases and prejudices, those considerations that influence the justices' thinking and, ultimately, the outcome of the case. At the end, there should be a short indication of the disposition or procedural resolution of the case (e.g., "Decision of the trial court for Mr. Smith (P) reversed").

The foregoing format is designed to help you "digest" the reams of case material with which you will be faced in your law school career. Once mastered by practice, it will place at your fingertips the information the authors of your casebooks have sought to impart to you in case-by-case illustration and analysis.

B. Be as Economical as Possible in Briefing Cases

Once armed with a format that encourages succinctness, it is as important to be economical with regard to the time spent on the actual reading of the case as it is to be economical in the writing of the brief itself. This does not mean "skimming" a case. Rather, it means reading the case with an "eye" trained to recognize into which "section" of your brief a particular passage or line fits and having a system for quickly and precisely marking the case so that the passages fitting any one particular part of

the brief can be easily identified and brought together in a concise and accurate manner when the brief is actually written.

It is of no use to simply repeat everything in the opinion of the court; record only enough information to trigger your recollection of what the court said. Nevertheless, an accurate statement of the "law of the case," i.e., the legal principle applied to the facts, is absolutely essential to class preparation and to learning the law under the case method.

To that end, it is important to develop a "shorthand" that you can use to make marginal notations. These notations will tell you at a glance in which section of the brief you will be placing that particular passage or portion of the opinion.

Some students prefer to underline all the salient portions of the opinion (with a pencil or colored underliner marker), making marginal notations as they go along. Others prefer the color-coded method of underlining, utilizing different colors of markers to underline the salient portions of the case, each separate color being used to represent a different section of the brief. For example, blue underlining could be used for passages relating to the rule of law, yellow for those relating to the issue, and green for those relating to the holding and decision, etc. While it has its advocates, the color-coded method can be confusing and time-consuming (all that time spent on changing colored markers). Furthermore, it can interfere with the continuity and concentration many students deem essential to the reading of a case for maximum comprehension. In the end, however, it is a matter of personal preference and style. Just remember, whatever method you use, underlining must be used sparingly or its value is lost.

If you take the marginal notation route, an efficient and easy method is to go along underlining the key portions of the case and placing in the margin alongside them the following "markers" to indicate where a particular passage or line "belongs" in the brief you will write:

N   (NATURE OF CASE)
RL   (RULE OF LAW)
I   (ISSUE)
HL   (HOLDING AND DECISION, relates to the RULE OF LAW behind the decision)
HR   (HOLDING AND DECISION, gives the RATIONALE or reasoning behind the decision)
HA   (HOLDING AND DECISION, APPLIES the general principle(s) of law to the facts of the case to arrive at the decision)

Remember that a particular passage may well contain information necessary to more than one part of your brief, in which case you simply note that in the margin. If you are using the color-coded underlining method instead of marginal notation, simply make asterisks or checks in the margin next to the passage in question in the colors that indicate the additional sections of the brief where it might be utilized.

The economy of utilizing "shorthand" in marking cases for briefing can be maintained in the actual brief writing process itself by utilizing "law student shorthand" within the brief. There are many commonly used words and phrases for which abbreviations can be substituted in your briefs (and in your class notes also). You can develop abbreviations that are personal to you and which will save you a lot of time. A reference list of briefing abbreviations can be found on page xii of this book.

C. Use Both the Briefing Process and the Brief as a Learning Tool

Now that you have a format and the tools for briefing cases efficiently, the most important thing is to make the time spent in briefing profitable to you and to make the most advantageous use of the briefs you create. Of course, the briefs are invaluable for classroom reference when you are called upon to explain or analyze a particular case. However, they are also useful in reviewing for exams. A quick glance at the fact summary should bring the case to mind, and a rereading of the rule of law should enable you to go over the underlying legal concept in your mind, how it was applied in that particular case, and how it might apply in other factual settings.

As to the value to be derived from engaging in the briefing process itself, there is an immediate benefit that arises from being forced to sift through the essential facts and reasoning from the court's opinion and to succinctly express them in your own words in your brief. The process ensures that you understand the case and the point that it illustrates, and that means you will be ready to absorb further analysis and information brought forth in class. It also ensures you will have something to say when called upon in class. The briefing process helps develop a mental agility for getting to the *gist* of a case and for identifying, expounding on, and applying the legal concepts and issues found there. The briefing process is the mental process on which you must rely in taking law school examinations; it is also the mental process upon which a lawyer relies in serving his clients and in making his living.

Abbreviations for Briefs

acceptance	acp	offer	O
affirmed	aff	offeree	OE
answer	ans	offeror	OR
assumption of risk	a/r	ordinance	ord
attorney	atty	pain and suffering	p/s
beyond a reasonable doubt	b/r/d	parol evidence	p/e
bona fide purchaser	BFP	plaintiff	P
breach of contract	br/k	prima facie	p/f
cause of action	c/a	probable cause	p/c
common law	c/l	proximate cause	px/c
Constitution	Con	real property	r/p
constitutional	con	reasonable doubt	r/d
contract	K	reasonable man	r/m
contributory negligence	c/n	rebuttable presumption	rb/p
cross	x	remanded	rem
cross-complaint	x/c	res ipsa loquitur	RIL
cross-examination	x/ex	respondeat superior	r/s
cruel and unusual punishment	c/u/p	Restatement	RS
defendant	D	reversed	rev
dismissed	dis	Rule Against Perpetuities	RAP
double jeopardy	d/j	search and seizure	s/s
due process	d/p	search warrant	s/w
equal protection	e/p	self-defense	s/d
equity	eq	specific performance	s/p
evidence	ev	statute	S
exclude	exc	statute of frauds	S/F
exclusionary rule	exc/r	statute of limitations	S/L
felony	f/n	summary judgment	s/j
freedom of speech	f/s	tenancy at will	t/w
good faith	g/f	tenancy in common	t/c
habeas corpus	h/c	tenant	t
hearsay	hr	third party	TP
husband	H	third party beneficiary	TPB
injunction	inj	transferred intent	TI
in loco parentis	ILP	unconscionable	uncon
inter vivos	I/v	unconstitutional	unconst
joint tenancy	j/t	undue influence	u/e
judgment	judgt	Uniform Commercial Code	UCC
jurisdiction	jur	unilateral	uni
last clear chance	LCC	vendee	VE
long-arm statute	LAS	vendor	VR
majority view	maj	versus	v
meeting of minds	MOM	void for vagueness	VFV
minority view	min	weight of authority	w/a
Miranda rule	Mir/r	weight of the evidence	w/e
Miranda warnings	Mir/w	wife	W
negligence	neg	with	w/
notice	ntc	within	w/i
nuisance	nus	without	w/o
obligation	ob	without prejudice	w/o/p
obscene	obs	wrongful death	wr/d

Table of Cases

Note: There are no principal cases in Chapter 1 of the casebook.

CHAPTER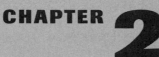

Trade Secret Protection

Quick Reference Rules of Law

Metallurgical Industries, Inc. v. Fourtek, Inc.

Metal processor (P) v. Competitor (D)

790 F.2d 1195 (5th Cir. 1986).

NATURE OF CASE: Appeal from directed verdict in favor of the defense in action for misappropriation of a trade secret.

FACT SUMMARY: Metallurgical Industries, Inc. (P) alleged that the modifications it had made on zinc recovery furnaces were trade secrets that were misappropriated by Fourtek, Inc. (D).

RULE OF LAW
A holder of a trade secret may divulge information to a limited extent without destroying its status as a trade secret.

FACTS: Metallurgical Industries, Inc. (Metallurgical) (P) expended time, money, and effort to modify zinc furnaces it had purchased from a company that became bankrupt. When a former employee (D) of the bankrupt company, who had been told the process was a secret, formed Fourtek, Inc. (D) and contracted with a third party to build a furnace incorporating the modifications, Metallurgical (P) sued, claiming misappropriation of a trade secret. The district court ruled that there was no misappropriation because no trade secret was involved since the basic zinc recovery process had been publicized in the trade. Metallurgical (P) appealed. It countered that its modifications gave it a clear advantage over its competitors. Metallurgical (P) also claimed that its modifications were trade secrets since the holder of a secret may communicate to employees and others pledged to secrecy without losing his protection.

ISSUE: May a holder of a trade secret divulge information to a limited extent without destroying its status as a trade secret?

HOLDING AND DECISION: (Gee, J.) Yes. A holder of a trade secret may divulge information to a limited extent without destroying its status as a trade secret. If disclosure to others is made to further the holder's economic interest, it should be considered a limited disclosure that does not destroy the requisite secrecy. In this case, the disclosures were not public announcements, Metallurgical (P) only divulged its information to two businesses with whom it was dealing, and the disclosures were made to further Metallurgical's (P) economic interests. Moreover, the modifications that led to the commercial operation of the zinc recovery furnace provided a clear advantage over the competition. That the scientific principles involved are generally known does not necessarily refute Metallurgical's (P) claim of trade secrets. The district court misconstrued the nature and elements of the cause of action and abused its discretion in excluding certain evidence. Affirmed in part, reversed in part, and remanded for a new trial.

ANALYSIS

This case reviewed the definition of a "trade secret." First of all, the subject matter must be a secret. Second, efforts must be made to keep the subject matter secret. Third, although the law requires secrecy, it need not be absolute.

Quicknotes

MISAPPROPRIATION The unlawful use of another's property or funds.

TRADE SECRET Consists of any formula, pattern, plan, process, or device known only to its owner and business that gives an advantage over competitors; a secret formula used in the manufacture of a particular product that is not known to the general public.

Rockwell Graphic Systems, Inc. v. DEV Industries, Inc.

Printing press manufacturer (P) v. Competitor (D)

925 F.2d 174 (7th Cir. 1991).

NATURE OF CASE: Appeal from summary judgment in favor of the defense in a suit for misappropriation of trade secrets.

FACT SUMMARY: When two former employees started working for a competitor, DEV Industries, Inc. (D), and using secret drawings, Rockwell Graphic Systems, Inc. (P) sued for misappropriation of trade secrets.

🏛 RULE OF LAW
Holders of trade secrets must take reasonable precautions to keep the secrets confidential.

FACTS: Rockwell Graphic Systems, Inc. (Rockwell) (P) manufactured printing presses and replacement parts based on secret piece part drawings. When two former employees of Rockwell (P) joined DEV Industries, Inc. (DEV) (D), a competitor, Rockwell (P) sued, alleging that they were using stolen secret piece part drawings. DEV (D) persuaded the district court that the piece part drawings were not really trade secrets at all because Rockwell (P) made only perfunctory efforts to keep them secret. DEV's (D) motion for summary judgment was granted. Rockwell (P) claimed that it had made reasonable efforts to maintain the secrecy and appealed.

ISSUE: Does the law of trade secrets require a plaintiff to show that he took reasonable precautions to keep the secret a secret?

HOLDING AND DECISION: (Posner, J.) Yes. Holders of trade secrets must take reasonable precautions to keep the secrets confidential. Only in an extreme case can what is a "reasonable" precaution be determined on a motion for summary judgment, because the answer depends on a balancing of costs and benefits that will vary from case to case and so will require estimation and measurement by persons knowledgeable in the particular field involved. Obviously Rockwell (P) could have taken more precautions, but at what cost? If trade secrets are protected only if their owners take extravagant, productivity-impairing measures to maintain their secrecy, the incentives to invest resources in discovering more efficient methods of production will be reduced. Reversed and remanded.

▶ ANALYSIS

Information that is in the public domain cannot be appropriated by one as a trade secret. The Uniform Trade Secrets Act defines a trade secret as information that is both "not generally known" and the subject of reasonable efforts to maintain secrecy. Most courts agree that reverse engineering of a product does not constitute misappropriation of a trade secret, although reverse engineering of a patented invention will not be allowed in most cases.

■━■

Quicknotes

MISAPPROPRIATION The unlawful use of another's property or funds.

TRADE SECRET Consists of any formula, pattern, plan, process, or device known only to its owner and business that gives an advantage over competitors; a secret formula used in the manufacture of a particular product that is not known to the general public.

■━■

Data General Corp. v. Digital Computer Controls, Inc.

Computer seller (P) v. Computer buyer (D)

Del. Ct. Chanc., 297 A.2d 433 (1971), *aff'd*, 297 A.2d 437 (Del. S. Ct. 1972).

NATURE OF CASE: Motions for an injunction and for summary judgment in a trade secrets action.

FACT SUMMARY: Data General Corp. (P) sought an order preliminarily enjoining Digital Computer Controls, Inc. (D) from making use of claimed trade secrets allegedly contained in design drawings.

🏛 RULE OF LAW

To prove violation of a trade secret, a plaintiff must demonstrate the existence of a trade secret, that the defendant improperly received the information in question in such a manner that its confidential nature should have been known, and that defendant proposes to misuse such information.

FACTS: Data General Corp. (P) sold Nova 1200 computers with accompanying design drawings bearing a legend that they contained proprietary information that was not to be used by the purchaser for manufacturing purposes. The Nova 1200 is not patented and its design drawings have not been copyrighted. The president of Digital Computer Controls, Inc. (Digital) (D) purchased a Nova 1200 computer and acquired a set of design drawings furnished to facilitate maintenance of the computer. Digital (D) thereafter proceeded to use such design drawings as a pattern for the construction of a competing machine, which it then prepared to market. Data General (P) sought to enjoin Digital (D) from making use of the alleged trade secrets contained in the design drawings. Digital (D) claimed that Data General (P) had not maintained that degree of secrecy that would preserve its right to relief and moved for summary judgment.

ISSUE: To prove violation of a trade secret, must a plaintiff demonstrate the existence of a trade secret, that the defendant improperly received the information in question in such a manner that its confidential nature should have been known to it, and that defendant proposes to misuse such information?

HOLDING AND DECISION: (Marvel, V. Chan.) Yes. To prove violation of a trade secret, a plaintiff must demonstrate the existence of a trade secret, that the defendant improperly received the information in question in such a manner that its confidential nature should have been known to it, and that defendant proposes to misuse such information. It cannot be held as a matter of law in this case that Data General's (P) precautions to safeguard its secrets were inadequate. The motions for summary judgment and for an injunction are denied. An order will issue with a provision that all drawings issued by Digital

Computer (D) in connection with the sale of its Nova-like computer contain a restrictive legend of the type now set forth on Data General's (P) drawings here in issue.

▶ ANALYSIS

This court came up with a compromise solution since trade secrets must remain secret to be protected, but computer manufacturers want to sell their computers to the public. In other similar cases, it has been held that unpatented articles sold to the public may be subject to examination and copying by anyone, but the manner of making them may still remain secret. Trade secret law does not protect against reverse engineering by purchasers.

Quicknotes

INJUNCTION A remedy imposed by the court ordering a party to cease the conduct of a specific activity.

SUMMARY JUDGMENT Judgment rendered by a court in response to a motion by one of the parties, claiming that the lack of a question of material fact in respect to an issue warrants disposition of the issue without consideration by the jury.

TRADE SECRET Consists of any formula, pattern, plan, process, or device known only to its owner and business that gives an advantage over competitors; a secret formula used in the manufacture of a particular product that is not known to the general public.

E.I. duPont deNemours & Co. v. Christopher

Chemical company (P) v. Photographers (D)

431 F.2d 1012 (5th Cir. 1970).

NATURE OF CASE: Appeal from award of damages and injunction in an action for misappropriation of trade secrets.

FACT SUMMARY: E.I. duPont deNemours & Co. (duPont) (P) alleged that the Christophers (D) had wrongfully obtained photos revealing duPont's (P) trade secrets.

🏛 RULE OF LAW

To obtain knowledge of a process without spending the time and money to discover it independently is improper unless the holder voluntarily discloses it or fails to take reasonable precautions to ensure its secrecy.

FACTS: E.I. duPont deNemours & Co. (duPont) (P) had developed a highly secret but unpatented process for producing methanol, which gave duPont (P) a competitive advantage over other producers. duPont (P) claimed that this process was a trade secret developed after much expensive and time-consuming research, one that duPont (P) had taken special precautions to safeguard. When the Christophers (D) deliberately flew over duPont (P) and took aerial photographs of new construction at one of duPont's (P) plants, which they then sold to undisclosed third parties, duPont (P) successfully sued for damages and an injunction. The Christophers (D) appealed claiming that there must be a trespass, other illegal conduct, or breach of a confidential relationship for any appropriation of a trade secret to be wrongful.

ISSUE: Is it improper to obtain knowledge of a process without spending the time and money to discover it independently if the holder does not voluntarily disclose it or fail to take reasonable precautions to ensure its secrecy?

HOLDING AND DECISION: (Goldberg, J.) Yes. To obtain knowledge of a process without spending the time and money to discover it independently is improper unless the holder voluntarily discloses it or fails to take reasonable precautions to ensure its secrecy. The rule found in the Restatement of Torts that has been specifically adopted by the Texas Supreme Court recognizes a cause of action for the discovery of a trade secret by any "improper" means. Aerial photography of plant construction is an improper means of deliberately obtaining another's trade secret. Commercial privacy must be protected from espionage that could not have reasonably been anticipated or prevented. Affirmed.

▶ ANALYSIS

This court also noted that the ruling in this case is in perfect accord with the Comments to the Restatement of Torts. The Comments state that the discovery of another's trade secret by improper means subjects the actor to liability independently of the harm to the interest in the secret. Fraudulent misrepresentation, wiretapping, and eavesdropping are other common means of commercial espionage that fall below the generally accepted standards of commercial morality and reasonable conduct.

Quicknotes

MISAPPROPRIATION The unlawful use of another's property or funds.

PATENT A limited monopoly conferred on the invention or discovery of any new or useful machine or process that is novel and nonobvious.

PERMANENT INJUNCTION A remedy imposed by the court ordering a party to cease the conduct of a specific activity until the final disposition of the cause of action.

TRADE SECRET Consists of any formula, pattern, plan, process, or device known only to its owner and business that gives an advantage over competitors; a secret formula used in the manufacture of a particular product that is not known to the general public.

Smith v. Dravo Corp.

Freight company (P) v. Competitor (D)

203 F.2d 369 (7th Cir. 1953).

NATURE OF CASE: Appeal from judgment for the defense in a suit for unlawful appropriation of trade secrets.

FACT SUMMARY: Safeway Containers (P), which had disclosed its secret design to enable Dravo Corp. (D) to appraise it, later alleged that the secret design had been unlawfully misappropriated by Dravo (D).

🏛 RULE OF LAW
A confidential relationship may be implied without any express promise of trust.

FACTS: Smith specially designed, constructed, sold, and leased uniformly sized steel freight containers that greatly facilitated the ship and shore handling and transportation of cargoes. At his death, Dravo Corp. (D) indicated an interest in purchasing some of the containers and possibly Smith's entire business, known as Safeway Containers (Safeway) (P). As a result of negotiations for the sale of the business, Safeway (P) provided Dravo (D) with its patent applications, blue prints, and other confidential information. Dravo (D) ultimately rejected Safeway's (P) offer but commenced building containers that differed from Smith's containers only in that they were four inches narrower. As a result, Safeway's (P) containers became obsolete because they could not be used interchangeably with Dravo's (D). Safeway (P), claiming that Dravo (P) had breached its confidential relationship of trust and used the information obtained to its own advantage and to Safeway's (P) detriment, sued. Dravo (D) successfully claimed in its defense that no express promise of trust had been exacted by Safeway (P) and that the information conveyed was not secret since transactions were at arm's length. Safeway (P) appealed.

ISSUE: May a confidential relationship be implied without any express promise of trust?

HOLDING AND DECISION: (Lindley, J.) Yes. A confidential relationship may be implied without any express promise of trust. Notwithstanding certain disclosures of information, Safeway's (P) information about how to design its containers remained a trade secret. There could be no question that Dravo (D) knew and understood that the information was being disclosed for the limited purpose of evaluating the business for possible purchase. Trust was reposed in Dravo (D) by Safeway (P) that the information thus transmitted was to be accepted subject to that limitation. Dravo (D) fraudulently abused the trust reposed in it since it did not begin construction of its containers until after it had access to Smith's plans. Reversed.

▶ ANALYSIS

This court did not focus on the existence of a trade secret as a starting point for the litigation. Other courts have held that the question is not whether there was a confidential relationship but rather whether there was a trade secret to be misappropriated. Some cases rely upon whether a party had "reason to know" that a confidential relationship existed at the time of the disclosure.

Quicknotes

CONFIDENTIAL RELATIONSHIP A relationship between a person who places his trust and confidence in another to act for his benefit, requiring a high degree of care in transactions between the parties.

TRADE SECRET Consists of any formula, pattern, plan, process, or device known only to its owner and business that gives an advantage over competitors; a secret formula used in the manufacture of a particular product that is not known to the general public.

Kadant, Inc. v. Seeley Machine, Inc.

Trade secret holder (P) v. Competitor (D)

244 F. Supp. 2d 19 (N.D.N.Y. 2003).

NATURE OF CASE: Motion for preliminary injunction in theft of trade secrets action.

FACT SUMMARY: Kadant, Inc. (Kadant) (P) claimed that its former employee, Corlew, stole design specifications for its products, which, it claimed, were trade secrets, and that Corlew turned the trade secrets over to his new employer, Seeley Machine, Inc. (D), which developed a new line of products based on Kadant's (P) trade secrets.

> 🏛 **RULE OF LAW**
> Trade secret protection is not appropriate where a plaintiff does not demonstrate that the defendant improperly obtained and reverse engineered its products.

FACTS: Corlew was an employee of Kadant, Inc. (Kadant) (P) in its AES division. Kadant (P) made products used in the pulp and papermaking industry. At AES, Corlew had access to Kadant's (P) design specifications for its products, as well as to its entire computer system. Throughout his employment with AES, Corlew was subject to a signed confidentiality agreement, in which he agreed not to disclose or use to his benefit any confidential information, including information about AES customers. Kadant (P) eventually terminated Corlew's employment, after which Corlew went to work for Seeley Machine, Inc. (Seeley) (D), one of Kadant's (P) competitors. At Seeley (D), Corlew was responsible for developing and marketing a new line of Seeley (D) products for sale to the pulp and papermaking industry. This new line came out soon after Corlew was employed with Seeley (D). Kadant (P) brought suit in federal district court, alleging, inter alia, that Corlew and Seeley (D) had misappropriated its trade secrets. According to Kadant (P), the only way Seeley (D) could have developed and put out for sale this new line of products in such a short time was by Corlew's theft of AES's trade secrets—its design specifications and customer databases. Seeley (D) claimed that it had reverse engineered the products from existing products that were freely available in the public domain and unprotected by published patent applications, in-force patents, or trade secrets. Kadant (P) argued that it was not possible for Seeley (D) to have reverse engineered the products, claiming that reverse engineering is time consuming, expensive, and requires technical skill. Specifically, Kadant (P) claimed that, using as a frame of reference Seeley's (D) own expert, it would take Seeley (D) 1.7 years to reverse engineer all of Kadant's (P) products. Seeley (D), however, maintained that only a small fraction, not all, of Kadant's (P) products were reverse engineered.

ISSUE: Is trade secret protection appropriate where a plaintiff does not demonstrate that the defendant improperly obtained and reverse engineered its products?

HOLDING AND DECISION: (Hurd, J.) No. Trade secret protection is not appropriate where a plaintiff does not demonstrate that the defendant improperly obtained and reverse engineered its products. If secrecy is lost when a product is placed on the market, there is no trade secret protection. Thus, trade secret law does not offer protection against reverse engineering where the means used were "honest" (in the public domain) and not obtained by virtue of a confidential relationship with an employer. Here, Kadant (P) has presented no evidence that the means used by Seeley (D) to obtain the alleged trade secret were improper or dishonest. In short, it has no evidence Corlew actually stole the design specifications. It instead necessarily relies upon an inference—that the only way Seeley (D) could develop, market, and sell its products in such a short time is if Corlew stole the design specification information. However, as far as the evidence to this point shows, such an inference is unjustified. Kadant (P) does not seem to argue that reverse engineering is impossible, just that it would take a great deal of time, skill, and expense, and that the lack thereof demonstrates that the design specifications must have been stolen. Seeley (D) has argued that Kadant's (P) products were simple, consisting of nontechnical and few parts, that reverse engineering would take little time, and that, in any event, they only reverse engineered a small fraction, not all, of Kadant's (P) products. Kadant (P) has not sufficiently rebutted these contentions. Thus, because Kadant (P) has failed to make a clear showing that Seeley (D) improperly obtained and reverse engineered its products, trade secret protection at this stage of the litigation is improper.

▌ *ANALYSIS*

Some courts have held that even where a product is out in the public domain, and is thus subject to being reverse engineered by a purchaser, trade secret status remains intact because the defendant's former employment with the plaintiff was the only basis for the defendants being "able to select particular items from a vast sea of public information." The court in this case rejected such a view because it "would effectively eviscerate any benefit reverse engineering would provide in the preliminary injunction analysis as applied to trade secrets, forestall healthy notions of commercial competitiveness, and heavily contribute to an

Continued on next page.

inert marketplace where products can only be developed and sold under an impenetrable cloak of originality."

■ ▬ ■

Quicknotes

INTER ALIA Among other things.

PUBLIC DOMAIN Works that are not protected by copyright and are free for the public to utilize.

TRADE SECRET Consists of any formula, pattern, plan, process, or device known only to its owner and business that gives an advantage over competitors; a secret formula used in the manufacture of a particular product that is not known to the general public.

■ ▬ ■

Edwards v. Arthur Andersen, LLP

Former professional employee (P) v. Former professional employer (D)

Cal. Sup. Ct., 81 Cal. Rptr. 3d 282 (2008).

NATURE OF CASE: Appeal from reversal of judgment for the defendant in an action for intentional interference with prospective economic advantage and anticompetitive business practices.

FACT SUMMARY: Edwards (P), a Certified Public Accountant who had been employed by Arthur Andersen, LLP (D), contended that the noncompetition agreement he had signed when hired was invalid because, in contravention of state statute, it restrained his ability to practice his accounting profession.

🏛 RULE OF LAW
A noncompetition agreement, even if it is narrowly drawn so it does not totally prohibit a former employee from engaging in his or her profession, trade, or business, violates a statute that prohibits the restraining of a former employee from practicing a profession, trade, or business, unless the agreement falls within an applicable statutory exception.

FACTS: Edwards (P), a Certified Public Accountant (CPA) who had been employed by Arthur Andersen, LLP (Andersen) (D) as a tax manager, had signed as a condition of his employment a noncompetition agreement that prohibited him, for an 18-month period, from performing professional services of the type that he had provided while at the firm, for any client on whose account he had worked during 18 months prior to his termination. The agreement also prohibited Edwards (P), for a year after termination, from soliciting any client of the firm's office where he worked. When Edward's (P) division was sold and purchased by another firm, as a condition of obtaining employment at the new firm, all employees were required to sign a termination of non-compete agreement (TONC) that Andersen (D) demanded as consideration to release employees from the noncompetition agreement. Edwards (P) refused to sign the TONC, and Andersen (D) terminated his employment. Edwards (P) sued Andersen (D) for intentional interference with prospective economic advantage and anticompetitive business practices, claiming, inter alia, that the noncompetition agreement was invalid under state statute (California Bus. & Prof. Code, § 16600), which states "[e]xcept as provided in this chapter, every contract by which anyone is restrained from engaging in a lawful profession, trade, or business of any kind is to that extent void." He argued it was invalid because it restrained his ability to practice his accounting profession. The trial court, finding that the noncompetition agreement was narrowly tailored and did not deprive Edwards (P) of his right to practice his profession, rendered judgment for Andersen

(D). The state's intermediate appellate court reversed, and the state's highest court granted review.

ISSUE: Does a noncompetition agreement, even if it is narrowly drawn so it does not totally prohibit a former employee from engaging in his or her profession, trade, or business, violate a statute that prohibits the restraining of a former employee from practicing a profession, trade, or business, unless it falls within an applicable statutory exception?

HOLDING AND DECISION: (Chin, J.) Yes. A noncompetition agreement, even if it is narrowly drawn so it does not totally prohibit a former employee from engaging in his or her profession, trade, or business, violates a statute that prohibits the restraining of a former employee from practicing a profession, trade, or business, unless it falls within an applicable statutory exception. The statute at issue rejects the common law "rule of reasonableness," which provides that contractual restraints on the practice of a profession, business, or trade, are valid as long as they are reasonably imposed. Instead, the statute evinces a settled legislative policy in favor of open competition and employee mobility. Under the statute's plain meaning, an employer cannot by contract restrain a former employee from engaging in his or her profession, trade, or business unless the agreement falls within one of the exceptions to the rule. Andersen (D) argues that the word "restrain" as used in the statute merely means "prohibit," so that only contracts that totally prohibit an employee from engaging in his or her profession, trade, or business are illegal. Under such an interpretation, mere limitation on an employee's ability to practice his or her vocation would be permissible as long as it was reasonably based. However, the cases cited by Andersen (D) to support its position only recognize that the statutory exceptions to the statute reflect the same exceptions to the rule against noncompetition agreements that were implied in the common law. Accordingly, the noncompetition at bar was invalid because it restrained his ability to practice his profession. The federal court of appeals for this circuit has adopted a "narrow-restraint" approach to noncompetition agreements whereby application of the statute is excepted where one is barred from pursuing only a small or limited part of a business, trade, or profession. The state's courts, however, have not adopted such an exception. The statute reflects a strong public policy of the state that should not be diluted by judicial fiat; if the legislature had intended the statute to apply only to restraints that were unreasonable or over-

Continued on next page.

broad, it could have included language to that effect. Non-competition agreements are invalid under the statute, even if narrowly drawn, unless they fall within the applicable statutory exceptions. Affirmed (as to this issue).

▶ ANALYSIS

The California statute at issue in this case takes a minority approach to noncompetition agreements and is stricter than the approach taken in the majority of states, which will uphold a noncompetition agreement if it is "reasonable" as to its duration, geographical area, and type of employment or line of business. Other states (e.g., New York) limit the enforcement of noncompetition agreements to situations where trade secrets are likely to be used or disclosed if an employee is allowed to compete.

■≡■

Quicknotes

FIAT A discretionary or authoritative decree.

INTER ALIA Among other things.

NONCOMPETE CLAUSE A provision, typically contained in an employment contract or a contract for the sale of a business, pursuant to which the promisor agrees not to compete with the promisee for a specified time period and/or within a particular geographic area.

■≡■

Warner-Lambert Pharmaceutical Co. v. John J. Reynolds, Inc.

Listerine manufacturer (P) v. Licensing company (D)

178 F. Supp. 655 (S.D.N.Y. 1959).

NATURE OF CASE: Action for a declaratory judgment that payments based on agreements providing for the licensing and use of a trade secret be discontinued.

FACT SUMMARY: The Warner-Lambert Pharmaceutical Co. (P) claimed that the formula for Listerine was no longer a trade secret and therefore it was no longer required to make payments to John J. Reynolds, Inc. (D) pursuant to earlier licensing agreements.

🏛 **RULE OF LAW**
Parties are free to contract with respect to a secret formula or trade secret in any manner.

FACTS: In 1881, Warner-Lambert Pharmaceutical Co. (Warner-Lambert) P) acquired the formula for Listerine and signed licensing agreements with John J. Reynolds, Inc. (Reynolds) (D). Warner-Lambert (P) subsequently contended that the formula was no longer a trade secret because it had gradually become a matter of public knowledge. Warner-Lambert (P) asked for a judgment declaring that it was no longer obligated to make periodic payments to Reynolds (D). Warner-Lambert (P) argued that despite the language of the contract, the court should imply a limitation upon its obligation to pay measured by the length of time that the Listerine formula remained secret. Reynolds (D) asserted that the terms of the contract should control.

ISSUE: Are parties free to contract with respect to a secret formula or trade secret in any manner?

HOLDING AND DECISION: (Bryan, J.) Yes. Parties are free to contract with respect to a secret formula or trade secret in any manner. One who acquires a trade secret or secret formula takes it subject to the risk that there may be a disclosure. If the parties desire the payments or royalties should continue only until the secret is disclosed to the public, it is easy enough for them to say so. But there is no justification for implying such a provision if the parties do not include it in their contract.

▶ *ANALYSIS*

This ruling differs from the cases regarding patents or copyrights. Federal law controls the length of time that a monopoly can be granted for a patent or a copyright. Since there is no statutory limit on the scope of trade secret protection, contract law overrides trade secret law. Other courts have ruled that agreements protecting information already in the public domain may be unreasonable restraints of trade.

Quicknotes

COPYRIGHT Refers to the exclusive rights granted to an artist pursuant to Article I, section 8, clause 8 of the United States Constitution over the reproduction, display, performance, distribution, and adaptation of his work for a period prescribed by statute.

PATENT A limited monopoly conferred on the invention or discovery of any new or useful machine or process that is novel and nonobvious.

TRADE SECRET Consists of any formula, pattern, plan, process, or device known only to its owner and business that gives an advantage over competitors; a secret formula used in the manufacture of a particular product that is not known to the general public.

■≡■

Winston Research Corp. v. 3M Corp.

Competitor (D) v. Trade secrets holder (P)

350 F.2d 134 (9th Cir. 1965).

NATURE OF CASE: Appeal from injunction in trade secrets action.

FACT SUMMARY: Mincom (P) argued that a two-year injunctive period protecting its trade secrets was too short, and that money damages should have been awarded for Winston Research Corp.'s (Winston's) (D) infringement of its trade secrets, whereas Winston (D) argued that an injunction was inappropriate because the definition of trade secrets used by the district court was too broad.

> ## 🏛 RULE OF LAW
> (1) A particular embodiment of a general approach to solving a problem can be a trade secret.
> (2) A court has discretion to enjoin disclosure of a trade secret for the duration of the period during which it would take a competitor to develop a competing product after the trade secret has been disclosed publicly by the trade secret holder.

FACTS: Mincom (P) developed an improved precision tape recorder and reproducer. Within fourteen months of Johnson and Tobias leaving Mincom (P), and forming Winston Research Corp. (Winston) (D), Winston (D) developed a similar machine. Mincom (P) alleged that the Winston (D) machine was developed by former employees of Mincom (P), including Johnson and Tobias, by using confidential information that they had acquired while working on the Mincom (P) machine. Mincom (P) brought suit in federal district court for damages and an injunction. The district court found that Johnson and the other former Mincom (P) employees based Winston's (D) development program upon the same approach to solving the problem posed by earlier versions of the recorder as they had pursued in developing the Mincom (P) machine. The district court further found that this general approach was not a trade secret of Mincom's (P). Finally, the district court found that the particular embodiment of these general concepts in the Mincom (P) machine was Mincom's (P) trade secret, and had been improperly utilized by the former Mincom (P) employees in developing the Winston (D) machine. The district court enjoined Winston (D), Johnson, and Tobias from disclosing or using Mincom's (P) trade secrets in any manner for a period of two years from the date of judgment, but denied damages. Both sides appealed, and the court of appeals granted review.

ISSUE: Can a particular embodiment of a general approach to solving a problem be a trade secret?

(2) Does a court have discretion to enjoin disclosure of a trade secret for the duration of the period during which it would take a competitor to develop a competing product after the trade secret has been disclosed publicly by the trade secret holder?

HOLDING AND DECISION: (Browning, J.)

(1) Yes. A particular embodiment of a general approach to solving a problem can be a trade secret. Mincom (P) contended that the court defined Mincom's (P) trade secrets too narrowly; Winston (D), that the court's definition was too broad. In describing Mincom's (P) trade secrets in the judgment, the district court first outlined the general approach that both Mincom (P) and Winston (D) followed in the development of their machines. The court then set out the detailed specifications of the various elements of the Mincom (P) machine. Winston (D) read the court's initial outline of the general approach as a determination that this was itself a Mincom (P) trade secret. However, this initial description of the general approach was merely introductory to, and limited by, the detailed specifications that followed. Thus, the district court correctly rejected Mincom's (P) assertion that the general approach itself was a Mincom (P) trade secret. This general approach was dictated by well-known principles of physics, so it was not "secret." However, there was substantial evidence that the specifications of the Mincom (P) machine's basic mechanical elements and their relationship to each other were not publicly known, and were arrived at by Mincom (P) only after painstaking research and extensive trial and error. It was these specifications and relationships that the district court correctly found to constitute Mincom's (P) trade secret.

(2) Yes. A court has discretion to enjoin disclosure of a trade secret for the duration of the period during which it would take a competitor to develop a competing product after the trade secret has been disclosed publicly by the trade secret holder. Mincom (P) was entitled to protection of its trade secrets for as long as they remained secret. The district court's decision to limit the duration of injunctive relief was necessarily premised upon a determination that Mincom's (P) trade secrets would shortly be fully disclosed, through no fault of Winston (D), as a result of public announcements, demonstrations, and sales and deliveries of Mincom (P) machines. This approach was sound. A permanent injunction, such as the one sought by

Continued on next page.

Mincom (P), would subvert the public's interest in allowing technical employees to make full use of their knowledge and skill and in fostering research and development. On the other hand, denial of any injunction at all would leave the faithless employee unpunished where, as here, no damages were awarded; and he and his new employer would retain the benefit of a head start over legitimate competitors who did not have access to the trade secrets until they were publicly disclosed. By enjoining use of the trade secrets for the approximate period it would require a legitimate Mincom (P) competitor to develop a successful machine after public disclosure of the secret information, the district court denied the employees any advantage from their faithlessness, placed Mincom (P) in the position it would have occupied if the breach of confidence had not occurred prior to the public disclosure, and imposed the minimum restraint consistent with the realization of these objectives upon the utilization of the employees' skills. Affirmed.

mula used in the manufacture of a particular product that is not known to the general public.

▶ ANALYSIS

The court also held that the former employees' knowledge of what not to do (negative know-how) could not be protected as a trade secret in this case (but could in other cases) because there would be no way to prohibit the former employees from using such knowledge without prohibiting them from using their general knowledge and experience at the same time. The court also affirmed the district court's decision to not award money damages, reasoning that Winston (D) had not profited from sales of its machines, and that possible future profits were too speculative. Finally, the court also affirmed the assignment of patents to Mincom (P), pursuant to an employment agreement, for inventions by former employees that were based on Mincom's (P) confidential information.

Quicknotes

ENJOIN The ordering of a party to cease the conduct of a specific activity.

INJUNCTIVE RELIEF A court order issued as a remedy, requiring a person to do, or prohibiting that person from doing, a specific act.

PATENT A limited monopoly conferred on the invention or discovery of any new or useful machine or process that is novel and nonobvious.

PERMANENT INJUNCTION A remedy imposed by the court ordering a party to cease the conduct of a specific activity until the final disposition of the cause of action.

TRADE SECRETS Consists of any formula, pattern, plan, process, or device known only to its owner and business that gives an advantage over competitors; a secret for-

Patent Law

Quick Reference Rules of Law

Diamond v. Chakrabarty

Patent office (D) v. Microbiologist (P)

447 U.S. 303 (1980).

NATURE OF CASE: Appeal of order reversing denial of patent application.

FACT SUMMARY: Chakrabarty (P) sought to patent a live, man-made microorganism.

🏛 RULE OF LAW
A live, man-made microorganism is a non-naturally occurring composition and thus may be patented.

FACTS: Chakrabarty (P) developed, through recombinant DNA processes, a new species of bacterium capable of metabolizing hydrocarbons in a manner unknown in naturally-occurring organisms. The microorganisms showed great promise in the treatment of oil spills. Chakrabarty (P) applied for a patent. The Patent Office (D) denied the application on the basis that the microorganisms were unpatentable products of nature. The Board of Appeals affirmed. The Court of Customs and Patent Appeals reversed, and the United States Supreme Court granted review.

ISSUE: May a live, man-made microorganism be patented?

HOLDING AND DECISION: (Burger, C.J.) Yes. A live, man-made microorganism is a non-naturally occurring composition and thus may be patented. Resolution of this issue is, despite its philosophical implications, strictly a matter of statutory construction. The relevant statute here, 35 U.S.C. § 101, defines as patentable any new and useful "manufacture" or "composition of matter," among other things. It is a basic rule of construction that words are given their natural, ordinary meanings. There can be little doubt that microorganisms produced by recombinant DNA technology may be said to be manufactured and to be compositions of matter. The fact they are alive is irrelevant for purposes of patent law. While it is true that naturally-occurring products may not be patented, a genetically-engineered microorganism is not naturally occurring. While this Court recognizes that recombinant DNA technology is a controversial field, it is ill-equipped to balance the competing values and interests manifested therein; this is Congress's task. Since the patent laws clearly include materials such as are at issue here within their ambit, and no specific law exists excluding it, the only appropriate holding is that recombinant DNA-produced microorganisms are patentable. Affirmed.

DISSENT: (Brennan, J.) Congress, in enacting the Plant Patent Act in 1930 and the Plant Variety Protection Act in 1970, has indicated that bacteria are excluded from patentability. Patent protection must be extended no further than intended by Congress. Congress has not left a legislative vacuum regarding the type of patent at issue. The Plant Patent Act affords patent protection to developers of certain asexually reproduced plants. The Plant Variety Protection Act extends protection to certain new plant varieties capable of sexual reproduction. Thus, contrary to the majority's assertion, the patent at issued does not pose the problem of "unanticipated inventions." In these two Acts, Congress has addressed the general problem of patenting animate inventions and has chosen carefully limited language granting protection to some kinds of discoveries, but specifically excluding others. These Acts strongly evidence a congressional limitation that excludes bacteria from patentability. The Acts evidence Congress's understanding, at least since 1930, that § 101 does not include living organisms. If newly developed living organisms not naturally occurring had been patentable under § 101, the plants included in the scope of the 1930 and 1970 Acts could have been patented without new legislation. Thus, Congress believed that it had to legislate in order to make agricultural "human-made inventions" patentable, and, because the legislation Congress enacted is limited, it follows that Congress never meant to make items outside the scope of the legislation patentable.

▶ ANALYSIS

The general rule is that things occurring naturally in the universe may not be patented. A type of plant occurring naturally could not be patented; neither could a natural principle. The laws of motion could not have been patented by Newton. This legal principle appears straightforward, but as the instant case demonstrates, modern science has made it less so.

■■■

Quicknotes

PATENT A limited monopoly conferred on the invention or discovery of any new or useful machine or process that is novel and nonobvious.

35 U.S.C. § 101 Defines the Categories of Patentable Inventions. It includes "any, ... process, machine, manufacture, composition of matter ... or improvement thereof."

■■■

Parke-Davis & Co. v. H.K. Mulford Co.

Medical product manufacturer (P) v. Competitor (D)

189 F. 95 (S.D.N.Y. 1911).

NATURE OF CASE: Appeal from holding that patents had been infringed.

FACT SUMMARY: Parke-Davis & Co. (P), the holder of patents for extracting crystals from animal glands to make a medically useful substance, sued H. K. Mulford Co. (D) for infringement.

🏛 RULE OF LAW
When the first person extracts a product and makes it available for any use, the product becomes a new thing commercially and therapeutically and is therefore patentable.

FACTS: Parke-Davis & Co. (Parke-Davis) (P) was the assignee of patents granted for adrenalin, a purified substance of significant medical use. Parke-Davis (P) successfully sued H. K. Mulford Co. (Mulford) (D) for infringement when Mulford (D) made and sold a similar product. Mulford (D) appealed, claiming that the patents were invalid because the patents were only for a degree of purity and not for a new "composition of matter."

ISSUE: When the first person extracts a product and makes it available for any use, does the product become a new thing commercially and therapeutically and is it therefore patentable?

HOLDING AND DECISION: (Hand, J.) Yes. When the first person extracts a product and makes it available for any use, the product becomes a new thing commercially and therapeutically and is therefore patentable. No product is patentable where it is merely separated by the patentee from its surrounding materials and remains unchanged, regardless of whether the process of extracting the product is patentable. Accordingly, the examiner correctly rejected the patentee's initial application to patent the underlying chemical extracted, or the "active principle." However, the patentee then submitted amended applications to cover the refined chemical in its crystal form. Those patent claims were broader than a mere claim to patent the active principle and cover the extracted, and thus purified, chemical. Therefore, Mulford (D) infringed the patents. The patents were not invalid. They did not protect a mere degree of purity, but protected an entirely new composition, i.e., the highly refined chemical based on the initial active principle. It is clear that, as a practical matter, the extracted product is now available for therapeutic and commercial uses, whereas before, the chemical in its unextracted form was not. The line between different substances and degrees of the same substance is to be made on the basis of common usage, rather than as a matter of theory. Affirmed.

▶ ANALYSIS

This case hinges on the "commercial and therapeutic" value of the extracted product. The invention of a new property or use is patentable. The discovery of an inherent property is not patentable.

━━■

Quicknotes

INFRINGEMENT Conduct in violation of statute or that interferes with another's rights pursuant to the law.

PATENT A limited monopoly conferred on the invention or discovery of any new or useful machine or process that is novel and nonobvious.

━━■

Mayo Collaborative Services v. Prometheus Laboratories, Inc.

Infringer (D) v. Diagnostic test manufacturer (P)

132 S. Ct. 1289 (2012).

NATURE OF CASE: Appeal from reversal of judgment that infringed patents were invalid.

FACT SUMMARY: Mayo Collaborative Services and Mayo Clinic Rochester (D) contended that processes claimed by patents exclusively licensed by Prometheus Laboratories, Inc. (P) effectively claimed natural laws or natural phenomena—i.e., the correlations between thiopurine metabolite levels and the toxicity and efficiency of thiopurine drugs—and, therefore, were not patentable.

🏛 RULE OF LAW
A patent is invalid as a natural law under § 101 of the Patent Act where steps in the claimed processes involve, in addition to natural laws themselves, well-understood, routine, conventional activity previously engaged in by researchers in the field and where upholding the patent would risk disproportionately tying up the use of the underlying natural laws, inhibiting their use in the making of further discoveries.

FACTS: Prometheus Laboratories, Inc. (Prometheus) (P) was the sole and exclusive licensee of two patents that concerned the use of thiopurine drugs to treat autoimmune diseases. When ingested, the body metabolizes the drugs, producing metabolites in the bloodstream. Because patients metabolize these drugs differently, doctors have found it difficult to determine whether a particular patient's dose is too high, risking harmful side effects, or too low, and so likely ineffective. The patent claims for the patents set forth processes embodying researchers' findings that identified correlations between metabolite levels and likely harm or ineffectiveness with precision. Each claim recited (1) an "administering" step—instructing a doctor to administer the drug to his or her patient; (2) a "determining" step—telling the doctor to measure the resulting metabolite levels in the patient's blood; and (3) a "wherein" step—describing the metabolite concentrations above which there is a likelihood of harmful side-effects and below which it is likely that the drug dosage is ineffective, and informing the doctor that metabolite concentrations above or below these thresholds "indicate a need" to decrease or increase (respectively) the drug dosage. Prometheus (P) sold diagnostic tests that incorporated these processes. For a while, Mayo Collaborative Services and Mayo Clinic Rochester (collectively "Mayo") (D) bought and used Prometheus' (P) tests, but then decided to market and sell its own similar tests using somewhat higher metabolite levels to determine toxicity. Prometheus (P) brought suit against Mayo (D) for patent infringement. The district court, although concluding that Mayo (D) infringed the patents at

issue, nevertheless held that the patents were invalid as laws of nature under § 101 of the Patent Act. The Federal Circuit reversed, holding that the processes were patent eligible under the "machine or transformation test" because they involved steps that involve the transformation of the human body or blood taken therefrom. That holding was appealed to the United States Supreme Court, and, on remand from the Supreme Court for reconsideration in light of *Bilski v. Kappos*, 130 S. Ct. 3218 (2010), which clarified that the "machine or transformation test" is not a definitive test of patent eligibility, the Federal Circuit reaffirmed its earlier conclusion. The United States Supreme Court granted certiorari.

ISSUE: Is a patent invalid as a natural law under § 101 of the Patent Act where steps in the claimed processes involve, in addition to natural laws themselves, well-understood, routine, conventional activity previously engaged in by researchers in the field and where upholding the patent would risk disproportionately tying up the use of the underlying natural laws, inhibiting their use in the making of further discoveries?

HOLDING AND DECISION: (Breyer, J.) Yes. A patent is invalid as a natural law under § 101 of the Patent Act where steps in the claimed processes involve, in addition to natural laws themselves, well-understood, routine, conventional activity previously engaged in by researchers in the field and where upholding the patent would risk disproportionately tying up the use of the underlying natural laws, inhibiting their use in the making of further discoveries. Because the laws of nature recited by Prometheus' patent claims—the relationships between concentrations of certain metabolites in the blood and the likelihood that a thiopurine drug dosage will prove ineffective or cause harm—are not themselves patentable, the claimed processes are not patentable unless they have additional features that provide practical assurance that the processes are genuine applications of those laws rather than drafting efforts designed to monopolize the correlations. The three additional steps in the claimed processes here are not themselves natural laws but neither are they sufficient to transform the nature of the claims. The "administering" step simply identifies the audience that will be interested in the correlations, namely, doctors who used thiopurine drugs to treat patents suffering from autoimmune disorders. Doctors had been using these drugs for this purpose long before these patents existed. Moreover, a prohibition against patenting abstract ideas cannot be

Continued on next page.

circumvented by attempting to limit the use of the formula to a particular technological environment. The "wherein" clauses simply tell a doctor about the relevant natural laws, adding, at most, a suggestion that they should consider the test results when making their treatment decisions. The "determining" step tells a doctor to measure patients' metabolite levels, through whatever process the doctor wishes to use. Because methods for making such determinations were well known in the art, this step simply tells doctors to engage in well-understood, routine, conventional activity previously engaged in by scientists in the field. Such activity is normally not sufficient to transform as unpatentable law of nature into a patent-eligible application of such a law. Finally, considering the three steps as an ordered combination adds nothing to the laws of nature that is not already present when the steps are considered separately. A more detailed consideration of the controlling precedents reinforces this conclusion. Precedents addressing processes using mathematical formulas held that, like laws of nature, such formulas are not themselves patentable. However, where additional steps of the process transformed the process into an inventive application of the formula, the overall process was patent eligible. But where the additional steps of the process did not limit the claim to a particular application, and the processes at issue were all "well known," to the point where, putting the formula to the side, there was no "inventive concept" in the claimed application of the formula, the process was held not patent eligible. Here, the claim presents a case for patentability that is weaker than under precedent finding a patent-eligible claim and no stronger than precedent where the process was held to be unpatentable. The three steps add nothing specific to the laws of nature other than what is well-understood, routine, conventional activity, previously engaged in by those in the field. Yet another concern that the Court has emphasized is that patent law not inhibit future discovery by improperly tying up the use of laws of nature and the like. Rewarding with patents those who discover laws of nature might encourage their discovery, but because those laws and principles form the basic tools of scientific and technological work, there is a danger that granting patents that tie up their use will inhibit future innovation. Such a danger becomes acute when a patented process is no more than a general instruction to "apply the natural law," or otherwise forecloses more future invention than the underlying discovery could reasonably justify. The patent claims at issue implicate this concern, notwithstanding that the laws of nature involved are narrow ones with limited applicability. In telling a doctor to measure metabolite levels and to consider the resulting measurements in light of the correlations they describe, they tie up her subsequent treatment decision regardless of whether she changes the dosage in light of the inference she draws using the correlations. They also threaten to inhibit the development of more refined treatment recommendations—such as those set forth by Mayo (D)—that combine Prometheus' (P) correlations with later discoveries. This reinforces the conclusion that the processes at

issue are not patent eligible, while eliminating any temptation to depart from case law precedent. Additional arguments supporting Prometheus' position must be rejected. The argument that the process is patent eligible because it passes the "machine or transformation test" fails for insufficient transformation of the body or its blood. Similarly, the argument that the process is patent eligible because the particular laws of nature that the claims embody are narrow and specific also fails because the underlying functional concern is a relative one that measures how much future innovation is foreclosed relative to the contribution of the inventor. Also unpersuasive is the argument that the Court should not invalidate these patents under § 101 because the Patent Act's other validity requirements will screen out overly broad patents; such an approach would make the "law of nature" exception to § 101 patentability a dead letter. Finally, the argument that a principle of law denying patent coverage here will discourage investment in discoveries of new diagnostic laws of nature is also unconvincing, because while protecting some discoveries, such a principle will also impede further scientific research and discovery by tying up critical scientific data. Reversed.

▌ ANALYSIS

This decision makes clear that once a law of nature is identified in a claim, the remaining elements, in order to satisfy § 101, cannot be as generic as "apply it," and they cannot be "well-understood, routine, conventional activity already engaged in by the scientific community" or "when viewed as a whole, add nothing significant beyond the sum of their parts taken separately." However, the decision fails to elucidate how the steps of a process might suffice to limit the application of a law of nature in a way to render a claim patent-eligible. This shortcoming can be seen in guidelines issued by the Patent & Trademark Office shortly after the Supreme Court's decision in *Mayo* was handed down. Those guidelines essentially direct examiners that if a claimed invention is a process that focuses on a law of nature, to be patent-eligible, it must include additional elements/steps or a combination of elements/steps that integrate the natural principle into the claimed invention such that the natural principle is practically applied, and are sufficient to ensure that the claim amounts to significantly more than the natural principle itself. However, other than providing some examples of sufficiency, it does not provide guiding principles for what constitutes sufficient additional steps or combination of elements. That determination will have to be made on a case-by-case, judgment-call basis by examiners and the courts in the absence of broad guidance from the Supreme Court.

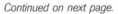

Continued on next page.

Quicknotes

CERTIORARI A discretionary writ issued by a superior court to an inferior court in order to review the lower court's decisions; the Supreme Court's writ ordering such review.

INFRINGEMENT Conduct in violation of a statute or contract that interferes with another's rights pursuant to law.

PATENT A limited monopoly conferred on the invention or discovery of any new or useful machine or process that is novel and non-obvious.

■▬■

Bilski v. Kappos

[Parties not identified.]

130 S. Ct. 3218 (2010).

NATURE OF CASE: Certiorari review of appeal from denial of patent on business method invention.

FACT SUMMARY: Petitioners applied to patent a business method using a mathematical algorithm to hedge against price changes in the energy market. The patent examiner rejected the application because it involved an abstract idea with no relationship to a specific apparatus.

🏛 RULE OF LAW
The machine-or-transformation test is not the sole test for patent eligibility under § 101 of the Patent Act.

FACTS: Petitioners developed a method to hedge against price fluctuations in the energy market. This method included a simple mathematical concept and familiar statistical approaches. Petitioners applied for a patent on their claimed invention, but the patent examiner rejected the application. The examiner claimed it related to an abstract idea and was not implemented on a specific apparatus. Petitioners appealed and the Federal Circuit affirmed. The Federal Circuit held the test for patentability under § 101 was the machine-or-transformation test: (1) the claimed process was tied to a particular machine; or (2) process transformed an article into something else. One dissenting judge argued it failed because it was a method of conduction business. A second dissenter argued the claimed invention was an unpatentable abstract idea. A third dissenter would have remanded to determine patentability under other provisions. Petitioners appealed and the United States Supreme Court granted certiorari.

ISSUE: Is the machine-or-transformation test the sole test for patent eligibility under § 101 of the Patent Act?

HOLDING AND DECISION: (Kennedy, J.) No. The machine-or-transformation test is not the sole test for patent eligibility under § 101 of the Patent Act. The Patent Act § 101 defines patent eligibility with exceptions for "laws of nature, physical phenomena, and abstract ideas." § 101 is a threshold test and the claimed invention must also be novel, nonobvious, and fully described. The instant invention is claimed to be a "process" under § 101. "Process" is defined within the Patent Act at § 100(b). The Federal Circuit adopted the machine-or-transformation test as the sole test for what constitutes a "process." § 100(b) explicitly defines "process," so the Federal Circuit's further definition and limitation is unnecessary and inapplicable here. Adopting such an exclusionary rule creates uncertainty for the patentability of computer software and other emerging technologies. Similarly, the definition of "process" does

not exclude business methods. Federal law explicitly contemplates at least some business method patents as a "method" eligible for patenting under § 101. The limitations of novelty, nonobviousness, and full description protects against unjustified patents. Petitioners' process, however, may not be a "process" under § 101 because it claims an abstract idea. The Court's precedent supports such a limitation. Affirmed.

CONCURRENCE: (Stevens, J.) While the majority is correct that the machine-or-transformation test is not the sole test for what constitutes a patentable process and that this test serves as a critical clue to patentability, the majority errs by suggesting that any series of steps that is not itself an abstract idea or law of nature may constitute a "process" within the meaning of § 101. The Court's holding should have been that the method at issue is not a "process" because it describes only a general method of engaging in business transactions. Because business methods are not patentable, the method here was patent-ineligible. The Court's opinion requires some clarifications. First, the Court's opinion should not be read literally to mean that the terms in the Patent Act must be read as lay speakers use those terms, and not as they have traditionally been understood in the context of patent law. To do otherwise would lead to absurd results. Also, the opinion should not be interpreted to mean that the machine-or-transformation test cannot be applied to digital technologies. Instead, it should be read as holding that few, if any, processes cannot effectively be evaluated using the test's criteria. Moreover, the Court does not provide a clear account of what constitutes an unpatentable abstract idea. Instead, the Court artificially limits the claims at bar to hedging, and then concludes that hedging is an abstract idea rather than a term that describes a category of processes including the claims. Thus, the Court fails to show how its conclusion follows clearly from precedents in this area. Accordingly, one might come to the conclusion that the Court's analysis means that any process that utilizes an abstract idea is itself an unpatentable, abstract idea, but such a rule has never been suggested; if this were the rule, it would undermine a host of patentable processes. Looking to the language of § 101, it is clear that it should not be interpreted to mean, in a lay sense, that the word "process" constitutes any series of steps. Instead, "process" has a distinctive, term-of-art meaning in patent law that does not encompass any series of steps or any way to do any thing. Therefore, the Court makes a serious interpretive error by its willingness to exclude general principles from

Continued on next page.

the provision's reach while apparently willing to include steps for conducting business. The history of patent law contains strong norms against patenting either of these two categories of subject matter, and such history provides a much clearer resolution to the issue presented. That history strongly supports the conclusion that a method of doing business is not a "process" under § 101. Early on, patents were used to protect industrial innovations, not those in business or finance, and by the early 20th century, it was established that a series of steps for conducting business could not be patented. This understanding was carried into the 1952 Patent Act. Moreover, the legislative history does not support an interpretation of the 1952 Act that means that anything created by man is patentable. To the contrary, the legislative history should be understood to mean that not everything created by man is patentable. Even though people have been devising better and better ways to conduct business throughout history, it has never been understood that these ways of conducting business were patentable. Although it may be difficult to define with precision what is a patentable "process" under § 101, the historical clues converge on one conclusion: A business method is not a "process." The constitutionally mandated purpose and function of the patent laws also bolster this conclusion. One of the purposes of patents, through the grant of a limited monopoly, is to promote innovation that would be stifled absent the grant of the patent. It is generally agreed that when innovation is expensive, risky, and easily copied, inventors are less likely to undertake the guaranteed costs of innovation in order to obtain the mere possibility of an invention that others can copy. These dynamics of cost, risk, and reward vary by the type of thing being patented. Where business is concerned, it is doubtful patents are necessary to encourage business innovation, given that the competitive marketplace rewards companies that use more efficient business methods. If business methods could be patented, then many business decisions, no matter how small, could be potential patent violations. Businesses would either live in constant fear of litigation or would need to undertake the costs of searching through patents that describe methods of doing business, attempting to decide whether their innovation is one that remains in the public domain. This would greatly inhibit business innovation and competition. For these and other reasons, the Court should have clearly stated that the claims at issue were not patentable because business methods are not patentable.

CONCURRENCE: (Breyer, J.) Justice Stevens is correct that this case should have been decided on the grounds that business methods are not patentable. Having said that, it is also important to clarify the patent law principles on which the majority of Justices agree. First, although the text of § 101 is broad, it is not without limit. Second, the transformation and reduction of an article to a different state or thing is the clue to the patentability of a process claim that does not include particular machines. Third,

although the machine-or-transformation test has always been a useful and important clue that helps in determining whether a process is patentable, this test has never been the "sole test" for determining patentability. Finally, although the machine-or-transformation test is not the only test for patentability, this by no means indicates that anything that produces a useful, concrete, and tangible result is patentable. Thus, in reemphasizing that the "machine-or-transformation" test is not necessarily the only test of patentability, the Court intends neither to deemphasize the test's usefulness nor to suggest that many patentable processes lie beyond its reach.

▌ANALYSIS

The Federal Circuit tried to create a strict test for patent eligibility but the Supreme Court maintained the fairly broad intent of Congress. The *Bilski* decision was met with approval by some because it left open the door for business method claimed inventions that did not strictly meet the "machine-or-transformation" test. Others bemoaned the opinion, however, because of a subsequent flood of "process" claims involving services such as legal counseling and arbitration. The supporters wanted more flexibility for patent applications and the detractors had hoped for greater insight into what constitutes an appropriate business method.

■■■

Quicknotes

CERTIORARI A discretionary writ issued by a superior court to an inferior court in order to review the lower court's decisions; the Supreme Court's writ ordering such review.

MONOPOLY A privilege or right conferred upon an individual or entity granting it the exclusive power to manufacture, sell and distribute a particular service or commodity; a market condition in which one or a few companies control the sale of a product or service thereby restraining competition in respect to that article or service.

PATENT A limited monopoly conferred on the invention or discovery of any new or useful machine or process that is novel and non-obvious.

■■■

Brenner v. Manson

Patent office (D) v. Inventor (P)

383 U.S. 519 (1966).

NATURE OF CASE: Review of order reversing denial of patent application.

FACT SUMMARY: Manson (P) sought to patent a chemical process whose only demonstrable utility was to aid in research.

🏛 RULE OF LAW
A process whose only demonstrable utility is to aid in research is not patentable.

FACTS: Manson (P) sought to patent a chemical process for synthesizing certain steroidal compounds. Although these compounds were not in themselves beneficial, they were useful in cancer research. The Patent Office (D) denied the application on the basis that the process was not useful. The Court of Customs and Patent Appeals reversed, and the United States Supreme Court granted review.

ISSUE: Is a process whose only demonstrable utility is to aid in research patentable?

HOLDING AND DECISION: (Fortas, J.) No. A process whose only demonstrable utility is to aid in research is not patentable. It has been the rule since the inception of patent law that, for an invention to be patentable, it must be useful. An invention must not only be harmless, it must also not be frivolous or insignificant. The question thus presents itself as to whether a product or process is useful if, rather than being useful in itself, it is the subject of serious scientific inquiry. While the Patent Act is silent on this issue, an examination of the purposes of the patent law reveals that the answer must be in the negative. The basis quid pro quo of patent law is that a monopoly is granted in exchange for a finished thing with substantial utility. A product or process useful as the subject of research does not fit this requirement. Further, to allow a monopoly on the research stage of innovation might well inhibit such innovation, in direct contravention to the purposes of patent law. Here, the process in question is capable only of synthesizing products suitable for research, not useful in themselves. The process is therefore not patentable. Reversed.

CONCURRENCE AND DISSENT: : (Harlan, J.) The Court's policy arguments against the patentability of processes that are useful in generating objects of study are not convincing. Further, decisional history tends to support such patentability.

▶ ANALYSIS

Utility is one of the basic requirements of patent law. Indeed, it is one of the characteristics relating to patents described in Art. I, § 8 of the Constitution. Congress, in its first Patent Act (enacted in 1790), mandated this requirement. It is now codified at 35 U.S.C. § 101.

Quicknotes

PATENT A limited monopoly conferred on the invention or discovery of any new or useful machine or process that is novel and nonobvious.

In re Fisher

[Parties not identified.]

421 F.3d 1365 (Fed. Cir. 2005).

NATURE OF CASE: Appeal from affirmance of a decision denying patentability for lack of utility and lack of enablement.

FACT SUMMARY: Fisher (P) contended that his claimed invention, relating to five purified nucleic acid sequences (genes), commonly referred to as expressed sequence tags (ESTs), that encoded proteins and protein fragments in maize plants, had a specific and substantial utility and that his patent application enabled one of ordinary skill in the art to use the invention.

RULE OF LAW
A patent application that discloses general, generic uses of a claimed invention, the claimed inventions of which are mere research intermediaries, lacks utility and lacks enablement.

FACTS: Fisher (P) submitted a patent application (the '643 application) that related to five purified nucleic acid sequences (genes), commonly referred to as expressed sequence tags (ESTs), that encoded proteins and protein fragments in maize plants. When Fisher (P) filed the '643 application, he did not know the precise structure or function of either the genes or the proteins encoded for by those genes. The '643 application disclosed that the five claimed ESTs could be used in a variety of ways. These included: (1) serving as a molecular marker for mapping the entire maize genome, which consists of ten chromosomes that collectively encompass roughly 50,000 genes; (2) measuring the level of mRNA in a tissue sample via microarray technology to provide information about gene expression; (3) providing a source for primers for use in the polymerase chain reaction (PCR) process to enable rapid and inexpensive duplication of specific genes; (4) identifying the presence or absence of a polymorphism; (5) isolating promoters via chromosome walking; (6) controlling protein expression; and (7) locating genetic molecules of other plants and organisms. The patent examiner found that none of the recited uses for the ESTs satisfied the "substantial utility" standard and "enablement" standard required for patentability. The Board of Appeals and Interferences affirmed, and the Federal Circuit granted review.

ISSUE: Does a patent application that discloses general, generic uses of a claimed invention, the claimed inventions of which are mere research intermediaries, lack utility and lack enablement?

HOLDING AND DECISION: (Michel, C.J.) Yes. A patent application that discloses general, generic uses of a

claimed invention, the claimed inventions of which are mere research intermediaries, lacks utility and lacks enablement. Fisher's (P) argument that the claimed ESTs provide seven specific and substantial uses, regardless whether the functions of the genes corresponding to the claimed ESTs are known, is not convincing. Essentially, the claimed ESTs act as no more than research intermediates that may help scientists to isolate the particular underlying protein-encoding genes and conduct further experimentation on those genes. The overall goal of such experimentation is presumably to understand the maize genome. Therefore, the claimed ESTs are mere "objects of use-testing," i.e., objects upon which scientific research could be performed with no assurance that anything useful will be discovered in the end. Fisher's (P) comparison of the ESTs to a patentable microscope is also unconvincing. A microscope can immediately reveal an object's structure, whereas the claimed ESTs can only be used to detect the presence of genetic material having the same structure as the EST itself. It is unable to provide any information about the overall structure let alone the function of the underlying gene. Accordingly, while a microscope can offer an immediate, real world benefit in a variety of applications, the same cannot be said for the claimed ESTs. The claimed ESTs themselves are not an end of Fisher's (P) research effort, but only tools to be used along the way in the search for a practical utility. Thus, while Fisher's (P) claimed ESTs may add a noteworthy contribution to biotechnology research, they are not of sufficient utility to merit patentability because Fisher (P) does not identify the function for the underlying protein-encoding genes. Absent such identification, the claimed ESTs have not been researched and understood to the point of providing an immediate, well-defined, real world benefit to the public meriting the grant of a patent. Therefore, Fisher's (P) asserted uses are insufficient to meet the standard for a "substantial" utility under § 101. The claimed inventions also lack enablement under § 112. Affirmed.

DISSENT: (Rader, J.) Although the Patent Office needs a tool to reject inventions that may advance the "useful arts" but not sufficiently to warrant the valuable exclusive right of a patent, the utility requirement is not the tool for this job. The utility requirement is inadequate for this task because it lacks any standard for assessing the state of the prior art and the contributions of the claimed advance. The proper tool for assessing sufficient contribution to the useful arts is the obviousness requirement § 103. Unfortunately, the Patent Office has been judicially

Continued on next page.

deprived of the obviousness requirement for genomic inventions. See *In re Deuel*, 51 F.3d 1552 (Fed. Cir. 1995). Nonetheless, rather than distort the utility test, the Patent Office should seek ways to apply the correct test, i.e., inventive step or obviousness.

▶ *ANALYSIS*

Judge Rader, in his dissent, also disagreed that the ESTs were not akin to a microscope. He found that "both take a researcher one step closer to identifying and understanding a previously unknown and invisible structure. Both supply information about a molecular structure. Both advance research and bring scientists closer to unlocking the secrets of the corn genome to provide better food production for the hungry world. If a microscope has § 101 utility, so too do these ESTs."

■═■

Quicknotes

PATENT A limited monopoly conferred on the invention or discovery of any new or useful machine or process that is novel and nonobvious.

■═■

Juicy Whip, Inc. v. Orange Bang, Inc.

Beverage dispenser manufacturer (P) v. Infringer (D)

185 F.3d 1364 (Fed. Cir. 1999).

NATURE OF CASE: Appeal of grant of summary judgment.

FACT SUMMARY: Juicy Whip, Inc. (P) sued Orange Bang, Inc. (Orange) (D), alleging it was infringing on its beverage-dispensing patent. Orange (D) alleged the dispenser was unpatentable because it lacked utility.

🏛 RULE OF LAW
The statutory requirement of utility is satisfied if one product can be altered to make it look like another because that in and of itself is a benefit. An invention does not lack utility for patent purposes simply because it can fool the public, through imitation, in a manner that is designed to increase product sales.

FACTS: Juicy Whip, Inc. (Juicy) (P) has a patent for a post-mix beverage dispenser that is designed to look like a pre-mix beverage dispenser. A post-mix dispenser stores beverage syrup concentrate and water in separate locations until the beverage is ready to be dispensed. A pre-mix beverage dispenser, on the other hand, pre-mixes the syrup concentrate and water and the beverage is stored in a display reservoir bowl until it is ready to be dispensed. A pre-mix dispenser's display bowl stimulates impulse buying. However, it creates the need to clean the bowl frequently because of bacterial build-up. The patented dispenser thus has the appearance of a pre-mix dispenser but functions as a post-mix dispenser, thereby alleviating the required maintenance. Juicy (P) sued Orange Bang, Inc. (Orange) (D), alleging it was infringing on the patent. The district court granted Orange's (D) motion for summary judgment and held the patent invalid for lack of utility.

ISSUE: Does the post-mix dispenser that looks like a pre-mix dispenser lack utility?

HOLDING AND DECISION: [Judge not stated in casebook excerpt.] No. The post-mix dispenser does not lack utility. The Patent Act provides that whoever invents any useful machine may obtain a patent for it. An invention is useful if it is capable of providing some identifiable benefit. Although inventions that are injurious to the well-being of society are considered unpatentable, the principle that inventions are invalid if they are principally designed to serve immoral purposes has not recently been applied broadly. The district court's reliance on the cases of *Rickard v. Du Bon*, 103 F. 868 (2d Cir. 1900), and *Scott & Williams v. Aristo Hosiery Co.*, 7 F.2d 1003 (2d Cir. 1925), is thus misplaced because they do not represent the correct view of the doctrine of utility under the Patent Act of 1952. The statutory requirement of utility is satisfied if one product can be altered to make it look like another, because that in and of itself is a benefit. It is common for a product to be designed to appear to viewers to be something that it is not and there are many patents directed at making one product imitate another. The value of such products is that they appear to be something that they are not. In this case, the post-mix dispenser has utility because it embodies the features of a post-mix dispenser while imitating the visual appearance of a pre-mix dispenser. Just because customers may believe that they are receiving fluid directly from the display tank does not mean the invention has no utility. Even if it was considered deceptive, that does not mean it is unpatentable. Other agencies, and not the Patent and Trademark Office, are delegated the task of protecting customers from fraud and deception in the sale of food products. Furthermore, it is up to Congress to declare particular types of inventions unpatentable. Reversed and remanded.

▶ ANALYSIS

This case centered on the reasoning that the invention was useful in and of itself because it was able to create more sales by fooling the public into believing that it was getting a certain product when it was really getting a different product. The real utility of the product was that it was increasing sales by providing customers with the appearance of the product but eliminating the work of cleaning and maintenance that would have been involved in creating the actual product.

■■■

Quicknotes

PATENT A limited monopoly conferred on the invention or discovery of any new or useful machine or process that is novel and nonobvious.

SUMMARY JUDGMENT Judgment rendered by a court in response to a motion made by one of the parties, claiming that the lack of a question of material fact in respect to an issue warrants disposition of the issue without consideration by the jury.

■■■

The Incandescent Lamp Patent

[Parties not identified.]

159 U.S. 465 (1895).

NATURE OF CASE: Patent infringement suit.

FACT SUMMARY: The Electric Light Company (P) filed suit to recover damages allegedly incurred for infringement of their letters of patent.

🏛 RULE OF LAW
A patent must state with specificity the composition of the materials to be mixed together to produce the result intended to be obtained and if they are not capable of such exact description, then the inventor is not entitled to a patent.

FACTS: The Electric Light Company (Electric) (P) filed suit against McKeesport (D) to recover damages for the infringement of letters patent issued to the Electro-Dynamic Light Company, assignee of Sawyer and Man, for an electric light. The defendants justified their actions under certain patents issued to Thomas Edison, denied their novelty and utility and claimed that they had been fraudulently and illegally obtained. The circuit court held the patent to be invalid and dismissed. Electric (P) appealed.

ISSUE: Must a patent state with specificity the composition of the materials to be mixed together to produce the result intended to be obtained and if they are not capable of such exact description, then is the inventor not entitled to a patent?

HOLDING AND DECISION: (Brown, J.) Yes. A patent must state with specificity the composition of the materials to be mixed together to produce the result intended to be obtained and if they are not capable of such exact description, then the inventor is not entitled to a patent. The two main defenses to the patent are: (1) that it is defective upon its face in attempting to monopolize use of all fibrous and textile materials for the purpose of electric illumination; and (2) that Sawyer and Man were not in fact the first to discover that these materials were better adapted than mineral carbons for such use. With respect to the first defense, had the patentees discovered in the fibrous and textile substances a quality distinguishing them from other materials adapting them particularly to incandescent conductors, such claim might prevail. Sawyer and Man presumed they discovered in carbonized paper the best material for an incandescent conductor. Instead of confining themselves to this material, they made a broad claim for every fibrous or textile material. Rev. Stat. § 4888 requires the application to contain a written description of the device and the manner and process of making and using it in full, clear, and concise terms. The purpose of this requirement is to apprise the public of what the patentee claims to hold a patent to. When the specification, however, only gives the names of the substances used without stating the relative proportions, the court must declare the patent void. If Sawyer and Man had discovered that a certain type of carbonized paper sufficed, then their claim to all carbonized paper might not fail; but the fact that such paper is a fibrous material does not allow them to limit other inventors to the entire domain of such materials. The claims of this patent are too indefinite. Affirmed.

▶ ANALYSIS

Rev. Stat. § 4888 is now found in 35 U.S.C. § 112. That section requires that a patent claim include a written description, clear claim and enablement requirement.

Quicknotes

INFRINGEMENT Conduct in violation of statute or that interferes with another's rights pursuant to law.

PATENT A limited monopoly conferred on the invention or discovery of any new or useful machine or process that is novel and nonobvious.

35 U.S.C. § 112 Requires that patent applicants disclose how to make and use the invention and include a written description.

The Gentry Gallery, Inc. v. The Berkline Corp.

Furniture manufacturer (P) v. Furniture manufacturer (D)

134 F.3d 1473 (Fed. Cir. 1998).

NATURE OF CASE: Patent infringement suit.

FACT SUMMARY: The Gentry Gallery, Inc. (P) brought suit against The Berkline Corp. (Berkline) (D) claiming patent infringement by Berkline's (D) manufacturing and selling of sectional sofas having two recliners facing in the same direction.

🏛 RULE OF LAW
Patent claims may be no broader than the supporting disclosure and, thus, a narrow disclosure will limit claim breadth.

FACTS: The Gentry Gallery, Inc. (Gentry) (P) owns the '244 patent to a sectional sofa in which two independent reclining seats face in the same direction. Gentry (P) filed suit alleging that The Berkline Corp. (Berkline) (D) infringed its patent by manufacturing and selling sofas having two recliners facing in the same direction. The district court granted Berkline's (D) motion for summary judgment of noninfringement, but denied its motions for invalidity and unenforceability. The court concluded that Berkline's (D) sofas did not contain a fixed console and thus did not infringe Gentry's (P) patent.

ISSUE: May patent claims may be broader than the supporting disclosure?

HOLDING AND DECISION: (Lourie, J.) No. Patent claims may be no broader than the supporting disclosure and, thus, a narrow disclosure will limit claim breadth. Berkline (D) argued that because the patent only described the sofas having controls on the console, the claimed consoles were not described within the meaning of § 112. This court agrees that the patent's disclosure does not support claims in which the location of the recliner controls is other than on the console. Whether a specification complies with the written description requirement of § 112 is a question of fact to be reviewed for clear error on appeal. To fulfill the written description requirement, the patent specification must "clearly allow persons of ordinary skill in the art to recognize that [the inventor] invented what is claimed." This requirement is met if the written description describes the invention, with all its claimed limitations. While a claim need not be limited to a preferred embodiment, the scope of a right to exclude may be limited by a narrow disclosure. Here the original disclosure clearly identifies the console as the only possible location for the controls. Locating the controls anywhere but on the consoles is outside the stated purpose of the invention. Claims may be no broader than the supporting disclosure; thus, a narrow disclosure will limit claim breadth. The

district court erred in finding that Gentry (P) was entitled to claims in which the recliner controls are not located on the console. Reversed.

▶ ANALYSIS

Gentry (P) relied on the position set forth in *Ethicon* that "an applicant . . . is generally allowed claims, when the art permits, which cover more than the specific embodiment shown." The court distinguishes that case from the present, however, indicating that while an applicant is free to draft claims broadly, within the restrictions imposed by the prior art, the inventor did so in *Ethicon* only because he did not, unlike Gentry (P), consider the element to be an essential part of his invention.

■═■

Quicknotes

INFRINGEMENT Conduct in violation of statute or that interferes with another's rights pursuant to law.

PATENT A limited monopoly conferred on the invention or discovery of any new or useful machine or process that is novel and nonobvious.

35 U.S.C. § 112 Requires that patent applicants disclose how to make and use the invention and include a written description.

■═■

Ariad Pharmaceuticals, Inc. v. Eli Lilly & Co.

Pharmaceutical patent holder (P) v. Pharmaceutical alleged infringer (D)

598 F.3d 1336 (Fed. Cir. 2010) (en banc).

NATURE OF CASE: Grant of petition for rehearing en banc of reversal of denial of defendant's motion for judgment as a matter of law in patent infringement action.

FACT SUMMARY: After a jury found that Eli Lilly & Company (Lilly) (D) had infringed patent '516 held by Ariad Pharmaceuticals, Inc., and others (collectively, "Ariad") (P), and found that none of the asserted claims were invalid, the district court denied Lilly's (D) motion for judgment as a matter of law (JMOL), but the court of appeals reversed, finding that the claims were invalid for lack of a sufficient written description. Ariad (P) petitioned for a rehearing, challenging the court of appeals' interpretation of 35 U.S.C. § 112, first paragraph, as containing a separate written description requirement.

☷ RULE OF LAW
35 U.S.C. § 112 contains a written description requirement separate from the enablement requirement.

FACTS: Ariad Pharmaceuticals, Inc., and others (collectively, "Ariad") (P) brought suit against Eli Lilly & Company (Lilly) (D) for infringement of patent '516. The inventors of the '516 patent were the first to identify NF-kB, a gene transcription factor, and to uncover the mechanism by which NF-kB activates gene expression underlying the body's immune responses to infection. The inventors discovered that NF-kB normally exists in cells as an inactive complex with a protein inhibitor, named I-kB, and is activated by extracellular stimuli through a series of biochemical reactions that release it from I-kB. Once free of its inhibitor, NF-kB travels into the cell nucleus where it binds to and activates the transcription of genes containing a NF-kB recognition site. The activated genes (cytokines) in turn help the body to counteract the extracellular assault. The production of cytokines can, however, be harmful in excess. Thus the inventors recognized that artificially interfering with NF-kB activity could reduce the harmful symptoms of certain diseases. They claimed methods for regulating cellular responses to external stimuli by reducing NF-kB activity in a cell. The claims were genus claims, encompassing the use of all substances that achieve the desired result of reducing the binding of NF-kB to NF-kB recognition sites. The specification also hypothesized three types of molecules with the potential to reduce NF-kB activity in cells: decoy, dominantly interfering, and specific inhibitor molecules. Lilly (D) argued that the asserted claims were not supported by a written description because the specification of the '516 patent failed to adequately disclose how the claimed reduction of NF-kB activity was

achieved. Ariad (P) responded that Lilly's (D) arguments failed as a matter of law because Ariad (P) did not actually claim the molecules. According to Ariad (P), because there was no term in the asserted claims that corresponded to the molecules, it was entitled to claim the methods without describing the molecules. Alternatively, Ariad (P) contended that the specification of the '516 patent and the testimony of its expert, Kadesch, provided the jury with substantial evidence of adequate written description of the claimed methods. The jury found that Lilly (D) had infringed patent '516 and also found that none of the asserted claims were invalid. The district court denied Lilly's (D) motion for judgment as a matter of law (JMOL), but the court of appeals reversed, finding that the claims were invalid for lack of an adequate written description as required by 35 U.S.C. § 112. Ariad (P) petitioned for a rehearing, challenging the court of appeals' interpretation of § 112, first paragraph, as containing a separate written description requirement. The court of appeals granted the petition.

ISSUE: Does 35 U.S.C. § 112 contain a written description requirement separate from the enablement requirement?

HOLDING AND DECISION: (Lourie, J.) Yes. 35 U.S.C. § 112 contains a written description requirement separate from the enablement requirement. The § 112 paragraph at issue provides: "The specification shall contain a written description of the invention, and of the manner and process of making and using it, in such full, clear, concise, and exact terms as to enable any person skilled in the art to which it pertains, or with which it is most nearly connected, to make and use the same, and shall set forth the best mode contemplated by the inventor of carrying out his invention." The plain language of this paragraph requires that the specification "shall contain a written description of the invention" and contains two separate description requirements: a written description (1) of the invention, and (2) of the manner and process of making and using the invention. Contrary to Ariad's (P) contention, there is nothing in the statute's language or grammar that unambiguously dictates that the adequacy of the "written description of the invention" must be determined solely by whether that description identifies the invention so as to enable one of skill in the art to make and use it. Thus, the written description requirement exists as an independent statutory requirement. Its purpose is not solely to identify the invention that must comply with the

Continued on next page.

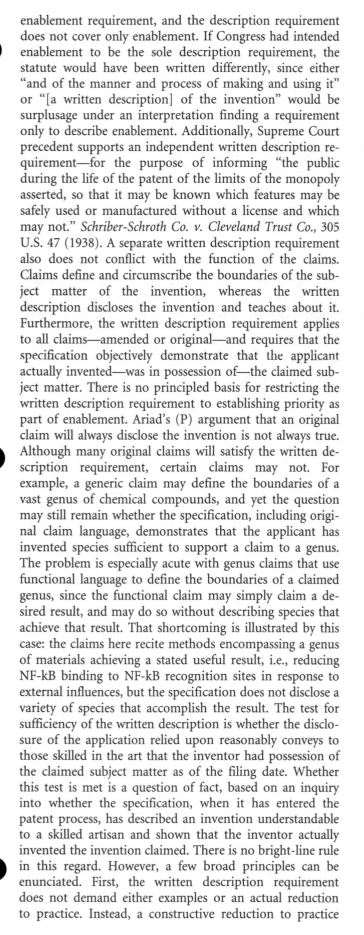

enablement requirement, and the description requirement does not cover only enablement. If Congress had intended enablement to be the sole description requirement, the statute would have been written differently, since either "and of the manner and process of making and using it" or "[a written description] of the invention" would be surplusage under an interpretation finding a requirement only to describe enablement. Additionally, Supreme Court precedent supports an independent written description requirement—for the purpose of informing "the public during the life of the patent of the limits of the monopoly asserted, so that it may be known which features may be safely used or manufactured without a license and which may not." *Schriber-Schroth Co. v. Cleveland Trust Co.*, 305 U.S. 47 (1938). A separate written description requirement also does not conflict with the function of the claims. Claims define and circumscribe the boundaries of the subject matter of the invention, whereas the written description discloses the invention and teaches about it. Furthermore, the written description requirement applies to all claims—amended or original—and requires that the specification objectively demonstrate that the applicant actually invented—was in possession of—the claimed subject matter. There is no principled basis for restricting the written description requirement to establishing priority as part of enablement. Ariad's (P) argument that an original claim will always disclose the invention is not always true. Although many original claims will satisfy the written description requirement, certain claims may not. For example, a generic claim may define the boundaries of a vast genus of chemical compounds, and yet the question may still remain whether the specification, including original claim language, demonstrates that the applicant has invented species sufficient to support a claim to a genus. The problem is especially acute with genus claims that use functional language to define the boundaries of a claimed genus, since the functional claim may simply claim a desired result, and may do so without describing species that achieve that result. That shortcoming is illustrated by this case: the claims here recite methods encompassing a genus of materials achieving a stated useful result, i.e., reducing NF-kB binding to NF-kB recognition sites in response to external influences, but the specification does not disclose a variety of species that accomplish the result. The test for sufficiency of the written description is whether the disclosure of the application relied upon reasonably conveys to those skilled in the art that the inventor had possession of the claimed subject matter as of the filing date. Whether this test is met is a question of fact, based on an inquiry into whether the specification, when it has entered the patent process, has described an invention understandable to a skilled artisan and shown that the inventor actually invented the invention claimed. There is no bright-line rule in this regard. However, a few broad principles can be enunciated. First, the written description requirement does not demand either examples or an actual reduction to practice. Instead, a constructive reduction to practice

that in a definite way identifies the claimed invention can satisfy the written description requirement. Conversely, actual "possession" or reduction to practice outside of the specification is not enough. Rather, the specification itself must demonstrate possession. Also, a description that merely renders the invention obvious does not satisfy the requirement. In some fields, it might be true that there is little difference between describing an invention and enabling one to make and use it, so that written description and enablement rise and fall together. However, in some fields (e.g., chemistry, biology) this is not always true, and requiring a written description of the invention plays a vital role in curtailing claims that do not require undue experimentation to make and use, and thus satisfy enablement, but that have not been invented, and thus cannot be described. The written description requirement also ensures that when a patent claims a genus by its function or result, the specification recites sufficient materials to accomplish that function. This helps to curtail claims that merely recite a description of the problem to be solved while claiming all solutions to it that as yet have not been invented. Finally, Ariad's (P) complaint that the written description doctrine unfairly disadvantages research universities is unavailing. Patents are aimed at the "useful arts." They are not awarded for academic theories, no matter how groundbreaking or necessary to the later patentable inventions of others. Requiring a written description of the invention limits patent protection to those who actually perform the difficult work of "invention," to those who conceive of the complete and final invention with all its claimed limitations, not to those who come up with just research hypotheses or plans that will later have to be turned into practical applications. Permitting claims to research plans would impose costs on downstream research, discouraging later invention. The written description doctrine appropriately incentivizes actual invention, not "attempt[s] to preempt the future before it has arrived."

An application of the written description requirement to the facts at bar leads to the conclusion that Ariad (P) failed to satisfy that requirement. Ariad's (P) specification suggested only the use of the three classes of molecules to achieve NF-kB reduction. Thus, to satisfy the written description requirement for the asserted claims, the specification must demonstrate that Ariad (P) possessed the claimed methods by sufficiently disclosing molecules capable of reducing NF-kB activity—but it failed to do so. As to specific inhibitor molecules, of which I-kB is one, I-kB was not disclosed with the initial application. Although one of ordinary skill could through experimentation isolate natural I-kB at the time of the application, in the context of the claimed invention, a vague functional description and an invitation for further research does not constitute written

Continued on next page.

disclosure of a specific inhibitor molecule. Dominantly interfering molecules are a truncated form of the NF-kB molecule and would block natural NF-kB from inducing the expression of its target genes. The specification provided no examples of this class of molecule, and it also did not disclose that requisite spatial separations in DNA domains required for the dominantly interfering molecules to work properly actually existed. Thus, if the inventors themselves did not know whether the domains were in fact separate and spatially distinct, one of ordinary skill in the art would be at best equally ignorant. The third class of molecules, decoy molecules, is designed to mimic a region of the gene whose expression would normally be induced by NF-kB, and NF-kB would bind the decoy, and thus, not be available to bind its natural target. Although the specification did propose example structures for decoy molecules, it failed to describe how to use those molecules to reduce NF-kB activity; there was no descriptive link between the table of decoy molecules and reducing NF-kB activity. Therefore, the '516 patent claims are invalid for lack of written description. Reversed in part and affirmed in part.

▶ ANALYSIS

In a concurring opinion, Judge Gajarsa articulated one of several key positions of many critics of the court's decision by stating that an independent written description requirement is not a necessity of patent law, since § 112's enablement requirement is a more than adequate vehicle for invalidating claims that are broader than their disclosure. He points out that the empirical evidence confirms that written description serves little practical purpose as an independent invalidity device and better serves the goals of the Patent Act when confined to the priority context. Similarly, in his dissent-in-part, Judge Linn asserts that any claim that uses purely functional language, or covers a broad genus without sufficient supporting examples, will not be enabled, so that the enablement requirement is an adequate policer, without the need for a separate written disclosure requirement. Judge Rader, in his dissent-in-part, goes further, and contends that the written description doctrine is a fabrication of the Federal Court of Appeals and that every case before the court's fabrication of the doctrine in 1997 actually applied the "written description" doctrine to police priority. In his rebuke of the court's activism, and on its invocation of the patent quid pro quo, he also says "this court's new creation offers the public nothing more in exchange for a patent than the statutory enablement requirement already ensures." He also asks, "what 'teaching function' does the court propagate by telling an inventor that a patent application must show 'possession as shown in the disclosure,' whatever that means? Inventors, to my knowledge, are always quite certain that they possess their invention." While disagreement over the policy and legal underpinnings of the *Ariad* decision is strong, as demonstrated by the non-majority

opinions, one thing that is fairly certain is that genus claims that recite function will be invalidated.

■═■

Quicknotes

BRIGHT-LINE RULE A legal rule of decision to help resolve ambiguous issues simply and in a straight-forward manner, sometimes sacrificing equity for certainty.

EN BANC The hearing of a matter by all the judges of the court, rather than only the necessary quorum.

INFRINGEMENT Conduct in violation of statute or that interferes with another's rights pursuant to law.

PATENT A limited monopoly conferred on the invention or discovery of any new or useful machine or process that is novel and nonobvious.

QUID PRO QUO What for what; in the contract context used synonymously with consideration to refer to the mutual promises between two parties rendering a contract enforceable.

■═■

Rosaire v. National Lead Co.

Oil prospectors (P) v. Competitor (D)

218 F.2d 72 (5th Cir. 1955).

NATURE OF CASE: Appeal from the trial court's decision that patents were invalid.

FACT SUMMARY: National Lead Co. (D) claimed that it had not infringed Rosaire's (P) patents because the patents had been invalidated by a prior reduction to practice of the same method.

🏛 RULE OF LAW
An invention is not patentable if it was known or used by others in this country before the patentee's invention.

FACTS: Rosaire (P) claimed to have invented a new method for oil prospecting and held two patents that National Lead Co. (D) had allegedly infringed. National Lead (D) claimed that the patents were invalidated because the alleged inventions had been known and used extensively by Teplitz for Gulf Oil prior to the date that Rosaire (P) first conceived of the invention. Rosaire (P) claimed that the work of Teplitz was an unsuccessful experiment that was not published or patented and therefore did not give the public the benefit of the experimental work. The trial court found that the work by Teplitz was a successful and adequate field trial of the prospecting method involved and a reduction to practice of that method. The trial court therefore held that the two patents involved in the litigation were invalid and void and that there had been no infringement by National Lead (D). Rosaire (P) appealed.

ISSUE: May an invention be patentable if it was known or used by others in this country before the patentee's invention?

HOLDING AND DECISION: (Tuttle, J.) No. An invention is not patentable if it was known or used by others in this country before the patentee's invention. The lack of publication of Teplitz's work did not deprive the alleged infringer, National Lead (D), of the defense of prior use. The work was done openly and in the ordinary course of the activities of the employer, a large producing company in the oil industry, and therefore no further affirmative act was necessary to bring the work to the attention of the public at large. Affirmed.

▶ ANALYSIS

The non-secret use of a claimed process in the usual course of producing articles for commercial purposes is considered a public use. "Public" in this case would seem to mean "not secret." This expansive view has been criticized by some who would require that the invention be generally known or used before creating a statutory bar.

◼═◼

Quicknotes

INFRINGEMENT Conduct in violation of statute or that interferes with another's rights pursuant to the law.

PATENT A limited monopoly conferred on the invention or discovery of any new or useful machine or process that is novel and nonobvious.

REDUCTION TO PRACTICE An invention is not patentable if it was known or used by others in this country.

◼═◼

In re Hall

[Parties not identified.]

781 F.2d 897 (Fed. Cir. 1986).

NATURE OF CASE: Appeal from a decision of the U.S. Patent and Trademark Office's former Board of Appeals sustaining rejection of patent claims.

FACT SUMMARY: An application for a patent was rejected by the Patent Office because a dissertation on the same topic had already been published overseas.

🏛 RULE OF LAW
Once an invention is in the public domain, it is no longer patentable.

FACTS: Hall's application for a patent was rejected because a doctoral thesis was available as a "printed publication" more than one year prior to the application's effective date. Hall appealed, claiming that there was no evidence that the dissertation was properly indexed in the library catalog prior to the critical date and that, even if it were, the presence of a single catalogued thesis in one university library does not constitute sufficient accessibility of the publication's teachings to those interested in the art exercising reasonable diligence.

ISSUE: Once an invention is in the public domain, is it any longer patentable?

HOLDING AND DECISION: (Baldwin, J.) No. Once an invention is in the public domain, it is no longer patentable. In this case, the dissertation had an effective date as prior art more than one year prior to the filing date of Hall's initial application. Competent evidence of the general library practice may be relied upon to establish an approximate time when a thesis becomes accessible. The dissertation was indexed and placed in the main collection at Freiburg University in Germany. Affirmed.

▶ ANALYSIS

This case demonstrates the rule that a publication becomes public as of the date it becomes available to at least one member of the general public. Magazine articles become public as of the date of their publication (when they are available to the public), not when they are sent to the publisher. In this case the statutory bar involved 35 U.S.C. § 102(b) because the publication occurred more than one year before applicant Hall filed for the patent.

Quicknotes

PATENT A limited monopoly conferred on the invention or discovery of any new or useful machine or process that is novel and nonobvious.

PUBLIC DOMAIN Works that are not protected by copyright and are free for the public to utilize.

35 U.S.C. § 102(b) Makes claim unpatentable if it has been published more than a year prior to filing the claim.

Egbert v. Lippmann

[Parties not identified.]

104 U.S. 333 (1881).

NATURE OF CASE: Review of dismissal of infringement action, holding that a patent claim was invalid.

FACT SUMMARY: Lippmann (D) contended that the inventor's gift of his invention—a set of corset-springs—to his girlfriend, Egbert (P), constituted public use, thereby invalidating the patent.

🏛 RULE OF LAW
If an inventor, having made his device, gives or sells it to another, to be used by the donee or vendee, without limitation or restriction, or injunction of secrecy, and it is so used, such use is public, even though the use and knowledge of the use may be confined to one person.

FACTS: In 1855, Samuel Barnes gave a set of corset-springs he had created to his girlfriend, Egbert (P), who had complained that hers were always breaking. She wore the corset-springs for many years. She and Barnes later married. In 1866, after the principle of his design had become the standard in the industry, he applied for a patent. After he died, Egbert (P) sued Lippmann (D) for infringement of Egbert's (P) reissued letters-patent. Lippmann (D) successfully denied any infringement, claiming that the patented invention had, with the consent of Barnes, the inventor, been publicly used for more than two years prior to his application for the original letters. Egbert (P) appealed.

ISSUE: If an inventor, having made his device, gives or sells it to another, to be used by the donee or vendee, without limitation or restriction, or injunction of secrecy, and it is so used, is such use public, even though the use and knowledge of the use may be confined to one person?

HOLDING AND DECISION: (Woods, J.) Yes. If an inventor, having made his device, gives or sells it to another, to be used by the donee or vendee, without limitation or restriction, or injunction of secrecy, and it is so used, such use is public, even though the use and knowledge of the use may be confined to one person. In this case, the invention was completed and put to use in 1855. The inventor slept on his rights for eleven years before applying for a patent. In the meantime, the invention had found its way into general, and almost universal, use. The defense of two years' public use, by the consent and allowance of the inventor, before he made application for letters-patent, is satisfactorily established by the evidence. Affirmed.

DISSENT: (Miller, J.) A private use with consent, which could lead to no copy or reproduction of the machine, which taught the nature of the invention to no one but the party to whom such consent was given, which left

the public at large as ignorant of this as it was before the author's discovery, was no abandonment to the public, and did not defeat his claim for a patent.

▶ ANALYSIS

This case concerning a pair of corset-springs demonstrates the rule that inventions that by their nature are only capable of being used where they cannot be seen or observed are considered to be used by the public if the inventor allows them to be used without any restrictions. If an invention is being used only for purposes of testing, however, that is not considered a public use. It is irrelevant whether or not the use was open to public view.

Quicknotes

INFRINGEMENT Conduct in violation of statute or that interferes with another's rights pursuant to the law.

PATENT A limited monopoly conferred on the invention or discovery of any new or useful machine or process that is novel and nonobvious.

City of Elizabeth v. Pavement Company

City (D) v. Pavement company (P)

97 U.S. 126 (1877).

NATURE OF CASE: Review of award of damages and injunction in infringement action.

FACT SUMMARY: American Nicholson Pavement Company (P) sued the city of Elizabeth, N.J. (D) for infringement of a patent for a new and improved wooden pavement.

🏛 RULE OF LAW
The experimental use of an invention by the inventor himself, or by any person under his direction has never been regarded as a public use.

FACTS: Nicholson (P) had obtained a patent for a process of constructing a wooden pavement and claimed that the city of Elizabeth, N.J. (D) had infringed his patent. The city of Elizabeth (D) claimed that the alleged invention of Nicholson (P) has been in public use, with his consent and allowance, for six years on an avenue in Boston before he applied for a patent and contended that said use constituted an abandonment of the pretended invention. Nicholson (P) countered that the pavement in Boston was 75 feet in length and constructed at his own expense to ascertain its durability, and therefore did not constitute abandonment by public use, the lower courts agreed, and the United States Supreme Court granted certiorari.

ISSUE: Has the experimental use of an invention by the inventor himself, or by any person under his direction ever been regarded as a public use?

HOLDING AND DECISION: (Bradley, J.) No. The experimental use of an invention by the inventor himself, or by any person under his direction has never been regarded as a public use. Here, Nicholson (P) merely intended the piece of pavement as an experiment, to test its usefulness and durability. So long as he did not voluntarily allow others to make it or use it, and so long as it was not on sale for general use, Nicholson (P) kept the invention under his own control and did not lose his title to a patent. Since Nicholson (P) kept the invention under his own eyes and never abandoned his intent to obtain a patent for it, it was still an experimental use and not a public one. The patent is valid. Affirmed.

▶ ANALYSIS

An abandonment of an invention to the public may be evinced by the conduct of the inventor at any time. If the invention is in public use or on sale, with the inventor's consent, at any time within one year (two years when the decision in the above case was handed down) before his application for a patent, it will be conclusive evidence of abandonment. The good faith of the inventor in experimenting or testing his invention is critical in such cases.

■■■

Quicknotes

INFRINGEMENT Conduct in violation of statute or that interferes with another's rights pursuant to the law.

PATENT A limited monopoly conferred on the invention or discovery of any new or useful machine or process that is novel and nonobvious.

■■■

Griffith v. Kanamaru

Patent applicant (P) v. Patent holder (D)

816 F.2d 624 (Fed. Cir. 1987).

NATURE OF CASE: Appeal from decision of the Board of Patent Appeals and Interferences denying priority to an inventor's patent claim.

FACT SUMMARY: Griffith (P) claimed to have priority over Kanamaru's (D) patent application, but the Board found that he had not established reasonable diligence in completing the reduction to practice of the invention.

🏛 RULE OF LAW
When evaluating excuses for inactivity in reduction to practice, courts may consider the reasonable everyday problems and limitations encountered by an inventor.

FACTS: Griffith (P), a Cornell University professor, applied for a patent on an aminocarnitine compound useful in the treatment of diabetes. He established conception of the invention by June 30, 1981, and a reduction to practice on January 11, 1984. Kanamaru (D) filed for a U.S. patent on the same compound on November 17, 1982. The Board of Patent Appeals and Interferences decided that Griffith (P) had failed to establish a prima facie case that he was entitled to an award of priority against the filing date of Kanamaru (D) for a patent. Griffith (P) claimed that the delay in reduction to practice was justified because he had to secure outside funding for the project as required by Cornell and he was waiting for a certain graduate student to matriculate so she could assist with the project. The Board concluded that Griffith's (P) explanation for his inactivity failed to provide a legally sufficient excuse to satisfy the "reasonable diligence" requirement of 35 U.S.C. § 102(g). Griffith (P) appealed on the issue of reasonable diligence.

ISSUE: When evaluating excuses for inactivity in reduction to practice, may courts consider the reasonable everyday problems and limitations encountered by an inventor?

HOLDING AND DECISION: (Nichols, J.) Yes. When evaluating excuses for inactivity in reduction to practice, courts may consider the reasonable everyday problems and limitations encountered by an inventor. But Griffith's (P) excuse sounded more in the nature of commercial development, which is not accepted as an excuse for delay, than in the nature of a "hardship" case. Delays in reduction to practice caused by an inventor's efforts to refine an invention to the most marketable and profitable form are not sufficient causes for inactivity. Griffith (P) was burdened with establishing a prima facie case of reasonable diligence from immediately before Kanamaru's (D)

filing date until Griffith's (P) reduction to practice. Waiting for outside funding or for the new semester to begin are not sufficient excuses for delay. It seems evident that Cornell consciously chose to assume the risk that priority in the invention might be lost to an outside inventor. Griffith (P) failed to establish a prima facie case of reasonable diligence or a legally sufficient excuse for inactivity to establish priority over Kanamaru (D). Affirmed.

▶ ANALYSIS

Note that the Board relied exclusively on Kanamaru's (D) filing date as the date that the Japanese inventor conceived and reduced his invention to practice. That is because this case was decided in 1987 and, at that time, foreign inventors could not introduce evidence of foreign conception and reduction to practice. In 1994, as part of the legislative package implementing the Trade Related Aspects of Intellectual Property (TRIPs) portion of the Uruguay Round negotiations, Congress changed 35 U.S.C. § 104 to permit such evidence. The Patent Office formerly collapsed the entire sequence of events leading to the foreign invention into the single date of the patent filing.

■━■

Quicknotes

REDUCTION TO PRACTICE The method of determining priority of patentability by assessing when the inventor's conception is rendered capable of use.

35 USC § 102(g) Establishes the guidelines for determining the priority of conflicting claims.

■━■

Graham v. John Deere Co.

Inventor (P) v. Tractor company (D)

383 U.S. 1 (1966).

NATURE OF CASE: Review of denial of patent application.

FACT SUMMARY: Graham (P) submitted for a patent a plow accessory that was an extension of the state-of-the-art design.

🏛 RULE OF LAW
A device that is an obvious extension of the state of the art for that type of device is not patentable.

FACTS: Graham (P) submitted for patenting a plow chisel that, because of its flexible nature, supposedly had certain advantages when used in certain types of soil. The Patent Office denied the patent application, finding the design a mere extension of the state of the art, and an obvious improvement on existing technology. The court of appeals affirmed, and the United States Supreme Court granted review.

ISSUE: Is a device that is an obvious extension of the state of the art for that type of device patentable?

HOLDING AND DECISION: (Clark, J.) No. A device that is an extension of the state of art for that type of device is not patentable. Section 103 of the Patent Act, enacted in 1952, mandates nonpatentability in the case of designs that would be obvious to a person having ordinary skill in the field related to the design in question. This section appears to be a codification of the long-standing judicial requirement that a device, to be patentable, must be the result of something more than the ordinary skill found in the field. Rather, a higher level of ingenuity is required. The work, in short, must be the product of an inventor, not a skillful mechanic. Here, the Patent Office found that the chisel in question did not represent a leap forward in design technology but rather was a logical improvement in design that could have been designed by anyone skilled in the field. This finding, not clearly erroneous, leads to the result that, under § 103 of the Patent Act, the chisel was not patentable. Affirmed.

▶ ANALYSIS

The enactment of § 103 constituted the first statutory addition of an element of patentability since the beginning of the republic. The 1790 Patent Act instituted the dual requirements of novelty and utility. These two requirements remained the cornerstones of patent law until the addition of § 103. Arguments were made that § 103 was an attempt to relax the judicially-imposed requirement of greater-than-ordinary skill in a device's creation, but the Court held the section to be a codification of the rule.

Quicknotes

PATENT ACT § 103 Makes an extension of prior art unpatentable if it would have been obvious to a person of skill.

PUBLIC DOMAIN Works that are not protected by copyright and are free for the public to utilize.

35 U.S.C. § 103 Disallows patents if the invention in the subject matter would have been obvious to a person based on prior inventions.

KSR International Co. v. Teleflex, Inc.

Alleged infringer (D) v. Patent license holder (P)

550 U.S. 398 (2007).

NATURE OF CASE: Writ of certiorari to resolve obviousness issue in patent infringement case.

FACT SUMMARY: Teleflex, Inc. (P) sued KSR International Co. (KSR) (D) for patent infringement based on an electronic sensor addition to an existing KSR (D) pedal design. KSR (D) argued the addition was obvious, so Teleflex's (P) patent claim was invalid.

> 🏛 **RULE OF LAW**
> In determining the obviousness of a patent claim, the courts must consider the prior art, the differences between the prior art and the subject matter of the claim, and the level of ordinary skill a person must have in the subject matter of the claim before considering secondary factors and the test for teaching, suggestion, or motivation of the patentee.

FACTS: Teleflex, Inc. (P) held the exclusive license to the patent entitled "Adjustable Pedal Assembly with Electronic Throttle Control." One claim of the patent involved the addition of an electronic sensor to the pedal that then transmitted information to the computer controlling the engine's throttle. KSR International Co. (KSR) (D) added an electronic sensor to its existing pedal design. Teleflex (P) sued KSR (D) for patent infringement. KSR (D) argued the Teleflex (P) claim was invalid under 35 U.S.C. § 103 because the addition of the electronic sensor was obvious. The district court granted summary judgment to KSR (D) and Teleflex (P) appealed. The court of appeals applied the "teaching, suggestion, or motivation" (TSM) test and reversed. KSR (D) filed for a writ of certiorari, which the United States Supreme Court granted to address the obviousness analysis.

ISSUE: In determining the obviousness of a patent claim, must the courts consider the prior art, the differences between the prior art and the subject matter of the claim, and the level of ordinary skill a person must have in the subject matter of the claim before considering secondary factors and the test for teaching, suggestion, or motivation of the patentee?

HOLDING AND DECISION: (Kennedy, J.) Yes. In determining the obviousness of a patent claim, the courts must consider the prior art, the differences between the prior art and the subject matter of the claim, and the level of ordinary skill a person must have in the subject matter of the claim before considering secondary factors and the test for teaching, suggestion, or motivation of the patentee. 35 U.S.C. § 103 prohibits issuance of a patent when the subject matter as a whole is obvious to a person with ordinary skill in the art to which the subject matter

pertains. [The Court reviewed the prior art of pedal and sensor technology.] The U.S. Patent and Trademark Office (PTO) rejected a prior patent application for a pedal technology that, unlike the Teleflex (P) licensed patent at issue, did not involve a fixed pivot point because the technology was "obvious." The Teleflex (P) licensed patent was granted because of the limitation of the fixed pivot point. The district court considered the prior art, examined the differences between the patent claim and the prior art, and then found the skill level to be that of a mechanical engineer familiar with pedal designs. The district court found little difference between the prior art and the patent claim and no secondary factors sufficient to overcome the obviousness. The district court then had to apply the TSM test and found KSR (D) satisfied it because the industry inevitably led to the combination of electronic sensors and adjustable pedals plus the prior art suggested the combination. The court of appeals reversed on the ground that the district court was not strictly applying the TSM test. The appellate court looked at the purpose of the two pedal designs and found them to be different. The appellate court also held that "obvious to try" the pedal and sensor combination did not rise to the level of obviousness. This Court's precedents reflect a broader, more general inquiry into obviousness. The TSM test encourages the PTO to consider the reason a person of ordinary skill in the field combined two known elements in such a way to result in a potentially new patent subject matter. The general principle of the TSM test, however, cannot be applied rigidly. The appellate court cannot consider solely the motivation for the joining of two known elements because the joining may have been obvious to the patentee but that does not make the claim obvious under § 103. The appellate court also wrongly asserted that a person of ordinary skill might not put known elements together in a new fashion even when those elements were designed to individually accomplish a specific, alternate purpose. Finally, the appellate court erred in stating "obvious to try" was not "obvious" because sometimes it might rise to that level if a known problem has a finite number of solutions. In consideration of the facts here, the patent claim does rise to the level of obviousness. [The Court considered the prior art and differences between the claims]. The district court carefully and appropriately applied this Court's precedent and the statutory elements of § 103 when determining the patent claim was obvious and thus invalid. The court of appeals erred in applying too rigid a TSM test. Reversed and remanded.

Continued on next page.

▶ *ANALYSIS*

The Supreme Court ignored the federal circuit's well-established precedent applying the TSM test although it retained the *Graham v. John Deere Co.,* 383 U.S. 1 (1966), elements for applying § 103 to a patent application. The impact of the decision, however, may be felt more by electrical and mechanical patent applicants than other applicants. The examiners can review the individual electrical/mechanical parts of the prior art to determine if the new claim would have been an obvious result even if it had not been accomplished previously.

■══■

Quicknotes

PRIOR ART Any prior knowledge or activity regarding a particular invention that may be considered by the Patent and Trademark Office in granting or denying a patent application or by the court in determining a patent infringement action.

35 U.S.C. § 103 Denies patent if the invention of the subject matter would have been obvious to a person based on prior inventions.

■══■

In re Kubin

[Parties not identified.]

561 F.3d 1351 (Fed. Cir. 2009).

NATURE OF CASE: Appeal from rejection of patent claims as obvious under 35 U.S.C. § 103.

FACT SUMMARY: Kubin and Goodwin claimed a patent on the isolation and sequencing of DNA molecules encoding a protein known as the Natural Killer Cell Activation Inducing Ligand (NAIL). The Board of Patent Appeals and Interferences (the Board) rejected their claim as obvious, finding that the claim was the product not of innovation but of ordinary skill and common sense, so that NAIL cDNA was not patentable as it would have been obvious to isolate it.

RULE OF LAW

A patent claim will be denied for obviousness where the prior art would lead a skilled artisan to seek the claimed invention, with every reasonable expectation of success in achieving it through conventional methodologies, thereby rendering the claim "obvious to try."

FACTS: Kubin and Goodwin claimed a patent on the isolation and sequencing of DNA molecules encoding a protein known as the Natural Killer Cell Activation Inducing Ligand (NAIL). NAIL is a specific receptor protein on the cell surface that plays a role in activating Natural Killer (NK) cells. They also claimed the discovery of a binding relationship between NAIL and a protein known as CD48. Thus, they claimed a genus of isolated polynucleotides encoding a protein that binds CD48 and is at least 80 percent identical to amino acids 22-221 of SEQ ID NO: 2—the disclosed amino acid sequence for the CD48-binding region of NAIL. Their specification also disclosed SEQ ID NO: 1, which recited the specific coding sequence of NAIL, and SEQ ID NO: 3, which recited the full NAIL gene. The specification also contemplated variants of NAIL that retained the same binding properties. The Board of Patent Appeals and Interferences (the Board) rejected the claims as obvious under 35 U.S.C. § 103, based on the teachings of U.S. Patent No. 5,688,690 (Valiante) and 2 Joseph Sambrook et al., Molecular Cloning: A Laboratory Manual 43-84 (2d ed. 1989) (Sambrook). Valiante disclosed a receptor protein called "p38" that is found on the surface of human NK cells. Valiante taught that the p38 receptor is present on virtually all human NK cells and also disclosed and claimed a monoclonal antibody specific for p38 called "mAB C1.7." The Board found that Valiante's p38 protein was the same protein as NAIL. A monoclonal antibody is an antibody that is mass produced in the laboratory from a single clone and that recognizes only one antigen. Monoclonal antibodies are useful as

probes for specifically identifying and targeting a particular kind of cell. Valiante also taught that "[t]he DNA and protein sequences for the receptor p38 may be obtained by resort to conventional methodologies known to one of skill in the art." Valiante further described a five-step cloning protocol for "isolating and identifying the p38 receptor," but did not disclose either the amino acid sequence of p38 recognized by mAb C1.7 or the polynucleotide sequence that encodes p38. Sambrook described methods for molecular cloning in general. The Board found that Kubin and Goodwin used conventional techniques described by Sambrook to isolate and sequence the gene that codes for NAIL, and also found that their claimed DNA sequence was "isolated from a cDNA library . . . using the commercial monoclonal antibody C1.7 . . . disclosed by Valiante." Regarding SEQ ID NO: 2, the Board found that Valiante's patent provided a reasonable expectation of success in obtaining a polynucleotide encoding p38, which was within the scope of the Kubin and Goodwin claim. Because of NAIL's important role in the human immune response, the Board further found that "one of ordinary skill in the art would have recognized the value of isolating NAIL cDNA, and would have been motivated to apply conventional methodologies, such as those disclosed in Sambrook and utilized in Valiante, to do so." Kubin and Goodwin appealed and the court of appeals granted review.

ISSUE: Will a patent claim be denied for obviousness where the prior art would lead a skilled artisan to seek the claimed invention, with every reasonable expectation of success in achieving it through conventional methodologies, thereby rendering the claim "obvious to try"?

HOLDING AND DECISION: (Rader, J.) Yes. A patent claim will be denied for obviousness where the prior art would lead a skilled artisan to seek the claimed invention, with every reasonable expectation of success in achieving it through conventional methodologies, thereby rendering the claim "obvious to try." First, there was ample evidence that Kubin and Goodwin used conventional techniques, as taught in Valiante and Sambrook, to isolate the NAIL gene sequence. Their arguments to the contrary are belied by their own disclosure to the extent that they disclose that the gene sequence can be derived and isolated by "standard biochemical methods." Their argument that other prior art, found in Mathew, teaches away from Valiante, also was properly rejected by the Board, since Mathew's disclosure, in light of Valiante's teachings regard-

Continued on next page.

ing the p38 protein and its role in NK cell activation, would have aroused a skilled artisan's curiosity to isolate the gene coding for p38. In fact, Mathew "exemplifies how the cDNA encoding 2B4, the mouse version of Valiante's p38, can be isolated and sequenced." Although this court previously held in *In re Deuel*, 51 F.3d 1552 (Fed. Cir. 1995) that "knowledge of a protein does not give one a conception of a particular DNA encoding it," and that "obvious to try" is an inappropriate test for obviousness, these aspects of *Deuel* were overturned by the United States Supreme Court in *KSR Int'l Co. v. Teleflex Inc.*, 550 U.S. 398 (2007). The Court repudiated as "error" the *Deuel* restriction on the ability of a skilled artisan to combine elements within the scope of the prior art, ruling that when there is a design need or market pressure to solve a problem and there are a finite number of identified, predictable solutions, a person of ordinary skill has good reason to pursue the known options within his or her technical grasp, and that if this leads to the anticipated success, the fact that a combination was obvious to try might show that it was obvious under § 103. This ruling, however, gives rise to two exceptions to the "obvious to try" test. The first is that, where a claimant merely throws metaphorical darts at a board filled with combinatorial prior art possibilities, courts should not succumb to hindsight claims of obviousness. The second is where what was "obvious to try" was to explore a new technology or general approach that seemed to be a promising field of experimentation, where the prior art gave only general guidance as to the particular form of the claimed invention or how to achieve it. Here, the claimed invention does not come within either of these exceptions. The record shows that the prior art teaches a protein of interest, a motivation to isolate the gene coding for that protein, and illustrative instructions to use a monoclonal antibody specific to the protein for cloning this gene. Therefore, the claimed invention is "the product not of innovation but of ordinary skill and common sense." In other words, the record shows that a skilled artisan would have had a resoundingly "reasonable expectation of success" in deriving the claimed invention in light of the teachings of the prior art. Moreover, *KSR* applies not only to the predictable arts, but also to the unpredictable arts, such as biotechnology, which is the art at issue here. One of skill in advanced art of biotechnology would find Kubin and Goodwin's claimed "results" profoundly "predictable" given the well-known and reliable nature of the cloning and sequencing techniques in the prior art, as well as the readily knowable and obtainable structure of an identified protein. The ease and predictability of cloning the gene that codes for that protein cannot be ignored as irrelevant to the question of obviousness. "This court cannot, in the face of *KSR*, cling to formalistic rules for obviousness, customize its legal tests for specific scientific fields in ways that deem entire classes of prior art teachings irrelevant, or discount the significant abilities of artisans of ordinary skill in an advanced area of art." Although Valiante did not explicitly supply an amino acid sequence for NAIL or a polynucleotide sequence for the NAIL gene, Kubin and Goodwin's disclosure, which therefore represents a minor advance in the art, cannot be given patent protection because it is an advance without innovation. To give their minor advance such protection would stifle, rather than promote, progress in the useful arts. Their claimed invention was reasonably expected in light of the prior art and "obvious to try." Affirmed.

▶ *ANALYSIS*

This important decision for the biotechnology field makes clear that the level of enablement of the prior art is very important to any obviousness conclusion, and revives the "obvious to try" test. However, it does not hold that an invention that was "obvious to try" is necessarily obvious under Section 103(a). Going forward, as the court itself observes, the question relating to obvious to try situations will be, "when is an invention that was obvious to try nevertheless nonobvious?" (quoting *In re O'Farrell*, 853 F.2d 894 (Fed. Cir. 1988)). *Kubin* does not mean that any patent claiming a cDNA is necessarily obvious if the encoded protein was known in the prior art. It simply means that one can no longer presume that the cDNA is never rendered obvious under those circumstances. Rather, the inquiry becomes whether there was any kind of suggestion or motivation to clone the cDNA, and if there was, whether there was a reasonable expectation of success.

Quicknotes

PATENT A limited monopoly conferred on the invention or discovery of any new or useful machine or process that is novel and nonobvious.

PRIOR ART Any prior knowledge or activity regarding a particular invention that may be considered by the Patent and Trademark Office in granting or denying a patent application or by the court in determining a patent infringement action.

Phillips v. AWH Corporation

Patent holder (P) v. Alleged infringer (D)

415 F.3d 1303 (Fed. Cir. 2005) (en banc).

NATURE OF CASE: En banc rehearing of appeal from summary judgment order of patent non-infringement.

FACT SUMMARY: Phillips (P), who sued AWH Corp. (D) for patent infringement, contended that the term "baffles" in claim 1 of his patented invention (the '798 patent) was not used in a restrictive manner so as to exclude structures that extend at a 90-degree angle from walls, and that the term should be given its plain meaning, rather than limiting the term to corresponding structures disclosed in the patent's specification, or their equivalents.

> ### 🏛 RULE OF LAW
> A term in a claim of a patented invention should not be restricted to corresponding structures disclosed in the specification, or their equivalents, where the term's plain meaning can be given effect without such limitation.

FACTS: Phillips (P) invented, and obtained a patent on, modular, steel-shell panels that could be welded together to form vandalism-resistant walls. Phillips (P) brought a patent infringement action against AWH Corp. (AWH) (D). Claim 1 of his patent (the '798 patent) stated: "further means disposed inside the shell for increasing its load bearing capacity comprising internal steel baffles extending inwardly from the steel shell walls." The district court found that the allegedly infringing product did not contain "baffles" as that term was used in claim 1, and, therefore, granted summary judgment of noninfringement. On appeal, the original court of appeals panel concluded that the patent used the term "baffles" in a restrictive manner so as to exclude structures that extend at a 90-degree angle from the walls. That panel noted that the specification repeatedly referred to the ability of the claimed baffles to deflect projectiles and that it described the baffles as being "disposed at such angles that bullets which might penetrate the outer steel panels are deflected." The panel also noted that the patent nowhere disclosed a right-angle baffle, and that baffles oriented at 90 degrees to the wall were found in the prior art. The panel added that the patent specification "is intended to support and inform the claims, and here it makes it unmistakably clear that the invention involves baffles angled at other than 90 [degrees]." The dissenting judge argued that the panel had improperly limited the claims to the particular embodiment of the invention disclosed in the specification, rather than adopting the "plain meaning" of the term "baffles." The court of appeals agreed to rehear the appeal en banc.

ISSUE: Should a term in a claim of a patented invention be restricted to corresponding structures disclosed in the specification, or their equivalents, where the term's plain meaning can be given effect without such limitation?

HOLDING AND DECISION: (Bryson, J.) No. A term in a claim of a patented invention should not be restricted to corresponding structures disclosed in the specification, or their equivalents, where the term's plain meaning can be given effect without such limitation. The issue of claim interpretation is framed by § 112 of the Patent Act (35 U.S.C. § 112). The second paragraph of that section directs the court to look to the language of the claims to determine what "the applicant regards as his invention." On the other hand, the first paragraph requires that the specification describe the invention set forth in the claims. The principal question presented, therefore, is the extent to which the court should resort to and rely on a patent's specification in seeking to ascertain the proper scope of its claims. First, it is a "bedrock principle" of patent law that "the claims of a patent define the invention to which the patentee is entitled the right to exclude." In addition, the words of a claim are given their ordinary and customary meaning, which is the meaning that the term would have to a person of ordinary skill in the art in question at the time of the invention. Importantly, the person of ordinary skill in the art is deemed to read the claim term not only in the context of the particular claim in which the disputed term appears, but in the context of the entire patent, including the specification. Where the ordinary meaning of claim language is readily apparent even to lay judges, general application dictionaries may be helpful. However, where such meaning is not apparent, the court must look to those sources available to the public that show what a person of skill in the art would have understood disputed claim language to mean. Those sources include the words of the claims themselves, the remainder of the specification, the prosecution history, and extrinsic evidence concerning relevant scientific principles, the meaning of technical terms, and the state of the art. Claims must be read in view of the specifications of which they are a part. Extrinsic evidence may comprise technical dictionaries and experts. However, an approach of claim language construction that places greater emphasis on technical dictionaries and encyclopedias than on the specification and prosecution history is inconsistent with rulings that the specification is the single best guide to the meaning of a disputed term and that the specification acts as a dictionary when it expressly defines terms used in the

Continued on next page.

claims or when it defines terms by implication. The main problem with elevating the dictionary to such prominence is that it focuses the inquiry on the abstract meaning of words rather than on the meaning of claim terms within the context of the patent. Properly viewed, the "ordinary meaning" of a claim term is its meaning to the ordinary artisan after reading the entire patent. The problem is that if the district court starts with the broad dictionary definition in every case and fails to fully appreciate how the specification implicitly limits that definition, the error will systematically cause the construction of the claim to be unduly expansive. The risk of systematic overbreadth is greatly reduced if the court focuses at the outset on how the patentee used the claim term in the claims, specification, and prosecution history, rather than starting with a broad definition and whittling it down. In cases in which it will be hard to determine whether a person of skill in the art would understand the embodiments to define the outer limits of the claim term or merely to be exemplary in nature, attempting to resolve that problem in the context of the particular patent is likely to capture the scope of the actual invention more accurately than either strictly limiting the scope of the claims to the embodiments disclosed in the specification or divorcing the claim language from the specification. Applying these principles, it is clear from claim 1 that the baffles must be made of steel, must be a part of the load-bearing means for the wall section, and must be pointed inward from the walls. Both parties stipulate that "baffles" refers to objects that check, impede, or obstruct the flow of something. The other claims of the '798 patent and the specification support the conclusion that persons of ordinary skill in the art would understand the baffles recited in the patent to be load-bearing objects that serve to check, impede, or obstruct flow. At several points, the specification discusses positioning the baffles so as to deflect projectiles. While the patent makes clear the invention envisions baffles that serve that function, it does not imply that in order to qualify as baffles within the meaning of the claims, the internal support structures must serve the projectile-deflecting function in all the embodiments of all the claims. The specification discusses several other purposes served by the baffles, e.g., providing structural support. The specification also provides for "overlapping and interlocking the baffles to produce substantially an intermediate barrier wall between the opposite [wall] faces" to create insulation compartments. The fact that the written description of the '798 patent sets forth multiple objectives to be served by the baffles recited in the claims confirms that the term "baffles" should not be read restrictively to require that the baffles in each case serve all of the recited functions. Here, although deflecting projectiles is one of the advantages of the baffles, the patent does not require that the inward extending structures always be capable of performing that function. Accordingly, a person of skill in the art would not interpret the disclosure and claims of the '798 patent to mean that a structure extending inward from one of the wall faces is a "baffle" if it is at an acute or obtuse angle, but is not a "baffle" if it is disposed at a right angle. Remanded.

DISSENT: (Mayer, J.) It is futile to conceive of claim construction as a matter of law devoid of any factual components. Instead, claim construction is, or should be, made in context: a claim should be interpreted both from the perspective of one of ordinary skill in the art and in view of the state of the art at the time of invention. These questions, which are critical to the correct interpretation of a claim, are inherently factual. They are hotly contested by the parties, not by resort to case law as one would expect for legal issues, but based on testimony and documentary evidence. Otherwise, by attempting to arrive at a conclusion from a purely legal view in the court of appeals, as the majority has done, and by not deferring to the district court's factual findings, "there is no reason why litigants should be required to parade their evidence before the district courts or for district courts to waste time and resources evaluating such evidence."

ANALYSIS

The effect of this case has been to limit exclusive reliance on dictionaries as an "objective" and presumptive source for meanings of claim terms. After *Phillips,* courts may still use dictionaries in conjunction with the specification, especially where there is no intrinsic evidence in the specification as to a term's specialized meaning, but the specification must be referenced to the extent possible.

■—■

Quicknotes

INFRINGEMENT Conduct in violation of statute or that interferes with another's rights pursuant to law.

PATENT A limited monopoly conferred on the invention or discovery of any new or useful machine or process that is novel and nonobvious.

SUMMARY JUDGMENT Judgment rendered by a court in response to a motion by one of the parties, claiming that the lack of a question of material fact in respect to an issue warrants disposition of the issue without consideration by the jury.

35 U.S.C. § 112 Requires that patent applicants disclose how to make and use the invention and include a written description.

■—■

Larami Corp. v. Amron

Toy manufacturer (P) v. Competitor (D)

27 U.S.P.Q.2d 1280 (E.D. Pa. 1993).

NATURE OF CASE: Motion for partial summary judgment of noninfringement of a patent in favor of the plaintiff.

FACT SUMMARY: Amron (D), a manufacturer of toy water guns, claimed that Larami Corp. (P), another manufacturer, had infringed on its patent.

🏛 RULE OF LAW
Literal infringement of a patent cannot be proved if the accused product is missing even a single element of the claim.

FACTS: Larami Corp. (P) manufactured toy water guns and held patents for four different models of toy guns. Amron (D) claimed that Larami's (P) guns infringed on a patent it held for toy water guns that included light and noise components. Claiming that there was no literal infringement nor any substantial equivalence of all the elements in the other patents, Larami (P) moved for partial summary judgment of noninfringement of Amron's (D) patent and for partial summary judgment on Amron's (D) counterclaim for infringement of its patent.

ISSUE: Does the absence of even one element of a patent's claim from the accused product mean there can be no finding of literal infringement?

HOLDING AND DECISION: (Reed, J.) Yes. Literal infringement of a patent cannot be proved if the accused product is missing even a single element of the claim. Additionally, in order to show infringement under the doctrine of equivalents, the patent owner must prove that the accused product has the "substantial equivalent" of every limitation or element of a patent claim. In patent cases, summary judgment is appropriate where the accused product does not literally infringe the patent and where the patent owner does not muster evidence that is sufficient to satisfy the legal standard for infringement under the doctrine of equivalents. Since Larami's (P) toy water pistol uses an external, detachable water reservoir that was found to be a dramatic improvement over the traditional design, it could not be held to be substantially equivalent to Amron's (D) claim in its patent. Motion granted.

▶ ANALYSIS

A patent owner's right to exclude others from making, using or selling the patented invention is defined and limited by the language in that patent's claims. Thus, in this case, the court was limited to interpreting the actual words used to describe the toy guns. Claim interpretation is a question of law for the court to decide.

Quicknotes

INFRINGEMENT Conduct in violation of statute or that interferes with another's rights pursuant to law.

PATENT A limited monopoly conferred on the invention or discovery of any new or useful machine or process that is novel and nonobvious.

SUMMARY JUDGMENT Judgment rendered by a court in response to a motion by one of the parties, claiming that the lack of a question of material fact in respect to an issue warrants disposition of the issue without consideration by the jury.

Festo Corp. v. Shoketsu Kinzoku Kogyo Kabushiki Co., Ltd.

Manufacturer (P) v. Competitor (D)

535 U.S. 722 (2002).

NATURE OF CASE: Appeal from decision holding that prosecution history estoppel precluded petitioner from asserting that accused device infringed its patents under the doctrine of equivalents.

FACT SUMMARY: Festo Corporation (P), which was the holder of two patents relating to magnetic rodless cylinders, sued Shoketsu Kinzoku Kogyo Kabushiki Co., Ltd. (Kabushiki) (D), a competitor, for infringement. The federal district court held for plaintiff, and Kabushiki (D) appealed. The court of appeals affirmed. On grant of writ of certiorari, the United States Supreme Court vacated and remanded. On remand, the court of appeals initially affirmed in part, vacated in part, and remanded, but on rehearing en banc reversed. The United States Supreme Court granted certiorari.

🏛 RULE OF LAW
Narrowing a claim to obtain a patent does not cause the patentee to surrender all equivalents to the amended claim element.

FACTS: Festo Corporation (P) owned two patents for an industrial device. When the patent examiner rejected the initial application for the first patent because of defects in description, the application was amended to add the new limitations that the device would contain a pair of one-way sealing rings and that its outer sleeve would be made of a magnetizable material. The second patent was also amended during a reexamination proceeding to add the sealing rings limitation. After Festo (P) began selling its device, Shoketsu Kinzoku Kogyo Kabushiki Co., Ltd. (Kabushiki) (D) entered the market with a similar device that uses one two-way sealing ring and a nonmagnetizable sleeve. Festo (P) filed suit, claiming that Kabushiki's (D) device was so similar that it infringed Festo's (P) patents under the doctrine of equivalents. The district court ruled for Festo (P), rejecting Kabushiki's (D) argument that the prosecution history estopped Festo (P) from saying that Kabushiki's (D) device was equivalent. The en banc federal circuit, reversing, held that prosecution history estoppel applied, noting that estoppel arises from any amendment that narrows a claim to comply with the Patent Act, not only from amendments made to avoid the prior art, as the district court had originally held. The federal circuit also held that, when estoppel applies, it bars any claim of equivalence for the element that was amended. Festo (P) appealed.

ISSUE: Does narrowing a claim to obtain a patent cause the patentee to surrender all equivalents to the amended claim element?

HOLDING AND DECISION: (Kennedy, J.) No. Prosecution history estoppel may apply to any claim amendment made to satisfy the Patent Act's requirements, not just to amendments made to avoid the prior art, but estoppel need not bar suit against every equivalent to the amended claim element. A patent holder's temporary monopoly is a property right, and the scope of the patent is not limited to its literal terms but instead embraces all equivalents to the claims described. As in this case, whether the amendment of a patent claim in response to an examiner objection bars a subsequent infringement claim based on the doctrine of equivalents requires an examination of the nature of the subject matter surrendered by the narrowing amendment. Furthermore, prosecution history estoppel requires that claims of patent be interpreted in light of the proceedings in the patent office during the application process. The circuit court erred in holding that when estoppel applies, it bars any claim of equivalence for the element that was amended. To the contrary, (1) prosecution history estoppel may apply to any claim amendment made to satisfy the Patent Act's requirements; (2) amendment is not an absolute bar to a claim of infringement under the doctrine of equivalents; and (3) the patentee has the burden of proving that amendment did not surrender the particular equivalent in question. Vacated and remanded.

▶ ANALYSIS

The Supreme Court noted that estoppel arises from any amendment that narrows a claim to comply with the Patent Act, not only from amendments made to avoid the prior art, as the district court had originally held.

Quicknotes

DOCTRINE OF EQUIVALENTS Rule that two inventions are the same for purposes of patent infringement if they achieve essentially the same result in the same manner despite trivial differences.

ESTOPPEL An equitable doctrine precluding a party from asserting a right to the detriment of another who justifiably relied on the conduct.

INFRINGEMENT Conduct in violation of statute or that interferes with another's rights pursuant to law.

PATENT A limited monopoly conferred on the invention or discovery of any new or useful machine or process that is novel and nonobvious.

Johnson & Johnston Associates Inc. v. R.E. Service Co., Inc.

Manufacturer (P) v. Competitor (D)

285 F.3d 1046 (Fed. Cir. 2002) (en banc).

NATURE OF CASE: Appeal of patent infringement case under the doctrine of equivalents.

FACT SUMMARY: Patentee Johnson & Johnston Associates, Inc. (P) sued competitor R.E. Service Co., Inc. (D) for patent infringement of aluminum/steel substrates used in the manufacture of circuit boards.

> ## 🏛 RULE OF LAW
> In a patent specification, under the doctrine of equivalents, there is no access to any subject matter that is disclosed but not claimed.

FACTS: The patent at issue, No. 5,153,050 ('050), relates to the manufacture of printed circuit boards. Johnson & Johnston Associates, Inc. (Johnston) (P) asserted its '050 patent against R.E. Services Co., Inc. (RES) (D), under the doctrine of equivalents and a jury found for Johnston (P). The '050 patent relates to the manufacture of printed circuit boards that are composed of very thin sheets of conductive copper foil pressed together in a press and heated to a point where a nonconductive resin bonds the sheets. Human workers participate in the process by manually handling the copper sheets during the layering process. The '050 patent prevents damage to the completed sheets by adhering aluminum substrates to the copper foils, as such aluminum substrates allow safe human handling during assembly. RES (D) manufactures steel substrates in the same process and argues that Johnston's (P) '050 patent relates only to aluminum substrates and not to steel substrates.

ISSUE: Can a patentee apply the doctrine of equivalents to cover subject matter that was disclosed but not claimed in the specification?

HOLDING AND DECISION: (Per curiam) No. A patentee may not apply the doctrine of equivalents to cover subject matter that is disclosed but not claimed in the specification. The claim requirement presupposes that a patent applicant defines the invention in the claims, not in the specification, since the claims provide the measure of a patentee's right to exclude infringement. Therefore, infringement law compares the accused infringing product with the claims as construed by a court. When a patent drafter discloses but fails to claim subject matter, as here, the unclaimed subject matter is dedicated to the public. Furthermore, a patentee cannot narrowly claim an invention, and then after patent issuance, use the doctrine of equivalents to establish infringement because the specification discloses equivalents. Johnston's (P) patent '050 specifically limits the claims to sheets of aluminum, but it does state that other metals, including stainless steel or

nickel alloys, may be used. Having disclosed the steel substrates but not claimed them, Johnston (P) cannot now utilize the doctrine of equivalents to extend the aluminum limitation to encompass steel substrates. A patentee who inadvertently fails to claim disclosed subject matter does have a remedy: within two years from the original patent grant, a patentee may file a reissue application to attempt to enlarge the scope of the original claims to include the unclaimed subject matter. Additionally, a patentee can file a separate application that claims the disclosed subject matter, which is what Johnston (P) actually did. Nevertheless, the district court erred as a matter of law in concluding RES (D) infringed the '050 patent under the doctrine of equivalents by using a steel substrate. Therefore, judgment of infringement is reversed.

CONCURRENCE: (Rader, J.) There is an alternative reasoning that reconciles the notice function of patent claims with the protective feature of the doctrine of equivalents. This simple principle: that the doctrine of equivalents does not capture subject matter that the patent drafter should have reasonably foreseen during the patent application process and, thus, should have included in the claims.

▶ ANALYSIS

The court sought to encourage competition. Otherwise someone submitting a patent application could cast too wide a net, prior to even anticipating new technology or new uses for a patent, by naming all future possibilities as to that product. Allowing someone to cast such a net would stifle someone else with an otherwise "original" invention.

■==■

Quicknotes

DOCTRINE OF EQUIVALENTS Rule that two inventions are the same for purposes of patent infringement if they achieve essentially the same result in the same manner despite trivial differences.

INFRINGEMENT Conduct in violation of statute or that interferes with another's rights pursuant to law.

PATENT A limited monopoly conferred on the invention or discovery of any new or useful machine or process that is novel and nonobvious.

■==■

C.R. Bard, Inc. v. Advanced Cardiovascular Systems, Inc.

Patent welder (P) v. Medical product manufacturer (D)

911 F.2d 670 (Fed. Cir. 1990).

NATURE OF CASE: Appeal from summary judgment entered for the plaintiff in a patent infringement suit.

FACT SUMMARY: C.R. Bard, Inc. (Bard) (P) contended that Advanced Cardiovascular Systems, Inc. (D) was a contributory infringer that had actively induced infringement of Bard's (P) method patent for medical treatment.

RULE OF LAW

A person induces infringement under 35 U.S.C. § 271 by actively and knowingly aiding and abetting another's direct infringement.

FACTS: Advanced Cardiovascular Systems, Inc. (ACS) (D) was marketing a perfusion catheter for use in coronary angioplasty. C.R. Bard, Inc. (Bard) (P) sued ACS (D), claiming that ACS's (D) catheter was especially adapted for use by a surgeon in a manner that infringed claim 1 of Bard's (P) method patent and that ACS (D) was therefore a contributory infringer and had actively induced infringement. Bard (P) successfully alleged that there was no evidence that any procedures using the ACS (D) catheter would be noninfringing. ACS (D) appealed, claiming that the catheter could be used in noninfringing procedures.

ISSUE: Does a person induce infringement under 35 U.S.C. § 271 by actively and knowingly aiding and abetting another's direct infringement?

HOLDING AND DECISION: [Judge not stated in casebook excerpt.] Yes. A person induces infringement under 35 U.S.C. § 271 by actively and knowingly aiding and abetting another's direct infringement. The statute requires that ACS (D) sell a catheter for use in practicing the patented process, which use constitutes a material part of invention, knowing that the catheter is especially made or adapted for use in infringing the patent, and that the catheter is not a staple article or commodity of commerce suitable for substantial noninfringing use. On this record a reasonable jury could find that there are substantial non-infringing uses for the ACS (D) catheter. It cannot be said that Bard (P) is entitled to judgment as a matter of law. Whether the ACS (D) catheter has no use except through practice of the patented method is a critical issue of fact in this case. Reversed and remanded.

▶ ANALYSIS

This case is between two rival manufacturers of catheters. The real infringer would seem to be, however, the doctor using the catheter. Congress amended the patent laws in 1996 to exempt doctors who perform medical processes from liability for infringement.

■■■■

Quicknotes

INFRINGEMENT Conduct in violation of statute or that interferes with another's rights pursuant to law.

35 U.S.C. § 271 A person induces infringement by actively and knowingly aiding and abetting another's direct infringement.

■■■■

Therasense, Inc. v. Becton, Dickinson and Co.

Biomedical patent holder (P) v. Competitor and alleged infringer (D)

649 F.3d 1276 (Fed. Cir. 2010) (en banc).

NATURE OF CASE: Petition for rehearing en banc of affirmance of judgment holding claims invalid and finding noninfringement in consolidated actions for declaratory judgment and patent infringement.

FACT SUMMARY: After the court of appeals affirmed the district court's judgment that Therasense, Inc.'s (P) '551 patent was unenforceable as a consequence of inequitable conduct, Therasense (P) and its parent company, Abbott (P), petitioned for a rehearing, arguing that the court of appeals had applied an overbroad legal standard for inequitable conduct.

🏛 RULE OF LAW
The standard for inequitable conduct must be tightly drawn, where the standard for intent is that the applicant knew of the reference, knew that it was material, and made a deliberate decision to withhold it, and the standard for materiality generally is but-for materiality except in cases of affirmative egregious misconduct, where such misconduct is deemed material.

FACTS: Therasense, Inc.'s (P) and its corporate parent, Abbott (P), held several patents, including the '551 patent, for disposable blood glucose test strips for diabetes management. Becton, Dickinson and Co. (Becton) (D), a competitor, sued for a declaratory judgment that the patents were invalid. Therasense (P) and Abbott (P) countersued for patent infringement. The cases were consolidated, and the district court held that all of the litigated patent claims were either invalid or not infringed. The court also ruled that the '551 patent was unenforceable due to Abbott's (P) inequitable conduct. Specifically, the '551 patent claimed a test strip with an electrochemical sensor for testing whole blood without a membrane over the electrode. For over thirteen years after Abbott (P) filed the original application leading to the '551 patent, that original application saw multiple rejections for anticipation and obviousness. Some of the rejections related to there being a protective membrane over the sensor. Then, Abbott's (P) patent attorney, Pope, and its director of research and marketing, Sanghera, presented new claims to the examiner based on a new sensor that did not require a protective membrane for whole blood. Pope asserted that this distinction would overcome the prior art found in another Abbott (P) patent (the '382 patent). To support this assertion, they submitted an affidavit to show that the prior art required a membrane for whole blood at the time of the invention. However, several years earlier, while prosecuting the European counterpart to the '382 patent, Abbott (P) made representations to the European Patent Office (EPO) that

disclosed sensors in which a protective membrane was optional in all cases except the case of live blood (as distinguished from whole blood), in which case the protective membrane was preferred—but not required. When Abbott (P) presented its new claims for the '551 patent, it failed to disclose to the U.S. Patent and Trademark Office (PTO) the briefs it had filed with the EPO. Accordingly, the district found that this failure constituted inequitable conduct. The court of appeals affirmed all of the district court's rulings. However, the court of appeals panel was divided on the inequitable conduct issue. Therasense (P) and Abbott (P) petitioned for an en banc rehearing. The court of appeals granted the petition.

ISSUE: Must the standard for inequitable conduct be tightly drawn, where the standard for intent is that the applicant knew of the reference, knew that it was material, and made a deliberate decision to withhold it, and the standard for materiality generally is but-for materiality except in cases of affirmative egregious misconduct, where such misconduct is deemed material?

HOLDING AND DECISION: (Rader, C.J.) Yes. The standard for inequitable conduct must be tightly drawn, where the standard for intent is that the applicant knew of the reference, knew that it was material, and made a deliberate decision to withhold it, and the standard for materiality generally is but-for materiality except in cases of affirmative egregious misconduct, where such misconduct is deemed material. Inequitable conduct is an equitable defense to patent infringement that, if proved, bars enforcement of a patent. This judge-made doctrine evolved over time from Supreme Court cases that applied the doctrine of unclean hands to dismiss patent cases involving egregious misconduct, including perjury, the manufacture of false evidence, and the suppression of evidence. The doctrine was broadened to encompass not only egregious affirmative acts of misconduct intended to deceive both the PTO and the courts but also the mere nondisclosure of information to the PTO. The remedy also became harsher: unenforceability of the entire patent, rather than mere dismissal of an action. In line with this wider scope and stronger remedy, the doctrine came to require a finding by clear and convincing evidence of both intent to deceive and materiality. Thus, for the accused infringer to prevail under the doctrine, it must be proved that the applicant misrepresented or omitted material information with the specific intent to deceive the PTO. However, the standards for intent and materiality have fluctuated over time, sometimes

Continued on next page.

being drawn broadly, and at other times being drawn narrowly. Given that the remedy for inequitable conduct is so strong, the standards for these elements must be drawn narrowly and tightly. Thus, the standard for intent is that the applicant knew of the reference, knew that it was material, and made a deliberate decision to withhold it. In other words, the evidence must show that the applicant made a deliberate decision to withhold a known material reference. A district court should not use a "sliding scale," where a weak showing of intent may be found sufficient based on a strong showing of materiality, and vice versa. Moreover, a district court may not infer intent solely from materiality. Instead, a court must weigh the evidence of intent to deceive independent of its analysis of materiality. Proving that the applicant knew of a reference, should have known of its materiality, and decided not to submit it to the PTO does not prove specific intent to deceive. Intent may be inferred from indirect and circumstantial evidence, but only where such intent is the single most reasonable inference able to be drawn from the evidence. Thus, if there are multiple reasonable inferences that may be drawn, intent to deceive cannot be found. The standard for materiality generally is but-for materiality. When an applicant fails to disclose prior art to the PTO, that prior art is but-for material if the PTO would not have allowed a claim had it been aware of the undisclosed prior art. Hence, in assessing the materiality of a withheld reference, the court must determine, based on a preponderance of the evidence, whether the PTO would have allowed the claim if it had been aware of the undisclosed reference. Where a district court invalidates a claim on the basis of a deliberately withheld reference, then ipso facto that reference is material, since the court is applying a higher evidentiary standard than used by the PTO. However, even if the court does not invalidate the claim on the basis of a deliberately withheld reference, the reference nevertheless may be material if it would have blocked patent issuance under the PTO's lower evidentiary standards. If the patent would have issued despite the deliberately withheld reference, the doctrine should not be applied, since the patentee will have obtained no advantage from its misconduct. One exception to this general requirement of but-for materiality arises where there is affirmative egregious misconduct. In such cases, the misconduct is material since it is unlikely that the patentee will have gone to great lengths to deceive the PTO with a falsehood unless it believes that the falsehood will affect issuance of the patent. Accordingly, applying these standards, on remand the district court should determine whether the PTO would not have granted the patent but for Abbott's (P) failure to disclose the EPO briefs. In particular, the district court must determine whether the PTO would have found Abbott's (P) agents' submissions unpersuasive in overcoming the obviousness rejection over the '382 patent if Abbott had disclosed the EPO briefs. In addition, the district court should determine whether there is clear and convincing evidence demonstrating that Sanghera or Pope knew of the EPO briefs, knew of their

materiality, and made the conscious decision not to disclose them in order to deceive the PTO. [Vacated and remanded as to the inequitable conduct issue.]

▶ ANALYSIS

The remedy for inequitable conduct is the "atomic bomb" of patent law. Unlike validity defenses, which are claim specific, inequitable conduct regarding any single claim renders the entire patent unenforceable. Unlike other deficiencies, inequitable conduct cannot be cured by reissue. Moreover, the taint of a finding of inequitable conduct can spread from a single patent to render unenforceable other related patents and applications in the same technology family. Thus, a finding of inequitable conduct may endanger a substantial portion of a company's patent portfolio. A finding of inequitable conduct may also spawn antitrust and unfair competition claims. Further, prevailing on a claim of inequitable conduct often makes a case "exceptional," leading potentially to an award of attorneys' fees under 35 U.S.C. § 285. Finally, a finding of inequitable conduct may also prove the crime or fraud exception to the attorney-client privilege.

■■■

Quicknotes

DECLARATORY JUDGMENT A judgment of the court establishing the rights of the parties.

EN BANC The hearing of a matter by all the judges of the court, rather than only the necessary quorum.

INFRINGEMENT Conduct in violation of a statute or contract that interferes with another's rights pursuant to law.

IPSO FACTO By the fact itself.

PATENT A limited monopoly conferred on the invention or discovery of any new or useful machine or process that is novel and non-obvious.

■■■

Motion Picture Patents Company v. Universal Film Manufacturing Company et al.

Patent licensor (P) v. Projector manufacturer (D)

243 U.S. 502 (1917).

NATURE OF CASE: Review of judgment in infringement action.

FACT SUMMARY: Universal Film Manufacturing Company (D) denied the validity of Motion Picture Patents Company's (P) patent, denied infringement, and claimed an implied license to use the patented machine without the restrictions imposed by the patent owner's terms in a notice attached to the machine.

🏛 RULE OF LAW
The exclusive right granted in every patent must be limited to the invention described in the claims of the patent and it is not competent for the owner to extend the scope of its patent monopoly by restricting the use of it to materials necessary in its operation that are not part of the patented invention.

FACTS: When Motion Picture Patents Company (MPPC) (P), the assignee of a patent, granted the right and a license to manufacture and sell machines embodying the invention described in the patent at suit, i.e., a mechanism for feeding film through a motion picture projector, MPPC (P) attached a notice to each machine limiting the use of the motion picture machines by the purchaser or by the purchaser's lessee to terms not stated in the notice but which were to be fixed after sale, by MPPC (P) at its discretion. The notice attempted to restrict the use of film supplies and the sale price and was not a restriction on the use of the machine itself. Universal Film Manufacturing Company (D) claimed that the owner's rights to control the materials to be used in operating the machine could not be derived from or protected by the patent law and that the notice was invalid.

ISSUE: Must the exclusive right granted in every patent be limited to the invention described in the claims of the patent and is it competent for the owner to extend the scope of its patent monopoly by restricting the use of it to materials necessary in its operation that are not part of the patented invention?

HOLDING AND DECISION: (Clarke, J.) Yes. The exclusive right granted in every patent must be limited to the invention described in the claims of the patent, but it is not competent for the owner to extend the scope of its patent monopoly by restricting the use of it to materials necessary in its operation that are not part of the patented invention. Nor may the owner send its machines forth into the channels of trade of the country subject to conditions as to use or royalty to be paid to be imposed thereafter at the discretion of the patent owner. The restriction contained in the notice attached to the machine sold by MPPC (P) is invalid because the film is obviously not a part of the invention of the patent in suit and because to enforce it would be to create a monopoly in the manufacture and use of moving picture films, wholly outside of the patent in suit and out of the patent law as we have interpreted it. Moreover, the owner of a patent is not authorized to fix, by notice, the price at which a patented article must be sold after the first sale of it.

DISSENT: (Holmes, J.) Since a patent owner can keep his patented machine wholly out of use, I cannot understand why he cannot keep it out of use unless the licensee, or, for that matter, the buyer, will use some unpatented thing in connection with it. Generally speaking, the measure of a condition is the consequence of a breach, and if that consequence is one that the owner may impose unconditionally, he may impose it conditionally upon a certain event.

▶ ANALYSIS

This enunciation of the doctrine of first sale coincided with antitrust legislation at the turn of the century. Resale price maintenance was made illegal under antitrust law. Later amendments to the patent laws clarified issues related to the tying of nonstaple products to patented products.

▰▬▰

Quicknotes

FIRST SALE DOCTRINE Once a copyright owner has transferred ownership of a particular copy of his work, the transferee may then lawfully dispose of that particular copy without permission of the copyright owner.

IMPLIED LICENSE A license that is presumed to have been given judging by the activities of the party that is authorized to give it.

INFRINGEMENT Conduct in violation of statute or that interferes with another's rights pursuant to law.

PATENT A limited monopoly conferred on the invention or discovery of any new or useful machine or process that is novel and nonobvious.

▰▬▰

eBay, Inc. v. MercExchange, LLC

Alleged infringer (D) v. Patentee (P)

547 U.S. 388 (2006).

NATURE OF CASE: Appeal from denial of permanent injunction.

FACT SUMMARY: eBay, Inc. (D) and MercExchange, LLC (P) could not agree on a license for MercExchange's (P) patent. When eBay (D) proceeded with its website, MercExchange (P) sued for patent infringement and won damages arising out of eBay's (D) liability. MercExchange (P) also sought a permanent injunction.

🏛 **RULE OF LAW**
The traditional four-part equitable test for injunctive relief applies to Patent Act cases.

FACTS: MercExchange, LLC (P) held a business method patent for an electronic sales market using a central authority. It attempted to license its patent to eBay, Inc. (D), but the parties could not reach an agreement. eBay (D) proceeded with its website that allowed private sellers to list goods for sale at auction or at a fixed price. MercExchange (P) filed suit for patent infringement. A jury found the patent valid and awarded damages to MercExchange (P) for eBay's (D) infringement. MercExchange (P) filed a motion for a permanent injunction, but the district court denied it. MercExchange (P) appealed and the federal circuit reversed based on the general rule that courts will grant permanent injunctions in patent infringement "absent exceptional circumstances." eBay (D) filed its petition for a writ of certiorari, which the United States Supreme Court granted to determine the appropriateness of the general rule on permanent injunctions in patent infringement cases.

ISSUE: Does the traditional four-part equitable test for injunctive relief apply to Patent Act cases?

HOLDING AND DECISION: (Thomas, J.) Yes. The traditional four-part equitable test for injunctive relief applies to Patent Act cases. A party seeking an injunction traditionally must establish four elements: (1) it has suffered an irreparable injury; (2) it has no adequate remedy at law; (3) an equitable remedy is warranted after balancing the hardships between plaintiff and defendant; and (4) a permanent injunction serves the public interest. These principles also apply to the Patent Act. The district court and the court of appeals failed to apply these principles when considering the appropriateness of a permanent injunction in this case. The district court impermissibly broadened the scope of the elements while the court of appeals applied a "general rule" for patent infringement cases. The district court must apply the four-part test in

patent cases as well as other equitable cases. Vacated and remanded.

CONCURRENCE: (Roberts, C.J.) Courts historically have granted injunctive relief in patent cases but that history does not guarantee a right to injunctive relief. The four-part test must still be applied to determine the appropriateness of relief.

CONCURRENCE: (Kennedy, J.) The four-part test is appropriate. Many companies now use patent protection as a means to secure licensing fees and the threat of injunctive relief as a means to secure exorbitant licensing fees. Courts should take the availability of money damages into account when considering injunctive relief.

▶ **ANALYSIS**

The Court considered MercExchange's (P) history of licensing the patent in determining that money damages were appropriate rather than injunctive relief. In 2008, after several years of litigation, the parties reached a settlement wherein MercExchange (P) assigned its patents to eBay (D).

■▬■

Quicknotes

CERTIORARI A discretionary writ issued by a superior court to an inferior court in order to review the lower court's decisions; the Supreme Court's writ ordering such review.

INJUNCTION A court order, requiring a person to do or prohibiting that person from doing, a specific act.

INJUNCTIVE RELIEF A court order issued as a remedy, requiring a person to do, or prohibiting that person from doing, a specific act.

■▬■

In re Seagate Technology, LLC

Alleged infringer (D)

497 F.3d 1360 (Fed. Cir. 2007) (en banc).

NATURE OF CASE: Writ of mandamus.

FACT SUMMARY: The trial court held Seagate Technology, LLC (Seagate) (D) waived its attorney-client privilege and work product protection for in-house, trial, and opinion counsel communications concerning the infringement, invalidity, and enforceability of Convolve patents. Seagate (D) sought a writ of mandamus to vacate the trial court's orders for document production.

RULE OF LAW
A patentee must show objective recklessness to recover enhanced damages on proof of willful infringement and a defendant no longer has an affirmative duty to obtain a legal opinion prior to action.

FACTS: Convolve, Inc. sued Seagate Technology, LLC (Seagate) (D) for willful violation of several patents. Just prior to the lawsuit, Seagate (D) hired opinion counsel, Gerald Sekimura, to evaluate the Convolve patents. Sekimura issued three opinion letters. Seagate (D) notified Convolve of its intent to rely on Sekimura's opinion letters as a defense, disclosed his work product, and produced him for deposition. Convolve then moved for disclosure of work product of all counsel, including trial counsel. The trial court held Seagate (D) waived attorney-client privilege concerning infringement, invalidity, and enforceability of the Convolve patents. It ordered the production of documents and testimony and provided for in camera review of trial strategy documents. Finally, the trial court held work product protection was waived. Seagate (D) moved for a stay and certification of an interlocutory appeal, which the trial court denied. Seagate (D) petitioned the federal court for a writ of mandamus to order the trial court to vacate its discovery production orders. The federal court sua sponte ordered en banc review.

ISSUE: Must a patentee show objective recklessness to recover enhanced damages on proof of willful infringement and does a defendant still have an affirmative duty to obtain a legal opinion prior to action?

HOLDING AND DECISION: (Mayer, J.) Yes and no. A patentee must show objective recklessness to recover enhanced damages on proof of willful infringement and a defendant no longer has an affirmative duty to obtain a legal opinion prior to action. A writ of mandamus is appropriate for a party who has no other method of obtaining the relief requested and the right to the writ is "clear and indisputable." In a discovery dispute regarding claims of privilege, mandamus is appropriate when: (1) an important issue of first impression is raised; (2) a delay until final judgment

means the loss of the privilege; (3) immediate resolution avoids doctrine development that would undermine the privilege. This case meets the criteria. Convolve can only obtain enhanced damages upon showing willful infringement. *Underwater Devices Inc. v. Morrison-Knudsen Co.*, 717 F.2d 1380 (Fed. Cir. 1983), set forth the analysis for willful infringement and enhanced damages. A potential infringer on actual notice of another's patent rights has the affirmative duty to obtain legal advice prior to initiating potentially infringing action. Thus developed the advice of counsel defense where alleged infringers claim reliance on legal opinions. "Willful" in *Underwater Devices*, however, is less stringent, more akin to negligence, than "willful" in the civil context and thus does not comply with Supreme Court precedent. *Underwater Devices* is overruled, a showing of objective recklessness is required, and the alleged infringer has no affirmative duty of due care. No duty to obtain legal opinion exists. Convolve argues it is improper to consider "willfulness" here but the proper legal standard informs the discovery scope, so this opinion is neither advisory nor hypothetical. Next, this court considers the attorney-client privilege waiver. The attorney-client privilege is meant to encourage frank communication and can only be waived by the client. The scope of a client's waiver has no bright-line rule. Here, trial counsel and opinion counsel serve vastly different functions and the Supreme Court has recognized the need to protect trial counsel's thoughts and strategy. Further, a claim of willfulness requires a good faith basis that the alleged infringer's pre-filing conduct was willful infringement. Thus, trial counsel's communications are not relevant to the pre-litigation willfulness. A claim of post-litigation willfulness can be addressed via a motion for preliminary injunction. Finally, a similar analysis applies to the waiver of work production protection. The waiver may be extended to trial counsel in some circumstances, but the general rule should be that waiver for reliance on opinion counsel work product as a defense to willful infringement does not extend to trial counsel. Writ granted.

CONCURRENCE: (Gajarsa, J.) The court should end the grafting of a willfulness standard onto 35 U.S.C. § 284. Even though the court itself has grafted such a standard onto the statute, the language of the statute unambiguously omits such a standard, and there is no principled reason for continuing to engraft a willfulness standard onto § 284. Instead, the plain meaning of the statute should be given effect, and the discretion to enhance damages should be left with the district courts, sans a willfulness standard.

Continued on next page.

ANALYSIS

This case set off waves in the patent litigation community because it nullified the affirmative duty to act with due care in willfulness cases. Prior to this opinion, defendants often waived the attorney-client privilege to establish the advice-of-counsel defense and the scope of the waiver was highly litigated. Now the prosecution of willful infringement becomes more difficult and the waiver issue less complicated.

■━■

Quicknotes

AFFIRMATIVE DUTY An obligation to undertake an affirmative action for the benefit of another.

ATTORNEY-CLIENT PRIVILEGE A doctrine precluding the admission into evidence of confidential communications between an attorney and his client made in the course of obtaining professional assistance.

DISCOVERY Pretrial procedure during which one party makes certain information available to the other.

DUE CARE The degree of care that can be expected from a reasonably prudent person under similar circumstances; synonymous with ordinary care.

EN BANC The hearing of a matter by all the judges of the court, rather than only the necessary quorum.

INTERLOCUTORY APPEAL The appeal of an issue that does not resolve the disposition of the case, but is essential to a determination of the parties' legal rights.

OBJECTIVE STANDARD A standard that is not personal to an individual, but is dependent on some external source.

PRELIMINARY INJUNCTION A judicial mandate issued to require or restrain a party from certain conduct; used to preserve a trial's subject matter or to prevent threatened injury.

RECKLESSNESS Conduct that is conscious and that creates a substantial and unjustifiable risk of harm to others.

STAY An order by a court requiring a party to refrain from a specific activity until the happening of an event or upon further action by the court.

SUA SPONTE An action taken by the court by its own motion and without the suggestion of one of the parties.

WILLFULLY An act that is undertaken intentionally, knowingly, and with the intent to commit an unlawful act without a justifiable excuse.

WORK PRODUCT Work performed by an attorney in preparation of litigation that is not subject to discovery.

WRIT OF MANDAMUS A court order issued commanding a public or private entity, or an official thereof, to perform a duty required by law.

■━■

Copyright Law

Quick Reference Rules of Law

Feist Publications v. Rural Telephone Service

Publishing company (D) v. Phone book publisher (P)

499 U.S. 340 (1991).

NATURE OF CASE: Appeal from grant of summary judgment to plaintiff in suit for copyright infringement.

FACT SUMMARY: After Feist Publications (Feist) (D) took 1,309 listings from Rural Telephone Service's (Rural) (P) white pages when compiling Feist's (D) own white pages, Rural (P) filed suit for copyright infringement.

🏛 RULE OF LAW
To be copyrightable, a work must be original and possess at least some minimal degree of creativity.

FACTS: As a certified telephone service provided in northwest Kansas, Rural Telephone Service (Rural) (P) published a typical telephone directory as a condition of its monopoly franchise. The white pages alphabetically listed the names, towns, and telephone numbers of Rural's (P) subscribers. Feist Publications (Feist) (D) was a publishing company specializing in area-wide telephone directories. The Feist (D) directory that was the subject of this litigation contained 46,878 white pages listings, compared to Rural's (P) approximately 7,700 listings. Feist (D) approached the 11 northwest Kansas telephone companies and offered to pay for the right to use their respective white pages listings. When only Rural (P) refused to license its listings, Feist (D) used them without Rural's (P) consent. A typical Feist (D) listing included each individual's street address, while most of Rural's (P) did not. Of the 46,878 listings in Feist's (D) 1983 directory, 1,309 of those listings were identical to listings in Rural's (P) white pages. Rural (P) sued for copyright infringement. The district court granted summary judgment to Rural (P), and the court of appeals affirmed. Feist (D) appealed.

ISSUE: To be copyrightable, must a work be original and possess at least some minimal degree of creativity?

HOLDING AND DECISION: (O'Connor, J.) Yes. To be copyrightable, a work must be original and possess at least some minimal degree of creativity. This case concerns the interaction of two well-established propositions. The first is that facts are not copyrightable; the other, that compilations of facts generally are. There is an undeniable tension between these two propositions. The key to resolving the tension lies in understanding why facts are not copyrightable. No one may claim originality as to facts because facts do not owe their origin to an act of authorship. Factual compilations, on the other hand, may possess the requisite originality. Compilations were expressly mentioned in the Copyright Acts of 1909 and 1976. Even a directory that contains absolutely no protectable written expression, only facts, meets the constitutional minimum for copyright protection if it features an original selection or arrangement. If the selection and arrangement are original, these elements of the work are eligible for copyright protection. No matter how original the format, though, the facts themselves do not become original through association. There is no doubt that Feist (D) took from the white pages of Rural's (P) directory a substantial amount of factual information. The question that remains is whether Rural (P) selected, coordinated, or arranged these uncopyrightable facts in an original way. It did not. Rural (P) simply took the data provided by its subscribers and listed it alphabetically by surname. There is nothing remotely creative about arranging names alphabetically in a white pages directory. Rural (P) expended sufficient effort to make the white pages directory useful, but insufficient creativity to make it original. Thus, because Rural's (P) white pages lack the requisite originality, Feist's (D) use of the listings cannot constitute infringement. Copyright rewards originality, not effort. Reversed.

▶ ANALYSIS

In the words of the Supreme Court, copyright assures authors the right to their original expression, but encourages others to build freely upon the ideas and information conveyed by a work. This principle, known as the idea/expression or fact/expression dichotomy, applies to all works of authorship. As applied to a factual compilation, assuming the absence of original written expression, only the compiler's selection and arrangement may be protected; the raw facts may be copied at will. This is the means by which copyright advances the progress of science and art by encouraging creativity with the reward of exclusive rights for the original creation.

■=■

Quicknotes

COPYRIGHT Refers to the exclusive rights granted to an artist pursuant to Article I, section 8, clause 8 of the United States Constitution over the reproduction, display, performance, distribution, and adaptation of his work for a period prescribed by statute.

COPYRIGHT INFRINGEMENT A violation of one of the exclusive rights granted to an artist pursuant to Article I, section 8, clause 8 of the United States Constitution over the reproduction, display, performance, distribution, and adaptation of his work for a period prescribed by statute.

Continued on next page.

FRANCHISE An agreement whereby one party (the franchisor) grants another (the franchisee) the right to market its product or service.

SUMMARY JUDGMENT Judgment rendered by a court in response to a motion by one of the parties, claiming that the lack of a question of material fact in respect to an issue warrants disposition of the issue without consideration by the jury.

Baker v. Selden

Alleged infringer (D) v. Writer (P)

101 U.S. 99 (1879).

NATURE OF CASE: Appeal from award of damages for copyright infringement.

FACT SUMMARY: Baker (D) sold forms similar to those Selden (P) had in his copyrighted book setting forth his system of bookkeeping.

🏛 RULE OF LAW
The protection afforded by a copyright on a book explaining an art or system extends only to the author's unique explanation thereof and does not preclude others from using the system or the forms necessarily incidental to such use.

FACTS: Selden (P) copyrighted a book in which he used an introductory essay explaining his system of bookkeeping followed by forms to put the system to use. He had arranged the columns and headings so that the entire operation of a day, week, or month was on a single page or on two pages facing each other. Baker (D) subsequently began selling forms with differently arranged columns and headings to achieve the same result. When Selden (P) successfully brought suit for copyright infringement, Baker (D) appealed. He argued that the forms were noncopyrightable.

ISSUE: Does a copyright on a book explaining an art or system preclude others from using the system or the forms incidental to such use?

HOLDING AND DECISION: (Bradley, J.) No. A copyright on a book explaining an art or system protects only the author's unique explanation thereof and does not preclude others from using the system or the forms incidental to such use. To find that a copyright protected against use of the system itself or the forms necessary to such use would be to grant patent-type protection without requiring a showing of novelty. Copyright is based on originality, not novelty, and protects the explanation and not the use of the system explained. Here, therefore, the copyright Selden (P) obtained could not give him the exclusive right to use the bookkeeping system or the forms necessary to such use. Reversed and remanded.

▌ ANALYSIS

Many have interpreted this case as allowing copying for use as opposed to copying for explanatory purposes. However, in applying this rule, some courts have gone a bit far and have allowed something to pass as copying for use when there were other arrangements of words available that could just as easily have been used to convey the noncopyrightable system or art. This has engendered much criticism of the aforementioned interpretation of the rule of this case.

◼▬◼

Quicknotes

COPYRIGHT Refers to the exclusive rights granted to an artist pursuant to Article I, section 8, clause 8 of the United States Constitution over the reproduction, display, performance, distribution, and adaptation of his work for a period prescribed by statute.

COPYRIGHT INFRINGEMENT A violation of one of the exclusive rights granted to an artist pursuant to Article I, section 8, clause 8 of the United States Constitution over the reproduction, display, performance, distribution, and adaptation of his work for a period prescribed by statute.

◼▬◼

Lotus Development Corp. v. Borland International

Computer program designer (P) v. Competitor (D)

49 F.3d 807 (1st Cir. 1995), *aff'd by an equally divided court,* 526 U.S. 233 (1996).

NATURE OF CASE: Appeal from finding of copyright infringement.

FACT SUMMARY: Borland International (Borland) (D) included in its own spreadsheet programs the commands used by the computer program Lotus 1-2-3 so that spreadsheet users who were already familiar with 1-2-3 could easily switch to the Borland (D) programs without learning new commands.

🏛 RULE OF LAW
A computer menu command hierarchy is not copyrightable subject matter.

FACTS: Lotus Development Corp. (Lotus) (P) marketed a computer spreadsheet program, Lotus 1-2-3. The program incorporated 469 menu commands, such as "Copy," "Print," etc. The program also enabled the user to write macros that would designate a series of commands with a single macro keystroke. Borland International (Borland) (D) subsequently released two versions of its own spreadsheet programs, called Quattro and Quattro Pro. Borland (D) included a virtually identical copy of the entire 1-2-3 menu tree in its Quattro programs. It did not copy any of Lotus's (P) underlying computer code, but it did copy the words and structures of Lotus's (P) menu command hierarchy so that consumers who used Borland's (D) programs would not have to relearn any commands or rewrite their Lotus (P) macros. Lotus (P) sued for copyright infringement and received a judgment in its favor. Borland (D) appealed, contending that the Lotus (P) menu command hierarchy was not copyrightable because it was a system, method of operation, process, or procedure foreclosed from protection by the Copyright Act.

ISSUE: Is a computer menu command hierarchy copyrightable subject matter?

HOLDING AND DECISION: (Stahl, J.) No. A computer menu command hierarchy is not copyrightable subject matter. A menu command hierarchy is an uncopyrightable "method of operation" as that term is used in § 102(b) of the Copyright Act. It provides the means by which users control and operate a program's functional capabilities. Just as it would be impossible to operate a VCR without buttons, it would be impossible to operate Lotus 1-2-3 without employing its menu command hierarchy. Thus, the Lotus (P) command terms are equivalent to the buttons themselves, which are an uncopyrightable method of operating the VCR. Therefore, Borland (D) did not infringe Lotus's (P) copyright when it copied its menu command hierarchy. Reversed.

CONCURRENCE: (Boudin, J.) Because computer programs, unlike literary works or works of art, are utilitarian, granting such programs copyright protection can have the same effect that granting a patent would have, i.e., limiting users' ability to perform a task in the most efficient manner. While utility does not bar copyrightability, it alters the calculus. While the incentive for the creator remains the same through the grant of a limited monopoly, the cost to users is great where the creation is the most efficient means of accomplishing a certain task. Copyright law has not extensively addressed utility, so there is not much precedent to go by. Where protection is sought for a computer menu, which may be a creative work, the importance of the menu over time may reside more in the investment that users have made in learning the menu and building macros based on it. Thus, to assume a computer program is just another form of expression, like a film, may be incorrect. While the expression of the computer program may look or feel like the familiar subject matter of copyright, its substance may be more suited to protection by patent law. The application of copyright law to computer programs does not quite "fit." Here, Borland's (D) rationale for wanting to incorporate the Lotus (P) menus rings true, i.e., to give Lotus (P) users who have invested time learning the Lotus (P) menu hierarchy a fallback option when they use Borland's (D) product. The issue is not whether Lotus (P) would lose money if its menu hierarchy were awarded copyright protection. The issue remains whether it should be awarded such protection. Given that the menu commands are largely for standard procedures that Lotus (P) did not invent and are common words that Lotus (P) cannot monopolize, copyrightability does not seem warranted, even for just the particular combination and subgrouping of the commands. Granting Lotus (P) copyright on this pattern of commands would lock users into using Lotus (P). If a better spreadsheet comes along, there is no reason why those customers who have learned the Lotus (P) menu and devised macros for it should be forced to remain captive of Lotus (P) merely because of an investment in learning made by them and not by Lotus (P). Under such a scenario, Lotus (P) will have already reaped the rewards of being first. Accordingly, Borland (D) should prevail, but the question remains on what basis. The choice seems to be between finding the menus not copyrightable or devising a new doctrine that renders Borland's (D) use privileged. Each approach has its pros and cons. In any event, the majority's approach is satisfactory.

Continued on next page.

▶ *ANALYSIS*

Judge Boudin suggested that an alternative analysis would be to say that Borland's (D) use of Lotus's (P) menu was privileged because it was merely trying to assist former Lotus (P) customers, not attract them. The closest analogy to that approach would be the fair use doctrine employed in conventional copyright law. However, he also admitted that a privileged use doctrine would cause a host of administrative problems and would also reduce the ability of the industry to predict outcomes.

■■■

Quicknotes

COPYRIGHT ACT § 102(b) Excludes systems, methods of operation, process, or procedure from copyright protection.

COPYRIGHT INFRINGEMENT A violation of one of the exclusive rights granted to an artist pursuant to Article I, section 8, clause 8 of the United States Constitution over the reproduction, display, performance, distribution, and adaptation of his work for a period prescribed by statute.

■■■

Morrissey v. Procter & Gamble

Copyright owner (P) v. Alleged infringer (D)

379 F.2d 675 (1st Cir. 1967).

NATURE OF CASE: Action for damages for copyright infringement.

FACT SUMMARY: Procter & Gamble (D) used a contest rule markedly similar to that which Morrissey (P) had copyrighted and used in a sales promotion contest.

🏛 RULE OF LAW

A rule incidental to the operation of a noncopyrightable contest cannot itself be copyrighted if the information it conveys is so simple that there are only a handful of ways in which it can be expressed.

FACTS: Morrissey (P) copyrighted the rules it had used in a sweepstakes contest revolving around the contestants' social security numbers. In conducting a similar-type contest, Procter & Gamble (D) used a substantially similar rule. It explained that a participant's name, address, and social security number should be printed on paper or a box top; that official rules were available at local dealers; that the social security number of another family member could be used if one did not have his own number, etc. When Morrissey (P) sued for copyright infringement, the district court found the contest itself was noncopyrightable. It then held that the rule springing therefrom contained no original creative authorship and was noncopyrightable. Morrissey (P) appealed.

ISSUE: If a rule incidental to the operation of a noncopyrightable contest conveys information so simple that it can be expressed only in a handful of ways, can the rule be copyrighted?

HOLDING AND DECISION: (Aldrich, C.J.) No. If the information conveyed in a rule incidental to the operation of a noncopyrightable contest is so simple that it can only be expressed in a handful of ways, the rule cannot be copyrighted. Permitting such rules to be copyrighted would be tantamount to giving a copyright on the contest itself to someone smart enough to simply copyright the handful of rule variations possible for running the contest. In this case, the rule at issue was of this nature and therefore was not copyrightable by Morrissey (P). Affirmed.

▶ ANALYSIS

The court relied on its interpretation of *Baker v. Selden*, 101 U.S. 99 (1879), as holding that certain kinds of expression are noncopyrightable, e.g., utilitarian forms. This flies in the face of commentators who continue to argue that *Baker v. Selden* held only that otherwise prohibited copying that is necessary to make use of a noncopyrightable system or art

does not constitute infringement, whereas copying for explanatory purposes does.

■■■

Quicknotes

COPYRIGHT Refers to the exclusive rights granted to an artist pursuant to Article I, section 8, clause 8 of the United States Constitution over the reproduction, display, performance, distribution, and adaptation of his work for a period prescribed by statute.

COPYRIGHT INFRINGEMENT A violation of one of the exclusive rights granted to an artist pursuant to Article I, section 8, clause 8 of the United States Constitution over the reproduction, display, performance, distribution, and adaptation of his work for a period prescribed by statute.

■■■

Brandir International, Inc. v. Cascade Pacific Lumber Co.

Bicycle rack designer (P) v. Competitor (D)

834 F.2d 1142 (2d Cir. 1987).

NATURE OF CASE: Appeal from denial of a claim of copyright violation.

FACT SUMMARY: A wire sculpture sold as a bicycle rack by Brandir International, Inc. (P) was deemed not to be copyrightable because it was an industrial design not subject to copyright protection.

> ## 🏛 RULE OF LAW
> Copyrightability ultimately depends on the extent to which the work reflects artistic expression uninhibited by functional considerations.

FACTS: After seeing undulating wire sculptures, a friend suggested to the artist, the chief owner of Brandir International, Inc. (Brandir) (P), that the sculptures would make excellent bicycle racks. Brandir International, Inc. (P) then began manufacturing and selling bicycle racks derived in part from one or more of the works of art. When Brandir (P) discovered that another company, Cascade Pacific Lumber (D), was selling a similar product, it included a copyright notice with its products and applied to the Copyright Office for registration. The Copyright Office denied the applications for registration because the bicycle racks did not contain any element that was capable of independent existence as a copyrightable pictorial, graphic, or sculptural work apart from the shape of the useful article. The Register of Copyright (D), named as a third party defendant in this action against Cascade Pacific Lumber (D), denied copyrightability, and the district court granted summary judgment on the copyright claim. Brandir (P) appealed.

ISSUE: Should copyrightability ultimately depend on the extent to which the work reflects artistic expression uninhibited by functional considerations?

HOLDING AND DECISION: (Oakes, J.) Yes. Copyrightability ultimately should depend on the extent to which the work reflects artistic expression uninhibited by functional considerations. If design elements reflect a merger of aesthetic and functional considerations, the artistic aspects of a work cannot be said to be conceptually separable from the utilitarian elements. The final form of the bicycle rack sold by Brandir (P) is essentially a product of industrial design. Form and function are inextricably intertwined in the rack, its ultimate design being as much the result of utilitarian pressures as aesthetic choices. The original aesthetic elements have clearly been adapted to accommodate and further a utilitarian purpose. Affirmed.

CONCURRENCE AND DISSENT: (Winter, J.) The relevant question should be whether the design of a

useful article, however intertwined with the article's utilitarian aspects, causes an ordinary reasonable observer to perceive an aesthetic concept not related to the article's use. The answer to this question is clear in the instant case since any reasonable observer would easily view the bicycle rack as an ornamental sculpture. The Copyright Act expressly states that the legal test is how the final article is perceived, not how it was developed through various stages.

▍ *ANALYSIS*

The majority in this case adopted a test suggested by Professor Denicola in his article "Applied Art and Industrial Design," 67 Minn. L. Rev. 707 (1983). The Winter dissent proposed applying a different test and another dissent suggested using a temporal displacement test. Generally speaking, if a work is a useful article, the artistic elements have to be separable in order for the work to be copyrightable.

Quicknotes

COPYRIGHT Refers to the exclusive rights granted to an artist pursuant to Article I, section 8, clause 8 of the United States Constitution over the reproduction, display, performance, distribution, and adaptation of his work for a period prescribed by statute.

17 U.S.C. § 101 Section 101 of the Copyright Act of 1976, setting forth the definitions for purposes of the Act.

Community for Creative Non-Violence et al. v. Reid

Art buyer (P) v. Sculptor (D)

490 U.S. 730 (1989).

NATURE OF CASE: Review of order adjudicating copyrights with respect to a sculpture.

FACT SUMMARY: Reid (D), who had created a sculpture on commission from the Community for Creative Non-Violence (P), contended that since he had not been an employee of it under common-law agency principles, he owned the copyright thereon.

⚖ RULE OF LAW
Under common-law agency principles, one who creates an artwork at the behest of another retains copyright thereon unless he was an employee of that other.

FACTS: The Community for Creative Non-Violence (CCNV) (P) was a nonprofit organization dedicated to advocacy for the cause of the homeless in the United States. It negotiated with Reid (D), a sculptor, for the latter to fashion a variation on the classic nativity scene, depicting homeless individuals. Agreement was finally made, and Reid (D) fashioned the sculpture out of a bronze-like material. The work was done by Reid (D) in his studio, with minimal direction from CCNV (P). After the unveiling, Reid (D) registered a copyright on the work. Subsequent to this, a disagreement arose between CCNV (P) and Reid (D) who had taken custody of the sculpture, over future exhibition thereof. CCNV (P) filed an action seeking to obtain possession of the work. The district court held CCNV (P) to have the right to exhibit the statue. The federal circuit of the court of appeals reversed, and the United States Supreme Court granted review.

ISSUE: Under common-law agency principles, does one who creates an artwork at the behest of another retain copyright thereon unless he had been an employee of that other?

HOLDING AND DECISION: (Marshall, J.) Yes. under common-law agency principles, one creating an artwork at the behest of another retains copyright thereon unless he had been an employee of that other. 17 U.S.C. § 201(a) provides that copyright ownership vests initially in the work's author, something Reid (D) in this instance indisputably was. Section 101 of the 1976 Copyright Act creates an exception to this in the case of works created "for hire." Section 101(2) mandates copyright vestiture in the case where the author is an independent contractor of another, in specific instances not applicable here. Section 101(1) provides that the work is one created "for hire" if the work is created by an employee within the scope of his employment, and this subsection is the only one that can

divest Reid (D) of copyright therein. "Employee" is not defined in the section. This being so, the rule comes into play that words used in a statute will be presumed to possess their normal meanings. Contrary to CCNV's (P) assertions, "employee" is a narrower term than one over whom another exercises a measure of control. Rather, "employee" has a particular meaning, derived from common-law agency principles, wherein one party performs labor for another under circumstances in which that other exerts substantial control over the work environment on the laborer, as well as the manner of performance. Numerous factors figure in this equation, such as the level of skill required, tax treatment of the putative employee, the singleness of the assignment, and the source of the instrumentalities of the labor. Here, the work was highly skilled; Reid (D) was retained only for this single assignment, was not treated as an employee for tax purposes, and supplied his own tools and work area. The conclusion is mandated that, under agency principles, Reid (D) was not an employee of CCNV (P). Therefore, the § 101(1) exception to § 201(a) does not apply, and the copyright belongs to Reid (D). Affirmed.

▶ ANALYSIS

Sections 101(1) and 101(2) were the result of lengthy debate and compromise in Congress. Prior to 1955, any commissioned work belonged to the hiring party. For the next several years, changes in this rule were proposed numerous times. Not until 1965 was the substantive embodiment of current law enacted.

■═■

Quicknotes

17 U.S.C. § 102 Defines the author of a work as person who actually creates work.

17 U.S.C. § 201(b) Makes employer the author of work prepared by employees.

1976 COPYRIGHT ACT § 101 Defines a "work made for hire" as a "work prepared by an employee within the scope of his or her employment."

■═■

Aalmuhammed v. Lee

Alleged copyright co-owner (P) v. Copyright holder (D)

202 F.3d 1227 (9th Cir. 2000).

NATURE OF CASE: Appeal from dismissal of a case for declaratory relief under the Copyright Act.

FACT SUMMARY: Aalmuhammed (P) sought a declaratory judgment that he was a co-owner of the copyright in a movie and thus entitled to an accounting of the profits from the movie.

🏛 RULE OF LAW
A person claiming to be a co-owner of a joint work must prove that both parties intended the work to be a joint work.

FACTS: Aalmuhammed (P) worked as a consultant on Lee's (D) film about Malcolm X. Aalmuhammed (P) reviewed the script, suggested revisions, and rewrote certain portions. When the film was released, Aalmuhammed (P) was listed in the credits as an "Islamic Technical Consultant." Aalmuhammed (P) sought a declaratory judgment that the movie was a "joint work" and that he was a co-owner of the copyright and entitled to an accounting of profits. Aalmuhammed (P) did not claim to be a co-author. The district court granted summary judgment to the defendants.

ISSUE: Does the contribution of independently copyrightable material to a work intended to be an inseparable whole make the work a joint work?

HOLDING AND DECISION: (Kleinfeld, J.) No. A joint work is one that was intended by both parties to be a joint work. That determination is fact specific. The courts will look to, among other things, the apportionment of decision-making authority and the billing accorded the various parties. Here, none of the parties made any objective manifestations of intent to be co-authors. Specifically, Aalmuhammed (P) had no supervisory authority over the film and signed a "work for hire" agreement that precluded him from being a co-author. Affirmed but remanded for further proceedings on a quantum meruit claim.

▶ *ANALYSIS*

A social consideration underlies limitations in the definitions of *author* and of *joint work*. The ability of an author to collaborate or consult with others without the risk of losing ownership in the work favors the progress of knowledge.

■━■

Quicknotes

COPYRIGHT ACT Copyright Act of 1976 extends copyright protection to "original works of authorship fixed in any tangible medium of expression, now known or later developed, from which they can be perceived, reproduced, or otherwise communicated, either directly or with the aid of a machine or device." 17 U.S.C. § 102.

DECLARATORY RELIEF A judgment of the court establishing the rights of the parties.

QUANTUM MERUIT Equitable doctrine allowing recovery for labor and materials provided by one party, even though no contract was entered into, in order to avoid unjust enrichment by the benefited party.

WORK FOR HIRE A work prepared by an employee in the scope of his employment or specially ordered and commissioned pursuant to a written agreement that the work constitute one made for hire.

■━■

Arnstein v. Porter

Songwriter (P) v. Songwriter (D)

154 F.2d 464 (2d Cir. 1946).

NATURE OF CASE: Appeal from summary judgment for defendant in copyright infringement suit.

FACT SUMMARY: Cole Porter (D) defended an infringement suit by denying having access to the songs or copying them.

🏛 RULE OF LAW
In a copyright infringement dispute, if there is evidence of access and similarities exist, then the trier of the facts must determine whether the similarities are sufficient to prove copying.

FACTS: Arnstein (P) alleged that Porter (D) had plagiarized some songs and sued for infringement of copyright. The district court considered Arnstein's (P) allegations that Porter (D) or his "stooges" had burglarized his room to gain access to his songs "fantastic," and accepted Porter's (D) denial of access and copying. When Porter's (D) motion for summary judgment was granted, Arnstein (P) appealed.

ISSUE: If there is evidence of access and similarities exist, then must the trier of the facts determine whether the similarities are sufficient to prove copying?

HOLDING AND DECISION: (Frank, J.) Yes. If there is evidence of access and similarities exist, then the trier of the facts must determine whether the similarities are sufficient to prove copying. If there are no similarities, no amount of evidence of access will suffice to prove copying. In this case, there are sufficient similarities between Arnstein's (P) and Porter's (D) compositions so that, if there is enough evidence of access to permit the case to go to the jury, the jury may properly infer that the similarities did not result from coincidence. The district court heard no oral testimony on the issue of access and Arnstein's (P) credibility, even as to the "fantastic" improbabilities, should be left to the jury. Since it is not "indubitable" that Porter (D) did not have access to Arnstein's (P) compositions, summary judgment was not proper. Reversed.

DISSENT: (Clark, J.) Since the musical compositions are of the simple and trite character where small repetitive sequences are not hard to discover, there is no legal basis for the claim of plagiarism.

▶ ANALYSIS

This case points out the two elements necessary to establish infringement. First, copying must be shown, either directly or circumstantially. Then, it must be shown that

the copying went so far as to constitute improper or unlawful appropriation.

◼◼

Quicknotes

APPROPRIATION The act of making something one's own or making use of something to serve one's own interest.

COPYRIGHT Refers to the exclusive rights granted to an artist pursuant to Article I, section 8, clause 8 of the United States Constitution over the reproduction, display, performance, distribution, and adaptation of his work for a period prescribed by statute.

COPYRIGHT INFRINGEMENT A violation of one of the exclusive rights granted to an artist pursuant to Article I, section 8, clause 8 of the United States Constitution over the reproduction, display, performance, distribution, and adaptation of his work for a period prescribed by statute.

SUMMARY JUDGMENT Judgment rendered by a court in response to a motion by one of the parties, claiming that the lack of a question of material fact in respect to an issue warrants disposition of the issue without consideration by the jury.

◼◼

Nichols v. Universal Pictures Corporation

Playwright (P) v. Producer (D)

45 F.2d 119 (2d Cir. 1930).

NATURE OF CASE: Copyright infringement suit.

FACT SUMMARY: Plaintiff, author of the play, "Abie's Irish Rose," brought suit against defendant, producer of the motion picture, "The Cohens and The Kellys," which plaintiff alleges was taken from his play.

🏛 RULE OF LAW
Two plays may correspond closely enough in plot for a finding of infringement.

FACTS: Plaintiff is the author of a play, "Abie's Irish Rose." Defendant produced a motion picture, "The Cohens and The Kellys," which the plaintiff alleges was taken from it. Both plays involve the stories of a Jewish and an Irish-Catholic family in which the children fall in love and are married, their parents are outraged, a grandchild is born, and there is a subsequent reconciliation.

ISSUE: May two plays correspond closely enough in plot for a finding of infringement?

HOLDING AND DECISION: (Hand, J.) Yes. Two plays may correspond closely enough in plot for a finding of infringement. Here it appears that defendant took no more of the plaintiff's work, assuming he took anything at all, than the law allowed. Both stories were very different, the only similarity being a quarrel between an Irish father and a Jewish father, the marriage of their children, the birth of grandchildren, and a reconciliation. The plaintiff's copyright did not cover all that might be drawn from her play; its content went to some extent into the public domain. The theme was essentially an idea and the characters were primarily stock figures, which have been used for many decades. Affirmed.

▶ ANALYSIS

This case involves the question of to what extent ideas may be subject to copyright protection. As a general rule, the "idea/expression dichotomy" holds that ideas are never copyrightable, though the expression of those ideas may be subject to copyright protection. While a plot falls more under the category of an idea, the court recognizes that in some instances the plot may nonetheless be copyrightable. This was not such a case.

■══■

Quicknotes

COPYRIGHT Refers to the exclusive rights granted to an artist pursuant to Article I, section 8, clause 8 of the United States Constitution over the reproduction, display, performance, distribution, and adaptation of his work for a period prescribed by statute.

COPYRIGHT INFRINGEMENT A violation of one of the exclusive rights granted to an artist pursuant to Article I, section 8, clause 8 of the United States Constitution over the reproduction, display, performance, distribution, and adaptation of his work for a period prescribed by statute.

PUBLIC DOMAIN Works that are not protected by copyright and are free for the public to utilize.

■══■

Computer Associates International v. Altai, Inc.

Computer programmer (P) v. Competitor (D)

982 F.2d 693 (2d Cir. 1992).

NATURE OF CASE: Appeal from award of damages for copyright infringement.

FACT SUMMARY: Upon discovering that Altai, Inc. (D) may have appropriated parts of its "Adapter" computer program, Computer Associates International (P) sued Altai (D) for copyright infringement and trade secret misappropriation.

🏛 RULE OF LAW
To warrant a finding of copyright infringement, the protectable, nonliteral elements of one computer program must be substantially similar to those elements in a second computer program.

FACTS: Computer Associates International (CA) (P) designed, developed, and marketed various types of computer programs, including "CA-Scheduler," a job scheduling program containing a subprogram entitled "Adapter." Adapter was a wholly integrated component of CA-Scheduler with no capacity for independent use. In 1982, Altai, Inc. (D) began marketing its own job scheduling program entitled "Zeke." Subsequently, Altai (D) decided to rewrite Zeke to run in conjunction with a different operating system, and Altai's (D) president, Williams, approached Arney, a computer programmer who worked for CA (P), about working for Altai (D). When Arney left CA (P) to work for Altai (D), he took with him copies of the source code for two versions of Adapter and used them to design Altai's (D) new component-program, "Oscar" (Version 3.4). Arney copied approximately 30% of Oscar's code from CA's (P) Adapter program. When CA (P) first learned that Altai (D) may have appropriated parts of Adapter, it brought this copyright and trade secret misappropriation action against Altai (D). A rewrite of Oscar was initiated, entitled Oscar 3.5. The district court awarded CA (P) $364,444 in actual damages and apportioned profits for copyright infringement regarding Oscar 3.4. However, the court denied relief on CA's (P) second claim, finding that Oscar 3.5 was not substantially similar to Adapter. The court further concluded that CA's (P) state law trade secret misappropriation claim against Altai (D) was preempted by the federal copyright act. On appeal, Altai (D) conceded liability for the copying of Adapter into Oscar 3.4 and raised no challenge to the award of damages. Thus, only CA's (P) second and third claims were addressed on appeal.

ISSUE: To warrant a finding of copyright infringement, must the protectable, nonliteral elements of one computer program be substantially similar to those in a second computer program?

HOLDING AND DECISION: (Walker, J.) Yes. To warrant a finding of copyright infringement, the protectable, nonliteral elements of one computer program must be substantially similar to those elements in a second computer program. It is now well settled that the literal elements of computer programs, i.e., their source and object codes, are the subject of copyright protection. Altai (D) made sure that the literal elements of its revamped Oscar program were no longer substantially similar to the literal elements of CA's (P) Adapter. If the nonliteral structures of literary works are protected by copyright (and by law computer programs are literary works), then the nonliteral structures of computer programs are also protected by copyright. It is a fundamental principle of copyright law that a copyright does not protect an idea, but only the expression of the idea. A three-step procedure, based on the abstractions test utilized by the district court, should be used to determine whether the nonliteral elements of two or more computer programs are substantially similar. As applied to computer programs, the abstractions test will comprise the first step in the examination for substantial similarity. Once the program's abstraction levels have been discovered, the substantial similarity inquiry moves from the conceptual to the concrete. This process entails examining the structural components at each level of abstraction to determine whether their particular inclusion at that level was dictated by considerations of efficiency; required by factors external to the program itself; or taken from the public domain, thus making them nonprotectable. Once a court has sifted out all those elements of the allegedly infringed program, there may remain a core of protectable expression. At this point, the court's substantial similarity inquiry focuses on whether Altai (D) copied any aspect of this protected expression, as well as an assessment of the copied portion's relative importance with respect to CA's (P) overall program. Upon a review of the record in this case, this court can discern no error on the part of the district court judge. Affirmed.

▶ ANALYSIS

One of the doctrines discussed by the court is the doctrine of merger. The doctrine's underlying principle is that when there is essentially only one way to express an idea, the idea and its expression are inseparable and copyright is no bar to copying that expression. In the computer context, this means that when specific instructions even though previously copyrighted are the only and essential means

Continued on next page.

of accomplishing a given task, their later use by another will not amount to infringement. When one considers the fact that programmers generally strive to create programs "that meet the user's needs in the most efficient manner," the applicability of the merger doctrine to computer programs becomes compelling.

■■■■

Quicknotes

COPYRIGHT INFRINGEMENT A violation of one of the exclusive rights granted to an artist pursuant to Article I, section 8, clause 8 of the United States Constitution over the reproduction, display, performance, distribution, and adaptation of his work for a period prescribed by statute.

MISAPPROPRIATION The unlawful use of another's property or funds.

TRADE SECRET Consists of any formula, pattern, plan, process, or device known only to its owner and business which gives an advantage over competitors; a secret formula used in the manufacture of a particular product that is not known to the general public.

■■■■

Anderson v. Stallone

Screenwriter (P) v. Actor (D)

11 U.S.P.Q.2d 1161 (C.D. Cal. 1989).

NATURE OF CASE: Copyright protection of movie characters.

FACT SUMMARY: Timothy Anderson (P), writer of a movie script treatment for the movie *Rocky IV*, using characters already developed in previous *Rocky* movies, sued scriptwriter/actor Sylvester Stallone (D) for copyright infringement.

🏛 RULE OF LAW
A treatment of a movie sequel that incorporates copyrighted characters who appeared in the prior movies is not itself entitled to copyright protection. It is an unauthorized derivative work.

FACTS: In May of 1982, Sylvester Stallone (D), following the success of three *Rocky* movies, described to reporters his general ideas for a future *Rocky IV* movie sequel. The ideas referenced having Rocky fight a Russian boxer in a "giant stadium in Moscow [with] everything in Russian Red." Timothy Anderson (P), after hearing Stallone (D) describe these ideas, wrote a thirty-one page treatment that he hoped Stallone (D) would use for the movie. Anderson (P) incorporated the characters created by Stallone (D) and cited Stallone (D) as co-author of the treatment. Later that year, Anderson (P) and his attorney met with representatives of MGM-UA Communications Co. (MGM), a movie production studio. Anderson (P) signed a release that relieved MGM of any liability stemming from the use of the treatment. Anderson (P) claims that at this meeting he was told that the treatment could be worth "big bucks" if Stallone/MGM used it. In April of 1984, Anderson's (P) attorney requested that MGM compensate Anderson (P) for the use of the treatment in the forthcoming *Rocky IV* movie. Meanwhile, Stallone (D) had finished his script for the movie, and *Rocky IV* was subsequently released in November 1985. Anderson (P) then filed suit.

ISSUE: Is a treatment of a movie sequel script that incorporates copyrighted characters who appeared in the prior movies itself entitled to copyright protection or is it an unauthorized derivative work?

HOLDING AND DECISION: (Keller, J.) No. A treatment of a movie sequel that incorporates copyrighted characters who appeared in the prior movies is not itself entitled to copyright protection. It is an unauthorized derivative work. Copyright protection is granted to a character if the character has been developed with enough specificity to constitute protected expression. Here, it is uncontested that Anderson (P) lifted the characters from prior *Rocky* movies in their entirety, retaining the names and relationships of those characters. These characters were developed by Stallone (D), who owns the copyrights to the first three *Rocky* movies and, therefore, has exclusive rights to prepare any derivative works based on those copyrights. Anderson (P) argues that, under 17 U.S.C. § 103(a), he is entitled to copyright protection for the non-infringing portions of his treatment. There is no such protection either in the House Report as to § 103(a) or in later case law interpreting § 103(a). Therefore, neither the House Report nor any cases support the conclusion that an infringing derivative work should be granted copyright protection. Summary judgment granted to the defendants. Plaintiff's action for copyright infringement against the defendant is precluded.

▶ ANALYSIS

Stallone (D) had already fully developed the basic personalities of the characters of the *Rocky* series. Anderson's (P) treatment, while perhaps somewhat "new" in that it related to a new movie, was based on Stallone's (D) general stated ideas about *Rocky IV*, which Anderson (P) of course heard prior to writing his treatment. It incorporated the same exact characters from *Rocky I, II,* and *III*. Anderson's (P) script was not original enough to withstand scrutiny under the derivative analysis.

Quicknotes

COPYRIGHT Refers to the exclusive rights granted to an artist pursuant to Article I, section 8, clause 8 of the United States Constitution over the reproduction, display, performance, distribution, and adaptation of his work for a period prescribed by statute.

DERIVATIVE WORK A work of authorship that is based on a previous work.

Sony Corporation of America v. Universal City Studios, Inc.

Videocassette recorder manufacturer (D) v. Movie studio (P)

464 U.S. 417 (1984).

NATURE OF CASE: Appeal from reversal of order dismissing copyright infringement action.

FACT SUMMARY: Movie studios (P) that owned copyrights in movies and other television programming contended that Sony (D) contributed to copyright infringement of their copyrighted works by marketing videocassette recorders (VCRs or VTRs) that enabled users to record the programs.

RULE OF LAW
One who supplies the means to accomplish an infringing activity and encourages that activity through advertisement is not liable for copyright infringement.

FACTS: Sony Corp. (Sony) (D) marketed Betamax videocassette recorders (VCRs or VTRs), which allowed home recording of televised programs. Several movie studios (P), holders of copyrights on televised movies and other televised programs, brought an action for contributory copyright infringement on the theory that Sony (D) was contributorily liable for infringement by consumers of VTRs of the studios' (P) copyrighted works on the basis of Sony's (D) marketing and distribution of the VTRs. The district court, finding, inter alia, that no Sony (D) employee had either direct involvement with the allegedly infringing activity or direct contact with purchasers of Betamax who recorded copyrighted works off-the-air, and that there was no evidence that any of the copies made by individuals were influenced or encouraged by Sony's (D) advertisements, held that Sony (D) was not liable for direct or contributory copyright infringement. The court of appeals reversed. The United States Supreme Court granted certiorari.

ISSUE: Is one who supplies the means to accomplish an infringing activity and encourages that activity through advertisement liable for copyright infringement?

HOLDING AND DECISION: (Stevens, J.) No. One who supplies the means to accomplish an infringing activity and encourages that activity through advertisement is not liable for copyright infringement. The protection given to copyrights is wholly statutory, and, in a case like this, in which Congress has not plainly marked the course to be followed by the judiciary, the Court must be circumspect in construing the scope of rights created by a statute that never contemplated such a calculus of interests based on technological advances. In proceeding, the Court must balance the encouraging and rewarding of authors to create new works with the public good. This case does not fall in the category of those in which it is manifestly just to

impose vicarious liability because the "contributory" infringer was in a position to control the use of copyrighted works by others and had authorized the use without permission from the copyright owner. Here, the only contact between Sony (D) and the users of the VTR's occurred at the moment of sale. However, there is no precedent for imposing vicarious liability on the theory that Sony (D) sold the VTR's with constructive knowledge that its customers might use the equipment to make unauthorized copies of copyrighted material. The sale of copying equipment, like the sale of other articles of commerce, does not constitute contributory infringement if the product is widely used for legitimate, unobjectionable purposes, or, indeed, is merely capable of substantial noninfringing uses. Here, a substantial portion of the public's use of VTRs does not implicate copyright at all, and also the most common use for the Betamax—time-shifting—constitutes a fair use. Reversed.

ANALYSIS

Justice Blackmun, in a dissent, faulted the majority for deferring to congressional action in the face of major technological advancements, saying that the Court was thereby "evad[ing] the hard issues when they arise in the area of copyright law." He instead proposed a test for indirect liability for copyright infringement based on whether the primary use of technology is infringing. Even under this test, however, Sony (D) would have prevailed given the majority's determination that the predominant use of VTRs (time-shifting) constituted fair use.

Quicknotes

COPYRIGHT Refers to the exclusive rights granted to an artist pursuant to Article I, section 8, clause 8 of the United States Constitution over the reproduction, display, performance, distribution, and adaptation of his work for a period prescribed by statute.

COPYRIGHT INFRINGEMENT A violation of one of the exclusive rights granted to an artist pursuant to Article I, section 8, clause 8 of the United States Constitution over the reproduction, display, performance, distribution, and adaptation of his work for a period prescribed by statute.

FAIR USE An affirmative defense to a claim of copyright infringement providing an exception from the copyright owner's exclusive rights in a work for the purposes of

Continued on next page.

criticism, comment, news reporting, teaching, scholarship, or research; the determination of whether a use is fair is made on a case-by-case basis and requires the court to consider: (1) the purpose and character of the use; (2) the nature of the work; (3) the amount and substantiality of the portion used; and (4) the effect of the use on the potential market for, or value of, the work.

17 U.S.C. § 107 Contains the fair use provisions of the Copyright Act.

■≡■

Harper & Row Publishers, Inc. v. Nation Enterprises

Book publisher (P) v. Magazine (D)

471 U.S. 539 (1985).

NATURE OF CASE: Review of reversal of award of damages for copyright infringement.

FACT SUMMARY: Nation Enterprises (D) contended that its use of quotes from a yet-unpublished set of memoirs constituted fair use.

🏛 RULE OF LAW
Publication of portions of a work soon to be published does not qualify as fair use.

FACTS: Harper & Row Publishers, Inc. (Harper) (P) obtained the rights to publish President Ford's memoirs, *A Time to Heal*. *Time* magazine contracted for the rights to preview the work immediately prior to publication. Prior to the publication of the article by *Time* magazine, Nation Enterprises (D), publisher of *The Nation* magazine, obtained a copy of the Ford manuscript. *The Nation* published an article that quoted the manuscript regarding the Nixon pardon. *Time* then declined to run the article it had planned and canceled its contract with Harper (P). Harper (P) sued Nation Enterprises (D) for copyright infringement. The district court awarded damages for infringement. The Second Circuit reversed, holding Nation Enterprises' (D) use to be a "fair use" under 17 U.S.C. § 107. The United States Supreme Court granted certiorari.

ISSUE: Is publication of portions of a work soon to be published fair use?

HOLDING AND DECISION: (O'Connor, J.) No. Publication of portions of a work soon to be published does not qualify fair use. The notion behind the fair use doctrine as it was formulated in the common law was that one using a copyrighted work should not have to obtain a copyright holder's permission to use the copyrighted work in a situation where a reasonable copyright holder would in fact grant permission. Section 107 of the Copyright Act, which codified the doctrine, expressly noted in its legislative history that it was not intended to modify the common law. In terms of reasonableness, it is not reasonable to expect a copyright holder to allow another person to "scoop" it by publishing his material ahead of time. With respect to § 107's language, the section lists four factors to be considered in applying the doctrine. The two factors most salient here are purpose of the use and effect on the market. Normally, a fair use will not be one of economic competition with the copyright holder, which is precisely what prior publication of a copyrighted work is. Further, the effect on the market of such a use is illustrated by what happened here: it greatly lessens the market value of the copyrighted work. The conclusion therefore presents itself

that, in almost all cases, prior publication of a work awaiting publication will not be a fair use. Such was the case here. Reversed.

▶ ANALYSIS

"Fair use" is a well-established common law doctrine. It was recognized by the Supreme Court as early as 1841. In *Folsom v. Marsh*, 9 F. Cas. 342 (1841), Justice Story permitted use of quotes by a reviewer as a "fair use." Use of quotes in criticism of a work has remained a major application of the doctrine.

Quicknotes

COPYRIGHT Refers to the exclusive rights granted to an artist pursuant to Article I, section 8, clause 8 of the United States Constitution over the reproduction, display, performance, distribution, and adaptation of his work for a period prescribed by statute.

COPYRIGHT INFRINGEMENT A violation of one of the exclusive rights granted to an artist pursuant to Article I, section 8, clause 8 of the United States Constitution over the reproduction, display, performance, distribution, and adaptation of his work for a period prescribed by statute.

FAIR USE An affirmative defense to a claim of copyright infringement providing an exception from the copyright owner's exclusive rights in a work for the purposes of criticism, comment, news reporting, teaching, scholarship or research; the determination of whether a use is fair is made on a case-by-case basis and requires the court to consider: (1) the purpose and character of the use; (2) the nature of the work; (3) the amount and substantiality of the portion used; and (4) the effect of the use on the potential market for, or value of, the work.

17 U.S.C. § 107 Contains the fair use provisions of the Copyright Act.

Sony Corporation of America v. Universal City Studios, Inc.

Videocassette recorder manufacturer (D) v. Movie studio (P)

464 U.S. 417 (1984).

NATURE OF CASE: Appeal from reversal of order dismissing copyright infringement action.

FACT SUMMARY: Movie studios (P) that owned copyrights in movies and other television programming contended that Sony Corporation of America (Sony) (D) contributed to copyright infringement of their copyrighted works by marketing videocassette recorders (VCRs or VTRs) that enabled users to record the programs. Sony (D) contended that consumers' predominant use was for time-shifting, i.e., making copies for later viewing, and that such use was a fair use.

🏛 RULE OF LAW
The use of a recording device to make a copy of a copyrighted work is a fair use where the device has significant commercial noninfringing uses.

FACTS: Sony Corporation of America (Sony) (D) marketed Betamax videocassette recorders (VCRs or VTRs), which allowed home recording of televised programs. Several movie studios (P), holders of copyrights on televised movies and other televised programs, brought an action for contributory copyright infringement on the theory that Sony (D) was contributorily liable for infringement by consumers of VTRs of the studios' (P) copyrighted works on the basis of Sony's (D) marketing and distribution of the VTRs. The district court, found, inter alia, that most consumers used Sony's (D) product for "time-shifting," i.e., recording shows for later viewing, and that relatively few consumers engaged in "archiving," recording and storing programs in a library. This was based on the studios' (P) survey that showed that 75.4% of the VTR owners used their machines to record for time-shifting purposes half or most of the time and on Sony's (D) survey that showed that 96% of the Betamax owners had used the machine to record programs they otherwise would have missed. When the studios (P) asked interviewees how many cassettes were in their library, 55.8% said there were 10 or fewer. In Sony's (D) survey, of the total programs viewed by interviewees in the past month, 70.4% had been viewed only that one time and for 57.9%, there were no plans for further viewing. Based on these surveys, the district court concluded that consumers' use was a fair use and that, therefore, Sony (D) could not be held liable for copyright infringements. The court had also held that Sony (D) could not be liable for direct or contributory copyright infringement (see Casenote at p. 66–67, supra, for a brief of the excerpt dealing with the contributory liability issue). The court of appeals reversed. The United States Supreme Court granted certiorari.

ISSUE: Is the use of a recording device to make a copy of a copyrighted work a fair use where the device has significant commercial noninfringing uses?

HOLDING AND DECISION: (Stevens, J.) Yes. The use of a recording device to make a copy of a copyrighted work is a fair use where the device has significant commercial noninfringing uses. The record and the district court's findings show that there is a significant likelihood that substantial numbers of copyright holders who license their works for broadcast on free television would not object to having their broadcast time-shifted by private viewers and that there is no likelihood that time-shifting would cause significant harm to the potential market for, or the value of, the studios' (P) copyrighted works. The VTR's are therefore capable of substantial noninfringing uses. Private, non-commercial time-shifting in the home satisfies this standard of noninfringing uses both because the studios (P) have no right to prevent other copyright holders from authorizing such time-shifting for their programs, and because the district court's findings reveal that even the unauthorized home time-shifting of respondents' programs is legitimate fair use. One of the fair-use factors is whether the use is commercial or for profit. Here, it is clear that time-shifting is neither, as it is used by private viewers to view a show they have been invited to watch at point in time later than originally shown. Thus, even the fact that the entire work is reproduced does not have its ordinary effect of militating against a finding of fair use. Another fair use factor that must be considered is whether the use, even if non-commercial, has a demonstrable effect upon the potential market for, or the value of, the copyrighted work. The studios (P) have not shown any deleterious effect on the market or value of their copyrighted works, as they have admitted no harm to date, and have not demonstrated that time-shifting will reduce the number of movie or television viewers in the future. In fact, the use of VTRs may increase the number of those viewing broadcasts and sponsors' advertisements. To the extent time-shifting expands public access to freely broadcast television programs, it yields societal benefits. Weighing these factors leads to the conclusion that on balance, time-shifting is a fair use and that the district court did not err in so ruling. Reversed.

▶ ANALYSIS

Arguably, the logical implication of the studios' (P) suit was that the Copyright Act conferred upon all copyright owners

Continued on next page.

collectively the exclusive right to distribute VTR's simply because they could be used to infringe copyrights, since the studios (P) effectively sought to declare VTRs contraband. The Court's decision seems to have protected the studios (P) from themselves, given that videotapes, and then DVDs, by greatly expanding the market for movie and television content, became the studios' (P) principal source of revenue.

■══■

Quicknotes

COPYRIGHT Refers to the exclusive rights granted to an artist pursuant to Article I, section 8, clause 8 of the United States Constitution over the reproduction, display, performance, distribution, and adaptation of his work for a period prescribed by statute.

COPYRIGHT INFRINGEMENT A violation of one of the exclusive rights granted to an artist pursuant to Article I, section 8, clause 8 of the United States Constitution over the reproduction, display, performance, distribution, and adaptation of his work for a period prescribed by statute.

FAIR USE An affirmative defense to a claim of copyright infringement providing an exception from the copyright owner's exclusive rights in a work for the purposes of criticism, comment, news reporting, teaching, scholarship or research; the determination of whether a use is fair is made on a case-by-case basis and requires the court to consider: (1) the purpose and character of the use; (2) the nature of the work; (3) the amount and substantiality of the portion used; and (4) the effect of the use on the potential market for, or value of, the work.

17 U.S.C. § 107 Contains the fair use provisions of the Copyright Act.

■══■

American Geophysical Union v. Texaco Inc.

Scientific journal (P) v. Oil company (D)

60 F.3d 913 (2d Cir. 1994).

NATURE OF CASE: Appeal from an interlocutory holding that there was a copyright infringement.

FACT SUMMARY: Texaco, Inc. (D) claimed that its unauthorized photocopying of scholarly articles was a fair use and therefore not a copyright infringement.

🏛 RULE OF LAW

Photocopying of copyrighted material converting scholarly articles into a useful format is not a transformative use of the material and therefore not a fair use.

FACTS: American Geophysical Union (P) and other publishers (P) of scientific and technical journals brought a class action claiming that Texaco's (D) unauthorized photocopying of articles from their journals constituted copyright infringement. Texaco (D) claimed that its copying was fair use under § 107 of the Copyright Act. After a limited-issue bench trial, the district court held that the photocopying of eight articles by one of Texaco's (D) researchers was not fair use. Texaco (D) appealed.

ISSUE: Is photocopying of copyrighted material converting the articles into a useful format a transformative use of the material?

HOLDING AND DECISION: (Newman, C.J.) No. Photocopying of copyrighted material converting the articles into a useful format is not a transformative use of the material and therefore not a fair use. The publishers (P) have demonstrated a substantial harm to the value of their copyrights through Texaco's (D) copying due to lost licensing and subscription revenue. Balancing the four non-exclusive considerations bearing on fair use enumerated in § 107 of the Copyright Act, Texaco's (D) use of the copyrighted material did not constitute a fair use. Affirmed.

DISSENT: (Jacobs, J.) The purpose and character of Texaco's (D) use is integral to transformative and productive ends of scientific research. The adverse effect of Texaco's (D) use upon the potential market for the work is illusory. For these reasons, Texaco's (D) photocopying of the articles constituted fair use and there was no copyright infringement.

▶ ANALYSIS

This court enumerated and discussed each of the four statutory factors. It found that the first factor, the purpose and character of the use, weighed against Texaco (D) because the dominant purpose of the copying was archival and not transformative. The second factor, the nature of the copy-righted work, favored Texaco (D) since the articles were all of a factual nature. The third factor, the amount and substantiality of the portion used, also weighed against Texaco (D), since all the articles were copied in their entirety. The fourth factor, the effect upon potential market or value, also was found to weigh against Texaco (D).

■━■

Quicknotes

COPYRIGHT Refers to the exclusive rights granted to an artist pursuant to Article I, section 8, clause 8 of the United States Constitution over the reproduction, display, performance, distribution, and adaptation of his work for a period prescribed by statute.

COPYRIGHT INFRINGEMENT A violation of one of the exclusive rights granted to an artist pursuant to Article I, section 8, clause 8 of the United States Constitution over the reproduction, display, performance, distribution, and adaptation of his work for a period prescribed by statute.

FAIR USE An affirmative defense to a claim of copyright infringement providing an exception from the copyright owner's exclusive rights in a work for the purposes of criticism, comment, news reporting, teaching, scholarship or research; the determination of whether a use is fair is made on a case-by-case basis and requires the court to consider: (1) the purpose and character of the use; (2) the nature of the work; (3) the amount and substantiality of the portion used; and (4) the effect of the use on the potential market for, or value of, the work.

17 U.S.C. § 107 Contains the fair use provisions of the Copyright Act.

■━■

Campbell v. Acuff-Rose Music, Inc.

Recording artist (D) v. Music publisher (P)

510 U.S. 569 (1994).

NATURE OF CASE: Review of reversal of summary judgment for the defense in copyright infringement action.

FACT SUMMARY: 2 Live Crew (D) contended that its parody of Roy Orbison's song, "Oh, Pretty Woman," was a fair use within the meaning of the Copyright Act of 1976, but the appellate court concluded that the commercial nature of the parody rendered it presumptively unfair.

🏛 RULE OF LAW
The commercial purpose of a work is only one element of the inquiry into the work's purpose and character for fair use purposes.

FACTS: 2 Live Crew (D) recorded a rap parody of the Roy Orbison hit "Oh, Pretty Woman." Acuff-Rose (P), the copyright holder of the original song, sued 2 Live Crew (D) for copyright infringement. The district court granted summary judgment for 2 Live Crew (D), having concluded that its song made fair use of Orbison's original. The appeals court reversed and remanded. It concluded that every commercial use is presumptively unfair and the blatantly commercial purpose of 2 Live Crew's (D) version prevented it from constituting fair use. 2 Live Crew (D) appealed.

ISSUE: Is the commercial purpose of a work the determining element of the inquiry into the work's purpose and character for fair use purposes?

HOLDING AND DECISION: (Souter, J.) No. The commercial purpose of a work is only one element of the inquiry into the work's purpose and character for fair use purposes. The other elements to be considered are the nature of the copyrighted work, the amount and substantiality of the portion used in relation to the copyrighted work as a whole, and the effect of the use upon the potential market for the copyrighted work. In this case, it was error for the court of appeals to conclude that the commercial nature of 2 Live Crew's (D) parody rendered it presumptively unfair. No such evidentiary presumption exists for either the first factor—the character and purpose of the use—or the fourth factor—market harm. The court also erred in holding that 2 Live Crew (D) had copied excessively from the Orbison original, considering the satiric purpose of their version. Reversed and remanded to evaluate the amount taken from the original, its transformative elements, and potential for market harm.

▶ ANALYSIS

Dictionaries define "parody" as a literary or artistic work that imitates the characteristic style of an author or a work for comic effect or ridicule. Copyright law recognizes that a parodist must use some elements of a prior author's composition in order to create a new one that comments on that author's work. Parody needs to mimic an original to make its point, but it may or may not be fair use depending on whether it could be perceived as commenting on, or criticizing, the original.

Quicknotes

COPYRIGHT Refers to the exclusive rights granted to an artist pursuant to Article I, section 8, clause 8 of the United States Constitution over the reproduction, display, performance, distribution, and adaptation of his work for a period prescribed by statute.

COPYRIGHT ACT Copyright Act of 1976 extends copyright protection to "original works of authorship fixed in any tangible medium of expression, now known or later developed, from which they can be perceived, reproduced, or otherwise communicated, either directly or with the aid of a machine or device." 17 U.S.C. § 102.

COPYRIGHT INFRINGEMENT A violation of one of the exclusive rights granted to an artist pursuant to Article I, section 8, clause 8 of the United States Constitution over the reproduction, display, performance, distribution, and adaptation of his work for a period prescribed by statute.

FAIR USE An affirmative defense to a claim of copyright infringement providing an exception from the copyright owner's exclusive rights in a work for the purposes of criticism, comment, news reporting, teaching, scholarship or research; the determination of whether a use is fair is made on a case-by-case basis and requires the court to consider: (1) the purpose and character of the use; (2) the nature of the work; (3) the amount and substantiality of the portion used; and (4) the effect of the use on the potential market for, or value of, the work.

SUMMARY JUDGMENT Judgment rendered by a court in response to a motion by one of the parties, claiming that the lack of a question of material fact in respect to an issue warrants disposition of the issue without consideration by the jury.

Bill Graham Archives v. Dorling Kindersley Ltd.

Copyright owner (P) v. Book publisher (D)

448 F.3d 605 (2d Cir. 2006).

NATURE OF CASE: Appeal from dismissal on summary judgment of copyright infringement action.

FACT SUMMARY: Bill Graham Archives, LLC (P), which owned the copyright in images on Grateful Dead event posters and tickets, contended that Dorling Kindersley Ltd. (D) infringed its copyright by publishing seven of the images in reduced size in a book on the history of the Grateful Dead.

🏛 RULE OF LAW
A book publisher's appropriation of copyrighted poster and ticket images in a biographical book in reduced-size format is a protected "fair use" under the copyright law where the balance of the statutory fair use factors favors the publisher.

FACTS: Bill Graham Archives, LLC (BGA) (P) owned the copyright in seven Grateful Dead (a rock band) event posters and ticket images that Dorling Kindersley Ltd. (DK) (D), in collaboration with Grateful Dead Productions, sought to reprint in reduced-size in a book titled *Grateful Dead: The Illustrated Trip* (*Illustrated Trip*), which was intended as a cultural history of the band. *Illustrated Trip* contains over 2000 images representing dates in the Grateful Dead's history, in chronological order with a timeline, with explanatory text. A typical page of the book features a collage of images, text, and graphic art designed to simultaneously capture the eye and inform the reader. DK (D) initially sought permission from BGA (P) to reprint the images, but, after it could not secure such permission, published the book with the images without a license or grant of permission. The images are displayed in significantly reduced form and are accompanied by captions describing the concerts they represent. When DK (D) refused to meet BGA's (P) post-publication license fee demands, BGA (P) filed suit for copyright infringement. The district court dismissed the action on summary judgment, and the court of appeals granted review.

ISSUE: Is a book publisher's appropriation of copyrighted poster and ticket images in a biographical book in reduced-size format a protected "fair use" under the copyright law where the balance of the statutory fair use factors favors the publisher?

HOLDING AND DECISION: (Restani, J.) Yes. A book publisher's appropriation of copyrighted poster and ticket images in a biographical book in reduced-size format is a protected "fair use" under the copyright law where the balance of the statutory fair use factors favors the publisher. Under 17 U.S.C. § 107(1), the first factor is "the purpose and character of the use, including whether such use is of a commercial nature or is for nonprofit educational purposes." Most important is whether the nature of the work is "transformative," i.e., "whether the new work merely supersede[s] the objects of the original creation, or instead adds something new, with a further purpose or different character, altering the first with new expression, meaning, or message." BGA (P) argues that as a matter of law merely placing poster images along a timeline is not a transformative use, contrary to the district court's finding. BGA's (P) argument must be rejected because here, *Illustrated Trip* is a biographical work documenting and commemorating the band's 30-year history, and courts have frequently afforded fair use protection to the use of copyrighted material in biographies, recognizing such works as forms of historic scholarship, criticism, and comment that require incorporation of original source material for optimum treatment of their subject. Moreover, DK's (D) purpose in using the images at issue is plainly different from the original purpose for which they were created. Originally, the images fulfilled the dual purposes of artistic expression and promotion, as the posters were distributed to generate public interest in the Grateful Dead and to convey information to a large number people about the band's forthcoming concerts. In contrast, DK (D) used each of BGA's (P) images as historical artifacts to document and represent the actual occurrence of Grateful Dead concerts featured on *Illustrated Trip*'s timeline. The images, in some instances, help the reader's understanding of the biographical text by marking important concerts. In sum, DK's (D) use of the disputed images is transformative both when accompanied by referencing commentary and when standing alone. This conclusion is strengthened by the manner in which they significantly reduced the size of the reproductions, which permits readers to recognize the historical significance of the posters, but is inadequate to offer more than a glimpse of their expressive value. The expressive value of the original images was further minimized by combining them with a timeline, textual material, and original graphical artwork to create a collage that ensures that the images at issue are employed only to enrich the presentation of the cultural history of the Grateful Dead, not to exploit copyrighted artwork for commercial gain. Yet another factor that supports the conclusion that the use was transformative is that the images constitute an inconsequential (less than one-fifth of one percent) portion of the book. Also, no BGA (P) image takes up more than one-eighth of a page in a book or is given more prominence than any other image on the

Continued on next page.

page. Finally, the commercial nature of the use also supports a finding that the use was transformative, since the book does not exploit the use of BGA's (P) images as such for commercial gain, i.e., they are not used in commercial advertising or in any other way to promote the sale of the book, and their use is merely incidental to the commercial biographical value of the book. The first factor weighs in favor of DK (D). The second fair use factor, under 17 U.S. C. § 107(2), is "the nature of the copyrighted work." In assessing this factor, the court considers "the protection of the reasonable expectations of one who engages in the kinds of creation/authorship that the copyright seeks to encourage." Here, the images are creative artworks, which are traditionally the core of intended copyright protection. The district court found this factor weighed in favor of BGA (P), but limited the weight it gave to it because the posters were published extensively. The district court was correct that creative works of art are the kind of works that weigh in favor of the copyright holder. However, the second fair use factor may be of limited usefulness where the creative work of art is being used for a transformative purpose, as here, where the images were used for their historical, rather than creative, qualities. The third fair use factor, under 17 U.S.C. § 107(3), is "the amount and substantiality of the portion used in relation to the copyrighted work as a whole." Although each image was reproduced in its entirety, courts have held that such copying does not necessarily weigh against fair use because copying the entirety of a work is sometimes necessary to make a fair use of the image. Because this reasoning is sound, the third-factor inquiry must take into account that "the extent of permissible copying varies with the purpose and character of the use." Applying this reasoning here, even though the copyrighted images are copied in their entirety, the visual impact of their artistic expression is significantly limited because of their reduced size. Therefore, such use by DK (D) was tailored to further its transformative purpose by ensuring the reader's recognition of the images as historical artifacts of Grateful Dead concert events. Accordingly, the third fair use factor does not weigh against fair use. Finally, the fourth fair use factor, under 17 U.S.C. § 107(4), is "the effect of the use upon the potential market for or value of the copyrighted work." Here, it is undisputed that DK's (D) use of the images did not impact BGA's (P) primary market for the sale of the poster images. Instead, the inquiry is whether DK's (D) use impacted BGA's (P) potential to develop a derivative market—in this case, the market for licensing BGA's (P) images for use in books. Although BGA (P) lost royalty revenues from DK (D), and it is indisputable that, as a general matter, a copyright holder is entitled to demand a royalty for licensing others to use its copyrighted work, and that the impact on potential licensing revenues is a proper subject for consideration in assessing the fourth factor, if the secondary user's failure to pay royalties was automatically held to constitute market harm, the fourth fair use factor would always favor the copyright holder. By defini-

tion, every fair use involves some loss of royalty revenue because the secondary user has not paid royalties. Therefore, it cannot be said that BGA (P) suffered market harm merely because DK (D) did not obtain and pay for a license to use the images. Instead, the inquiry focuses on the impact on potential licensing revenues for "traditional, reasonable, or likely to be developed markets." Even though DK (D) paid other copyright owners to reproduce their copyrighted works, and even though BGA (P) licensed its images to others and was willing to license images to DK (D) (but for a fee that was unacceptable to DK (D)), neither of these arguments shows impairment to a traditional, as opposed to a transformative market. The market at issue is the transformative one of using the images for their historical significance, and because copyright owners may not preempt exploitation of transformative, fair use, markets, BGA (P) did not suffer market harm due to the loss of license fees. The balance of the fair use factors weighs in DK's (D) favor, so its use was a fair use and did not infringe BGA's (P) copyrights. Affirmed.

▶ ANALYSIS

The fair use doctrine was first codified in the Copyright Act of 1976, which describes the four non-exclusive factors that must be considered in determining fair use. The ultimate test of fair use, however, has been said to be whether the copyright law's goal of "promoting the Progress of Science and useful Arts," would be better served by allowing the use than by preventing it. Thus, by concluding that the fair use factors favored DK's (D) use is essentially a conclusion that progress of the arts was better served by permitting such use.

■━■

Quicknotes

COPYRIGHT Refers to the exclusive rights granted to an artist pursuant to Article I, section 8, clause 8 of the United States Constitution over the reproduction, display, performance, distribution, and adaptation of his work for a period prescribed by statute.

COPYRIGHT ACT Copyright Act of 1976 extends copyright protection to "original works of authorship fixed in any tangible medium of expression, now known or later developed, from which they can be perceived, reproduced, or otherwise communicated, either directly or with the aid of a machine or device." 17 U.S.C. § 102.

COPYRIGHT INFRINGEMENT A violation of one of the exclusive rights granted to an artist pursuant to Article I, section 8, clause 8 of the United States Constitution over the reproduction, display, performance, distribution, and adaptation of his work for a period prescribed by statute.

Continued on next page.

FAIR USE An affirmative defense to a claim of copyright infringement providing an exception from the copyright owner's exclusive rights in a work for the purposes of criticism, comment, news reporting, teaching, scholarship or research; the determination of whether a use is fair is made on a case-by-case basis and requires the court to consider: (1) the purpose and character of the use; (2) the nature of the work; (3) the amount and substantiality of the portion used; and (4) the effect of the use on the potential market for, or value of, the work.

SUMMARY JUDGMENT Judgment rendered by a court in response to a motion by one of the parties, claiming that the lack of a question of material fact in respect to an issue warrants disposition of the issue without consideration by the jury.

Blanch v. Koons

Photographer/copyright owner (P) v. Artist (D)

467 F.3d 244 (2d Cir. 2006).

NATURE OF CASE: Appeal from summary judgment for defendants in a copyright infringement action.

FACT SUMMARY: Blanch (P), a professional photographer, contended that Koons (D), a well-known artist, infringed her copyright in an ad image, a part of which Koons (D) adapted and used in a commissioned collage painting.

🏛 RULE OF LAW
An artist's appropriation of a copyrighted image in a collage painting is a protected "fair use" under the copyright law where the balance of the statutory fair use factors favors the artist.

FACTS: Koons (D), a well-known visual artist, was commissioned to create a series of seven billboard-sized paintings for $2 million. He is known for incorporating into his artwork objects and images taken from popular media and consumer advertising, a practice that has been referred to as "neo-Pop art," or "appropriation art." In creating one of the paintings, titled "Niagara," Koons (D) incorporated a part of an ad that he had seen in *Allure* magazine. The ad, titled "Silk Sandals," a photograph taken by Blanch (P), a professional photographer, shows a woman's lower legs and feet, adorned with bronze nail polish and glittery Gucci sandals, resting on a man's lap in what appears to be a first-class airplane cabin. Koons (D) scanned the image into his computer and incorporated a version of it into "Niagara." He included in the painting only the legs and feet from the photograph, discarding the background of the airplane cabin and the man's lap on which the legs rest. He inverted the orientation of the legs so that they dangle vertically downward above the other elements of "Niagara" rather than slant upward at a 45-degree angle as they appear in the photograph. He added a heel to one of the feet and modified the photograph's coloring. The legs from the ad are second from the left among the four pairs of legs that form the focal images of "Niagara," which depicts four pairs of women's feet and lower legs dangling prominently over images of confections—a large chocolate fudge brownie topped with ice cream, a tray of donuts, and a tray of apple danish pastries—with a grassy field and Niagara Falls in the background. Koons (D) did not seek permission from Blanch (P) or anyone else before using the image. Blanch (D) brought suit, claiming that Koons (D) had infringed her copyright in the image. Koons (D) claimed fair use, and the district court granted summary judgment to him. The court of appeals granted review.

ISSUE: Is an artist's appropriation of a copyrighted image in a collage painting a protected "fair use" under the copyright law where the balance of the statutory fair use factors favors the artist?

HOLDING AND DECISION: (Sack, J.) Yes. An artist's appropriation of a copyrighted image in a collage painting is a protected "fair use" under the copyright law where the balance of the statutory fair use factors favors the artist. Under 17 U.S.C. § 107(1), the first factor is "the purpose and character of the use, including whether such use is of a commercial nature or is for nonprofit educational purposes." Koons (D) asserts, without contest from Blanch (P), that his purposes in using Blanch's (P) image are sharply different from Blanch's (P) goals in creating it. Blanch (P) wanted to add sexiness to the sandals; Koons (D) wanted "the viewer to think about his/her personal experience with these objects, products, and images and at the same time gain new insight into how these affect our lives." The greatly different purpose of each use supports a finding that the use was transformative. Here, the copyrighted work is being used as "raw material" in the furtherance of distinct creative or communicative objectives, and, therefore, the use is transformative. The test for whether "Niagara's" use of "Silk Sandals" is "transformative" is whether it merely supersedes the objects of the original creation, or instead adds something new, with a further purpose or different character, altering the first with new expression, meaning, or message. Koons's (D) use of the image in his painting fits this test almost perfectly; the use is thus transformative. Although Koons (D) profited from his paintings, which were publicly exhibited, his economic gains were not to the exclusion of broader public benefits of having the paintings exhibited. Also, Koons's (D) use of the image was satirical, and, therefore, the use must be justified by a genuine creative rationale for borrowing the image, rather than using it merely "to get attention or to avoid the drudgery in working up something fresh." Koons (D) explained that the rationale for his use, which was not challenged by Blanch (P), was to use the image to satirize life as it appears when seen through the prism of slick fashion photography and to give the image veracity so the viewer could understand his commentary. Thus, Koons (D) established the needed justification for his borrowing. Finally, as to the first factor, there is an issue of whether Koons's (D) use was made in good faith. The only conduct of his challenged as made in bad faith is that he did not seek Blanch's (P) permission to reprint the image. There is no precedent, however, that the failure to seek

Continued on next page.

permission to use a copyrighted work is an act of bad faith where the use is otherwise fair. For these reasons, the first fair use factor strongly favors Koons (D). The second fair use factor, under 17 U.S.C. § 107(2), is "the nature of the copyrighted work." If the work is creative, rather than factual, that weighs in favor of the copyright holder, and if the work has been published, that weighs against the copyright holder. Here, the work was creative in nature, which weighs in Blanch's (P) favor, but it was published, which weighs in Koons's (D) favor. Nevertheless, where a use is transformative, as here, the second fair use factor may be of limited usefulness since the use is not exploiting the work's creative virtues. The third fair use factor, under 17 U.S.C. § 107(3), is "the amount and substantiality of the portion used in relation to the copyrighted work as a whole." The question becomes whether the quantity and value of the materials used are reasonable in relation to the purpose of the copying. By extracting only the image of the leg, feet, and sandals, rather than also including the other components of Blanch's (P) photo, Koons (D) made a reasonable use of the image that was not excessive for the purpose for which he wanted it; Koons (D) copied only that portion of the image necessary to evoke "a certain style of mass communication." This factor favors Koons (D). Finally, the fourth fair use factor, under 17 U.S.C. § 107(4), is "the effect of the use upon the potential market for or value of the copyrighted work." Here, the question is whether the secondary use usurps the market for the original. Blanch (P) acknowledged that she had not published or licensed "Silk Sandals" subsequent to its appearance in *Allure*, that she has never licensed any of her photographs for use in works of graphic or other visual art, that Koons's (D) use of her photograph did not cause any harm to her career or upset any plans she had for "Silk Sandals" or any other photograph, and that the value of "Silk Sandals" did not decrease as the result of Koons's (D) alleged infringement. Accordingly, it is clear that "Niagara" had no deleterious effect "upon the potential market for or value of the copyrighted work," and the fourth fair use factor greatly favors Koons (D). Thus, the balance of the factors favors Koons (D) and permitting the use, rather than preventing it, promotes the sciences and useful arts. Affirmed.

▶ *ANALYSIS*

The relevancy of bad faith in fair use determinations is a subject of considerable controversy. Judge Katzmann, in a concurring opinion, while not disagreeing with the majority that there is no precedent that the failure to seek permission to use a copyrighted work is an act of bad faith (if it were, there would be an element of bad faith in every fair use case), would have instead concluded that "whatever bad faith Koons (D) may have exhibited in this case, as well as the limited commercial nature of his use, would not outweigh the much stronger considerations pointing toward a finding of fair use." He would thus have avoided ruling that failure to seek authorization, even where doing

so would have been feasible, is not relevant to the fair use inquiry.

Quicknotes

COPYRIGHT Refers to the exclusive rights granted to an artist pursuant to Article I, section 8, clause 8 of the United States Constitution over the reproduction, display, performance, distribution, and adaptation of his work for a period prescribed by statute.

COPYRIGHT INFRINGEMENT A violation of one of the exclusive rights granted to an artist pursuant to Article I, section 8, clause 8 of the United States Constitution over the reproduction, display, performance, distribution, and adaptation of his work for a period prescribed by statute.

FAIR USE An affirmative defense to a claim of copyright infringement providing an exception from the copyright owner's exclusive rights in a work for the purposes of criticism, comment, news reporting, teaching, scholarship or research; the determination of whether a use is fair is made on a case-by-case basis and requires the court to consider: (1) the purpose and character of the use; (2) the nature of the work; (3) the amount and substantiality of the portion used; and (4) the effect of the use on the potential market for, or value of, the work.

SUMMARY JUDGMENT Judgment rendered by a court in response to a motion by one of the parties, claiming that the lack of a question of material fact in respect to an issue warrants disposition of the issue without consideration by the jury.

Sega Enterprises Ltd. v. Accolade, Inc.

Video game maker (P) v. Game maker (D)

977 F.2d 1510 (9th Cir. 1992).

NATURE OF CASE: Appeal from preliminary injunction issued in a copyright infringement case.

FACT SUMMARY: Accolade, Inc. (D) copied and then disassembled Sega Enterprises Ltd.'s (Sega's) (P) video game programs in order to discover the requirements for compatibility with Sega's (P) console.

🏛 RULE OF LAW
Disassembly of a copyrighted object code is a fair use of the material if it is the only means of access to uncopyrighted elements of the code and there is a legitimate reason for seeking such access.

FACTS: Sega Enterprises Ltd. (Sega) (P) and Accolade, Inc. (D) manufactured and marketed video game cartridges. In order to render its own games compatible with Sega's (P) console, Accolade (D) "reverse engineered" Sega's (P) video game programs to discover the requirements for compatibility with the console. To do this, it first copied Sega's (P) copyright code in its entirety and then disassembled it to see how it worked. Accolade (D) then created its own games for use with Sega's (P) console, but did not copy Sega's (P) programs or use any of its codes. Sega (P) sued for copyright infringement. The district court granted Sega's (P) motion for a preliminary injunction preventing Accolade (D) from further disassembly of Sega's (P) object codes. Accolade (D) appealed.

ISSUE: Is disassembly of a copyrighted object code a fair use of the material if it is the only means of access to uncopyrighted elements of the code and there is a legitimate reason for seeking such access?

HOLDING AND DECISION: (Reinhardt, J.) Yes. Disassembly of a copyrighted object code is a fair use of the material if it is the only means of access to uncopyrighted elements of the code and there is a legitimate reason for seeking such access. Section 107 of the Copyright Act of 1976 lists four factors to be considered in determining whether a particular use is a fair one: (1) the purpose and character of the use; (2) the nature of the copyrighted work; (3) the amount and substantiality of the portion used in relation to the copyrighted work as a whole; and (4) the effect of the use upon the market for the copyrighted work. First, Accolade (D) sought only to become a legitimate competitor in the field of Sega (P) compatible video games. Therefore, it had a legitimate, nonexploitative purpose for copying Sega's (P) code. Second, Sega's (P) video game programs must be afforded a lower degree of protection than more traditional literary works because they contain unprotected aspects that cannot be examined with-

out copying. Third, the fact that Accolade (D) disassembled entire programs written by Sega (P) should receive little weight. Fourth, Accolade's (D) copying may have affected the market, but not significantly, since consumers tend to buy many video games rather than just one. Accordingly, Accolade (D) has the better case on the fair use issue. Affirmed in part, reversed in part, and remanded.

▶ ANALYSIS

An issue similar to reverse engineering was raised in *Triad Systems Corp. v. Southeastern Express Co.,* 64 F.3d 1330 (9th Cir. 1995). In that case, Southeastern copied Triad's software into Triad's computer as part of an attempt to service the computer. The Ninth Circuit concluded that such copying was not fair use because it was neither creative nor transformative and did not provide the marketplace with new creative works. Instead, the copies made by Southeastern undoubtedly diminished the value of Triad's copyright.

■▭■

Quicknotes

17 U.S.C. § 101 Section 101 of the Copyright Act of 1976; sets forth the definitions for purposes of the act.

COPYRIGHT ACT § 117 Limits a copyright owner's exclusive rights by allowing computer program copies without permission under certain circumstances.

■▭■

Viacom Int'l, Inc. v. YouTube

Copyright holder (P) v. Online video sharing provider (D)

679 F.3d 19 (2d Cir. 2012).

NATURE OF CASE: Appeal from grant of summary judgment to defendants in action for direct and secondary copyright infringement.

FACT SUMMARY: Viacom International, Inc. (Viacom) and other copyright holders (collectively, "plaintiffs") (P) alleged direct and secondary copyright infringement based on the public performance, display, and reproduction of approximately 79,000 audiovisual "clips" that appeared on the website of YouTube (D), an online video sharing service. The plaintiffs (P) contended that YouTube (D) was not entitled to safe harbor protection under the Digital Millennium Copyright Act (DMCA) for the airing of these clips because, the plaintiffs (P) contended, YouTube (D) was aware—or was willfully blind to the fact—that these clips actually infringed the plaintiffs' (P) copyrights.

🏛️ **RULE OF LAW**
(1) The § 512 safe harbor of the Digital Millennium Copyright Act (DMCA) requires knowledge or awareness of specific infringing activity.
(2) The common law willful blindness doctrine may be applied to demonstrate knowledge or awareness of specific instances of infringement under the DMCA.
(3) Item-specific knowledge of infringing activity is not required for a service provider to have the "right and ability to control" infringing activity under § 512(c)(1)(B) of the DMCA.

FACTS: Viacom International, Inc. (Viacom) and other copyright holders (collectively, "plaintiffs") (P) alleged direct and secondary copyright infringement based on the public performance, display, and reproduction of approximately 79,000 audiovisual "clips" that appeared on the website of YouTube (D), an online video sharing service, over a period of three years. The plaintiffs brought suit against YouTube (D) and related entities (collectively, "YouTube") (D) seeking, inter alia, statutory damages pursuant to 17 U.S.C. § 504(c) or, in the alternative, actual damages from the alleged infringement, as well as declaratory and injunctive relief. The YouTube (D) website permits users to "upload" and view video clips free of charge. Before uploading a video to YouTube (D), a user must register and create an account with the website. The registration process requires the user to accept YouTube's (D) Terms of Use agreement, which provides, inter alia, that the user "will not submit material that is copyrighted . . . unless [he is] the owner of such rights or ha[s] permission from their

rightful owner to post the material and to grant YouTube all of the license rights granted herein." During the upload process, YouTube (D) makes one or more exact copies of the video in its original file format. YouTube (D) also makes one or more additional copies of the video in "Flash" format, a process known as "transcoding." The transcoding process ensures that YouTube (D) videos are available for viewing by most users at their request. YouTube (D) allows users to gain access to video content by "streaming" the video to the user's computer in response to a playback request, and it uses a computer algorithm to identify clips that are "related" to a video the user watches and display links to the "related" clips. At the time of the litigation, the YouTube (D) website had more than 1 billion daily video views, with more than 24 hours of new video uploaded to the site every minute. YouTube (D) claimed safe harbor protection under § 512 of the Digital Millennium Copyright Act (DMCA). The DMCA created several safe harbors for service providers who transmit potentially infringing material over their networks. To qualify for any of these, a service provider must meet several threshold criteria, including that the provider actually meets the definition of being a service provider; that the provider has adopted and reasonably implemented certain policies; and that the provider can accommodate "standard technical measures" that are used by copyright owners to identify or protect copyrighted works. Beyond the threshold criteria, a service provider must satisfy the requirements of a particular safe harbor. In this case, the safe harbor at issue was § 512(c), which covers infringement claims that arise "by reason of the storage at the direction of a user of material that resides on a system or network controlled or operated by or for the service provider." Section 512(c) specifies that actual knowledge of infringing material, awareness of facts or circumstances that make infringing activity apparent, or receipt of a takedown notice from a copyright holder will each trigger an obligation to expeditiously remove the infringing material. The district court determined that YouTube (D) came within the § 512 safe harbor, primarily because it had insufficient notice of the particular infringements in suit as required by the statute. The district court held that the replication, transmittal, and display of videos on YouTube (D) constituted activity "by reason of the storage at the direction of a user" within the meaning of § 512(c)(1). In construing § 512, the district court concluded that the "actual knowledge" or "aware[ness] of facts or circumstances" that would disqualify an online service provider from safe harbor protection under § 512(c)(1)(A) refer to "knowledge of specific and identifiable infringements."

Continued on next page.

The district court further held that item-specific knowledge of infringing activity is required for a service provider to have the "right and ability to control" infringing activity under § 512(c)(1)(B). The court of appeals granted review.

ISSUE:

(1) Does the § 512 safe harbor of the Digital Millennium Copyright Act (DMCA) require knowledge or awareness of specific infringing activity?

(2) May the common law willful blindness doctrine be applied to demonstrate knowledge or awareness of specific instances of infringement under the DMCA?

(3) Is item-specific knowledge of infringing activity required for a service provider to have the "right and ability to control" infringing activity under § 512(c)(1)(B) of the DMCA?

HOLDING AND DECISION: (Carbranes, J.)

(1) Yes. The § 512 safe harbor of the Digital Millennium Copyright Act (DMCA) requires knowledge or awareness of specific infringing activity. The text of the statute compels this conclusion, as the basic operation of § 512(c) requires knowledge or awareness of specific infringing activity. Under § 512(c)(1)(A), knowledge or awareness alone does not disqualify the service provider. Instead, under § 512(c)(1)(A)(iii), the provider that gains knowledge or awareness of infringing activity retains safe-harbor protection if it "acts expeditiously to remove, or disable access to, the material." Thus, it can be inferred that the nature of the removal obligation itself contemplates knowledge or awareness of specific infringing material, because expeditious removal would not be possible if the provider did not know with specificity which items to remove. To hold otherwise would impose a generalized obligation on providers to take commercially reasonable steps to remove infringing materials. However, such a reading cannot be reconciled with the statute. Contrary to the plaintiffs' (P) position, § 512(c)(1)(A)(ii), the so-called "red flag" knowledge provision, does not require a different conclusion. According to the plaintiffs (P), the use of the phrase "facts or circumstances" demonstrates that Congress did not intend to limit the red flag provision to a particular type of knowledge, and that requiring awareness of specific infringements would render the red flag provision superfluous because that provision would be satisfied only when the "actual knowledge" provision is also satisfied. This reading misconstrues the relationship between "actual" knowledge and "red flag" knowledge. That is because the phrase "actual knowledge" in § 512(c)(1)(A)(i) is being used to denote subjective belief, whereas the use of the phrase "facts or circumstances" in § 512(c)(1)(A)(ii), is being used to denote an objective reasonableness standard. The difference between actual and red flag knowledge is thus not between specific and generalized knowledge, but instead between a subjective and an objective standard. The

actual knowledge provision turns on whether the provider actually or "subjectively" knew of specific infringement, whereas the red flag provision turns on whether the provider was subjectively aware of facts that would have made the specific infringement "objectively" obvious to a reasonable person. Under both provisions, specific instances of infringement are at issue. The few cases interpreting the knowledge provisions of the § 512(c) safe harbor support this specificity requirement. Those cases have indicated that service providers do not have the burden of determining whether materials are actually illegal to be precluded from taking shelter in the § 512 safe harbor; they must have specific knowledge of particular infringing activity. In any event, no court has held that the red flag provision requires less specificity than the actual knowledge provision. Accordingly, the standard enunciated by the district court was correct. However, applying that standard here, the district court erred in granting summary judgment to YouTube (D). Survey evidence was adduced that suggested that YouTube (D) was generally aware that significant quantities of material on the YouTube (D) website were infringing—estimated at as much as 60% to 85%. Such estimates alone are insufficient, standing alone, to create a triable issue of fact as to whether YouTube (D) actually knew, or was aware of facts or circumstances that would indicate, the existence of particular instances of infringement. However, other evidence, including YouTube (D) emails and communications about specific clips or groups of clips, suggests that YouTube (D) was aware of specific instances of infringement. These clips were taken from various specifically identified sports broadcasts, popular television shows, news broadcasts, and commercials. The communications suggest that YouTube (D) executives were aware that these particular clips were in fact infringing, or "blatantly illegal" as one email said. Notwithstanding that the executives seemed to be aware of the infringing nature of specific content, some of the executives seemed to want to keep the content on YouTube (D) as long as possible before receiving an official cease and desist takedown notification, presumably to enhance the YouTube (D) site's popularity. Based on this evidence, the plaintiffs (P) may have raised a material issue of fact regarding YouTube's (D) knowledge or awareness of specific instances of infringement, so that a reasonable juror could conclude that YouTube (D) had actual knowledge of specific infringing activity, or was at least aware of facts or circumstances from which specific infringing activity was apparent. Accordingly, the district court's grant of summary judgment to YouTube (D) was premature. Affirmed as to the district court's holding of law as to this issue; judgment vacated

Continued on next page.

and remanded as to the district court's application of the law to the facts.

(2) Yes. The common law willful blindness doctrine may be applied to demonstrate knowledge or awareness of specific instances of infringement under the DMCA. This is an issue of first impression. The inquiry is whether the DMCA abrogates the common law doctrine of willful blindness, which equates willful blindness with knowledge. A person is "willfully blind" or engages in "conscious avoidance" amounting to knowledge where the person is aware of a high probability of the fact in dispute and consciously avoids confirming that fact. A statute abrogates the common law where the statute directly speaks to the issue addressed by the common law. Although the DMCA does not mention willful blindness, § 512(m) provides that safe harbor protection cannot be conditioned on affirmative monitoring by a service provider. Thus, the DMCA is incompatible with a broad monitoring duty. However, willful blindness cannot be defined as an affirmative duty to monitor, so the DMCA cannot be said to abrogate the willful blindness doctrine, even though it may limit it. The district court did not address the willful blindness issue, and, on remand, it must consider whether YouTube (D) made a "deliberate effort to avoid guilty knowledge." Remanded as to this issue.

(3) No. Item-specific knowledge of infringing activity is not required for a service provider to have the "right and ability to control" infringing activity under § 512(c)(1)(B) of the DMCA. Section 512(c)(1)(B), the so-called "control and benefit" provision, provides that an eligible service provider must "not receive a financial benefit directly attributable to the infringing activity, in a case in which the service provider has the right and ability to control such activity." The district court erroneously held that the right and ability to control the activity requires item-specific knowledge of it. The position adopted by the district court is problematic because importing a specific knowledge requirement into § 512(c)(1)(B) renders the control provision duplicative of § 512(c)(1)(A). Any service provider that has item-specific knowledge of infringing activity and thereby obtains financial benefit would already be excluded from the safe harbor under § 512(c)(1)(A) for having specific knowledge of infringing material and failing to effect expeditious removal. Because statutory interpretations that render language superfluous are disfavored, this construction must be rejected. An alternative construction, advocated by the plaintiffs (P), is that the control provision codifies the common law doctrine of vicarious copyright liability. Such an interpretation must also be rejected because it would render § 512(c) internally inconsistent. Section 512(c) presumes that service providers have the ability to block access to infringing material. By blocking or removing infringing content, the service provider would be admitting the "right and ability to control" the infringing

material under a vicarious copyright liability standard. Thus, the prerequisite to safe harbor protection under §§ 512(c)(1)(A)(iii) & (C) would at the same time be a disqualifier under § 512(c)(1)(B). Moreover, if Congress had intended § 512(c)(1)(B) to be coextensive with vicarious liability, it could have accomplished that result in a more direct manner. Accordingly, the "right and ability to control" infringing activity under § 512(c)(1)(B) requires something more than the ability to remove or block access to materials posted on a service provider's website. The few courts that have considered what constitutes that additional element have found sufficient control where the service provider exerted substantial influence on the activities of users, without necessarily—or even frequently—acquiring knowledge of specific infringing activity. Accordingly, on remand, the district court should consider whether the plaintiffs (P) have adduced sufficient evidence to allow a reasonable jury to conclude that YouTube (D) had the right and ability to control the infringing activity and received a financial benefit directly attributable to that activity. Finally, the district court held that YouTube's (D) software functions fell within the safe harbor for infringements that occur "by reason of" user storage. That holding is affirmed with respect to three of the challenged software functions: (1) the conversion (or "transcoding") of videos into a standard display format, (2) the playback of videos on "watch" pages, and (3) the "related videos" function. As to a fourth software function, involving the third-party syndication of videos uploaded to YouTube (D), the issue is remanded to the district court for further fact finding. Reversed and remanded as to the issue of item-specific knowledge under § 512(c)(1)(B); affirmed as to three software functions; remanded as to a fourth software function.

▶ ANALYSIS

This is a very important DMCA case that will likely be looked to as precedent for years to come. The court addressed numerous points of DMCA law, which points out the numerous factors a service provider must meet under the DMCA to qualify for safe harbor protection under § 512. This aspect of the DMCA has been criticized as a structural deficiency, because even if a service provider meets all but one of these many factors, the provider will not be entitled to safe harbor protection. Thus, there has been a call for Congress to streamline the act. Here, if YouTube (D) fails to satisfy even one of these elements on remand, it will have lost all safe harbor protection and will be exposed to significant liability. One of the court's straightforward, unbelabored rulings in this case was that the DMCA § 512 (c) safe harbor applies to all affirmative

Continued on next page.

claims of relief, regardless of whether the infringement is claimed to be direct or secondary, thus settling that issue, at least in the Second Circuit. Thus, if YouTube (D) loses safe harbor protection on remand, its liability will be for both direct and secondary copyright infringement. The case may be significant enough for it to be accepted on certiorari by the United States Supreme Court, especially since it diverges from the Ninth Circuit as to the "control" provision. The court in this case held that item-specific knowledge of infringing activity is not required for a servicer provider to have control over infringing activity, whereas the Ninth Circuit, in *UMG Recordings, Inc. v. Shelter Capital Partners LLC,* 667 F.3d 1022, 1041 (9th Cir. 2011), held that until the service provider becomes aware of specific unauthorized material, it cannot exercise its power or authority over the specific infringing item, and that, in practical terms, it does not have the kind of ability to control infringing activity the statute contemplates. The Supreme Court may want to resolve this split among the circuits.

■═■

Quicknotes

CEASE AND DESIST ORDER An order from a court or administrative agency prohibiting a person or business from continuing a particular course of conduct.

COPYRIGHT INFRINGEMENT A violation of one of the exclusive rights granted to an artist pursuant to Article I, Section 8, clause 8 of the United States Constitution over the reproduction, display, performance, distribution, and adaptation of his work for a period prescribed by statute.

INJUNCTIVE RELIEF A court order issued as a remedy, requiring a person to do, or prohibiting that person from doing, a specific act.

INTER ALIA Among other things.

SUMMARY JUDGMENT Judgment rendered by a court in response to a motion made by one of the parties, claiming that the lack of a question of material fact in respect to an issue warrants disposition of the issue without consideration by the jury.

■═■

Metro-Goldwyn-Mayer Studios Inc. v. Grokster, Ltd.

Copyright holders (P) v. Software distributors (D)

545 U.S. 913 (2005).

NATURE OF CASE: Appeal from affirmance of summary judgment in favor of defendants in copyright infringement action.

FACT SUMMARY: Copyright holders, including MGM Studios, Inc. (collectively "MGM") (P) contended that Grokster, Ltd. and StreamCast Networks, Inc. (collectively "the distributors") (D), distributors of free software that permitted users to share electronic files through peer-to-peer networks, were contributorily liable for the users' copyright violations because the distributors knew that the software was being used primarily for infringement purposes and because the distributors benefited from such activity.

RULE OF LAW
One who distributes a device with the object of promoting its use to infringe copyright, as shown by clear expression or other affirmative steps taken to foster infringement, going beyond mere distribution with knowledge of third-party action, is liable for the resulting acts of infringement by third parties using the device, regardless of the device's lawful uses.

FACTS: Grokster, Ltd. and StreamCast Networks, Inc. (collectively "the distributors") (D) distributed free software that permitted users to share electronic files through peer-to-peer networks. Although peer-to-peer networks can be used to share any type of digital file, recipients of the distributors' (D) software mostly used them to share copyrighted music and video files without authorization. Copyright holders, including MGM Studios, Inc. (collectively "MGM") (P) sued the distributors (D) for their users' copyright infringements, alleging that they knowingly and intentionally distributed their software to enable users to infringe copyrighted works. Discovery revealed that billions of files were being shared across peer-to-peer networks each month, and that the distributors (D) were aware that users employed the software primarily to download copyrighted files, although the decentralized networks revealed neither which files were copied nor when. The distributors (D) sometimes learned about the infringement directly when users e-mailed questions regarding copyrighted works, and the distributors (D) replied with guidance. The distributors (D) were not merely passive recipients of information about infringement. The record clearly showed that when they began to distribute their free software, each of them clearly voiced the objective that recipients use the software to download copyrighted works and took active steps to encourage infringement. After the notorious file-sharing service, Napster, was sued

by copyright holders for facilitating copyright infringement, both distributors (D) promoted and marketed themselves as Napster alternatives. The distributors (D) received no revenue from users, but, instead, generated income by selling advertising space, then streaming the advertising to their users. As the number of users increases, advertising opportunities were worth more and the distributors (D) made more money. There was no evidence that either of the distributors (D) made an effort to filter copyrighted material from users' downloads or otherwise to impede the sharing of copyrighted files. Both sides cross-moved for summary judgment. While acknowledging that the distributors' (D) users had directly infringed MGM's (P) copyrights, the district court nonetheless granted summary judgment to the distributors (D) as to liability arising from distribution of their software. The court of appeals affirmed, and the United States Supreme Court granted certiorari.

ISSUE: Is one who distributes a device with the object of promoting its use to infringe copyright, as shown by clear expression or other affirmative steps taken to foster infringement, going beyond mere distribution with knowledge of third-party action, liable for the resulting acts of infringement by third parties using the device, regardless of the device's lawful uses?

HOLDING AND DECISION: (Souter, J.) Yes. One who distributes a device with the object of promoting its use to infringe copyright, as shown by clear expression or other affirmative steps taken to foster infringement, going beyond mere distribution with knowledge of third-party action, is liable for the resulting acts of infringement by third parties using the device, regardless of the device's lawful uses. The principal focus of this case is the tension between the competing values of supporting creativity through copyright protection and promoting technological innovation by limiting infringement liability. Despite offsetting considerations, the argument for imposing indirect liability here is powerful, given the number of infringing downloads that occurred daily using distributors' (D) software. When a widely shared product is used to commit infringement, it may be impossible to enforce rights in the protected work effectively against all direct infringers, so that the only practical alternative is to go against the device's distributor for secondary liability on a theory of contributory or vicarious infringement. One infringes contributorily by intentionally inducing or encouraging direct infringement, and infringes vicariously by profiting from

Continued on next page.

direct infringement while declining to exercise the right to stop or limit it. Although "the Copyright Act does not expressly render anyone liable for [another's] infringement," these secondary liability doctrines emerged from common law principles and are well established in the law. *Sony Corp of America v. Universal City Studios, Inc.*, 464 U.S. 417 (1984), addressed a claim that secondary liability for infringement can arise from the very distribution of a commercial product. There, copyright holders sued Sony, the manufacturer of videocassette recorders, claiming that it was contributorily liable for the infringement that occurred when VCR owners taped copyrighted programs. The evidence showed that the VCR's principal use was "time-shifting," i.e., taping a program for later viewing at a more convenient time, which the Court found to be a fair, noninfringing use. Moreover, there was no evidence that Sony had desired to bring about taping in violation of copyright or taken active steps to increase its profits from unlawful taping. On those facts, the only conceivable basis for liability was on a theory of contributory infringement through distribution of a product. Because the VCR was "capable of commercially significant noninfringing uses," the Court held that Sony was not liable. This theory reflected patent law's traditional staple article of commerce doctrine, which holds that distribution of a component of a patented device will not violate the patent if it is suitable for use in other ways. The doctrine absolves the equivocal conduct of selling an item with lawful and unlawful uses and limits liability to instances of more acute fault. However, in the instant case, the court of appeals misread *Sony* to mean that when a product is capable of substantial lawful use, the producer cannot be held contributorily liable for third parties' infringing use of it, even when an actual purpose to cause infringing use is shown, unless the distributors had specific knowledge of infringement at a time when they contributed to the infringement and failed to act upon that information. Nonetheless, *Sony* did not displace other secondary liability theories. Nothing in *Sony* requires courts to ignore evidence of intent to promote infringement if such evidence exists. It was never meant to foreclose rules of fault-based liability derived from the common law. Where evidence goes beyond a product's characteristics or the knowledge that it may be put to infringing uses, and shows statements or actions directed to promoting infringement, *Sony*'s staple-article rule will not preclude liability. At common law, a copyright or patent defendant who "not only expected but invoked [infringing use] by advertisement" was liable for infringement. The rule on inducement of infringement as developed in the early cases is no different today. Evidence of active steps taken to encourage direct infringement, such as advertising an infringing use or instructing how to engage in an infringing use, shows an affirmative intent that the product be used to infringe, and overcomes the law's reluctance to find liability when a defendant merely sells a commercial product suitable for some lawful use. A rule that premises liability

on purposeful, culpable expression and conduct does nothing to compromise legitimate commerce or discourage innovation having a lawful promise. On the record, the distributors' (D) unlawful objective is unmistakable. The classic instance of inducement is by advertisement or solicitation that broadcasts a message designed to stimulate others to commit violations. Three features of the evidence of intent are particularly notable. First, each of the distributors (D) showed itself to be aiming to satisfy a known source of demand for copyright infringement, the market comprising former Napster users. The distributors' (D) efforts to supply services to former Napster users indicated a principal, if not exclusive, intent to bring about infringement. Second, neither distributor (D) attempted to develop filtering tools or other mechanisms to diminish the infringing activity using their software. While the court of appeals treated that failure as irrelevant because the distributors (D) lacked an independent duty to monitor their users' activity, this evidence underscores their intentional facilitation of their users' infringement. Third, the distributors (D) made money by selling advertising space, then by directing ads to the screens of computers employing their software. The more their software was used, the more ads were sent out and the greater the advertising revenue. Since the extent of the software's use determines the gain to the distributors (D), the commercial success of their enterprise turned on high-volume use, which the record showed was infringing. This evidence alone would not justify an inference of unlawful intent, but its import is clear in the entire record's context. In addition to intent to bring about infringement and distribution of a device suitable for infringing use, the inducement theory requires evidence of actual infringement by recipients of the device, the software in this case. There was evidence of such infringement on a gigantic scale. Because substantial evidence supported MGM (P) on all elements, summary judgment for the distributors (D) was error. Vacated and remanded.

CONCURRENCE: (Ginsburg, J.) This case is distinguishable from *Sony* because here there was no evidence of fair use. Fairly appraised, the evidence was insufficient to demonstrate, beyond genuine debate, a reasonable prospect that substantial or commercially significant noninfringing uses were likely to develop over time.

CONCURRENCE: (Breyer, J.) The Court is incorrect to enter into a factual debate about whether this case passes the *Sony* test, because the record shows that at least 10 percent of use was noninfringing—a number very close to the number of noninfringing uses in *Sony*. Thus, this case does meet the *Sony* test. Importantly, *Sony* asked whether a product was "capable of" substantial noninfringing uses. Here, the record revealed a significant future market for noninfringing uses of peer-to-peer software. In

Continued on next page.

fact, such uses have already begun. Examples include the swapping of research, photos, public domain films, historical recordings, digital educational materials, etc. Thus, the foreseeable development of such uses, when taken together with an estimated 10 percent noninfringing material, is sufficient to meet *Sony*'s standard.

▶ *ANALYSIS*

This case demonstrates the difficulty of applying pre-digital copyright law and constructs to file-sharing and other digital technologies. One proposal that has been made on how to reform copyright law to more effectively treat peer-to-peer technology is to replace the staple article of commerce standard (i.e., *Sony*) with a predominant use standard that considers whether noninfringing uses can be achieved for most users through other means without significant added expense, inconvenience, or loss of functionality; considers the extent to which copyright owners can protect themselves without significant added expense; and considers the cost and efficacy of enforcement against direct infringers.

■≡■

Quicknotes

CONTRIBUTORY INFRINGEMENT The intentional assisting of another in the unlawful appropriation of a patented work.

COPYRIGHT INFRINGEMENT A violation of one of the exclusive rights granted to an artist pursuant to Article I, Section 8, clause 8 of the United States Constitution over the reproduction, display, performance, distribution, and adaptation of his work for a period prescribed by statute.

SUMMARY JUDGMENT Judgment rendered by a court in response to a motion made by one of the parties, claiming that the lack of a question of material fact in respect to an issue warrants disposition of the issue without consideration by the jury.

■≡■

Perfect 10, Inc. v. Amazon.com, Inc.

Web porn publisher (P) v. Internet company (D)

487 F.3d 701 (9th Cir. 2007).

NATURE OF CASE: Appeal from preliminary injunction in copyright infringement action.

FACT SUMMARY: Google, Inc. ((D) claimed that even if its transmission of thumbnail images of Perfect 10, Inc.'s (P) copyrighted nude images, or its in-line linking to or framing of full-size images that infringed Perfect 10's (P) copyright in the images constituted infringement of Perfect 10's (P) display or distribution rights, its use nevertheless constituted a fair use.

🏛 RULE OF LAW

(1) A computer owner that stores an image as electronic information and serves that electronic information directly to a user displays the electronic information in violation of a copyright holder's exclusive display right in the image.

(2) A computer owner that in-line links to or frames a full-size image does not infringe the distribution right of the image's copyright owner when the image is displayed on a user's computer screen.

(3) A search engine's owner's appropriation of a copyrighted image for use as an indexed thumbnail picture is a protected "fair use" under the copyright law where the balance of the statutory fair use factors favors the search engine owner.

FACTS: Perfect 10, Inc. (P) markets and sells copyrighted images of nude models, and operates a subscription website on the Internet whereby subscribers pay a monthly fee to view Perfect 10 (P) images in a "members' area" of the site. Subscribers must use a password to log into the members' area. Perfect 10 (P) has also licensed reduced-size copyrighted images for download and use on cell phones. Google, Inc. (D) operates a search engine, a software program that automatically accesses thousands of websites (collections of web pages) on the Internet and indexes them within a database stored on Google's (D) computers. When a Google (D) user accesses the Google (D) website and types in a search query, Google's (D) software searches its database for websites responsive to that search query. Google (D) then sends relevant information from its index of websites to the user's computer. Google's (D) search engines can provide results in the form of text, images, or videos. The Google (D) search engine that provides responses in the form of images is called "Google Image Search." Google Image Search identifies text in its database responsive to the query and then communicates to users the images associated with the relevant text. Google's (D) software cannot

recognize and index the images themselves. Google Image Search provides search results as a web page of small images called "thumbnails," which are stored in Google's (D) servers. The thumbnail images are reduced, lower-resolution versions of full-sized images stored on third-party computers. When a user clicks on a thumbnail image, Google (D)'s software directs the user's browser to create on the user's computer screen a small rectangular box that contains the Google (D) thumbnail and a larger box that contains the full-size image, which the user's computer has been instructed to access from the third-party site that houses that image. Google (D) does not store the images that fill this larger box and does not communicate the images to the user. The two boxes together appear to be coming from the same source, since they are in the same frame, but actually come from two sources—Google (D) and the third-party website. The process by which the web page directs a user's browser to incorporate content from different computers into a single window is referred to as "in-line linking." The term "framing" refers to the process by which information from one computer appears to frame and annotate the in-line linked content from another computer. Google (D) also stores web page content in its cache, which ultimately means that Google's (D) cache copy can provide a user's browser with valid directions to an infringing image even though the updated web page no longer includes that infringing image. In addition to its search engine operations, Google (D) generates revenue through a business program called "AdSense." Under this program, a website owner can register with Google (D) to become an AdSense "partner." The owner then places HTML instructions on its web pages that signal Google's (D) server to place advertising on the web pages that is relevant to the web pages' content. Google's (D) computer program selects the advertising automatically by means of an algorithm, and the AdSense participants share the revenues that flow from such advertising with Google (D). Some website publishers pirated Perfect 10's (P) images and Google's (D) search engine automatically indexed the web pages containing the pirated images and provided thumbnail versions of the images in response to user inquiries. Perfect 10 (P) repeatedly sent Google (D) that its thumbnail images and in-line linking to the full-size images infringed Perfect 10's (P) copyright and when Google (D) continued its search engine practices, Perfect 10 (P) filed a copyright infringement action against Google (D), and sought a preliminary injunction to prevent Google (D) from infringing Perfect 10's (P) copyright

Continued on next page.

in its images and linking to websites that provide full-size infringing versions of Perfect 10's (P) photographs. The district court granted the preliminary injunction, finding harm to the derivative market for Perfect 10's (P) reduced-size images. The court also ruled that Google's (D) search engine likely infringed Perfect 10's (P) display right with respect to the infringing thumbnails, but that Perfect 10 (P) was not likely to prevail on its claim that Google (D) violated either Perfect 10's (P) display or distribution right with respect to its full-size infringing images. In reaching these conclusions, the district court used what it called a "server test," reasoning that a computer owner that stores an image as electronic information and serves that electronic information directly to the user is displaying the electronic information in violation of a copyright holder's exclusive display right. Conversely, the court reasoned that the owner of a computer that does not store and serve the electronic information to a user is not displaying that information, even if such owner in-line links to or frames the electronic information. The district court also reasoned that distribution requires an "actual dissemination" of a copy, and since Google (D) did not communicate the full-size images to the user's computer, Google (D) did not distribute these images. Google (D) raised the affirmative defense that its use was a fair use, but the district court rejected this defense. The court of appeals granted review.

ISSUE:

(1) Does a computer owner that stores an image as electronic information and serves that electronic information directly to a user display the electronic information in violation of a copyright holder's exclusive display right in the image?

(2) Does a computer owner that in-line links to or frames a full-size image infringe the distribution right of the image's copyright owner when the image is displayed on a user's computer screen?

(3) Is a search engine's owner's appropriation of a copyrighted image for use as an indexed thumbnail picture a protected "fair use" under the copyright law where the balance of the statutory fair use factors favors the search engine owner?

HOLDING AND DECISION: (Ikuta, J.)

(1) Yes. A computer owner that stores an image as electronic information and serves that electronic information directly to a user displays the electronic information in violation of a copyright holder's exclusive display right in the image. The district court's reasoning and "server test" comport with the language in the Copyright Act, and, therefore, its ruling is correct with respect to Perfect 10's (P) display rights. Based on the plain language of the statute, a person displays a photographic image by using a computer to fill a computer screen with a copy of the photographic image fixed in the computer's memory. Google's (D) computers store thumbnail versions of Perfect 10's (P) copy-

righted images and communicate copies of those thumbnails to Google's (D) users. Therefore, Perfect 10 (P) has made a prima facie case that Google's (D) communication of its stored thumbnail images directly infringes Perfect 10's (P) display right. Conversely, Google's (D) computers do not store the full-size photographic images, but merely in-line links to, and frames, those images. Therefore, Google (D) does not have a copy of the images for purposes of the Copyright Act, i.e., it does not have any "material objects . . . in which a work is fixed . . . and from which the work can be perceived, reproduced, or otherwise communicated" and thus Google (D) cannot communicate a copy as defined under 17 U.S.C. § 101. While Google (D) may facilitate access to infringing copies, such assistance only implicates contributory liability—not direct liability—for copyright infringement. Even if such in-line linking and framing may cause some computer users to believe they are viewing a single Google (D) web page, the Copyright Act, unlike the Trademark Act, does not protect a copyright holder against acts that cause consumer confusion. Finally, the same analysis is applicable to Google's (D) cache.

(2) No A computer owner that in-line links to or frames a full-size image does not infringe the distribution right of the image's copyright owner when the image is displayed on a user's computer screen. Again, the district court's ruling is consistent with the Copyright Act's language. Under § 106(3), a copyright owner has the exclusive right "to distribute copies. . . ." "Copies" means "material objects . . . in which a work is fixed," and the Supreme Court has indicated that in the electronic context, copies may be distributed electronically. Because the full-size images are not on Google's (D) computers, it cannot "distribute" them. It is the third-party website publisher's computer that distributes copies of the images by transmitting the photographic image electronically to the user's computer. Moreover, Perfect 10's (P) argument that merely making the images "available" constitutes distribution is unsupported. A "deemed distribution" rule that is applicable in other contexts is inapplicable to Google (D) because Google (D) does not own a collection of Perfect 10's (P) full-size images and does not communicate these images to the computers of people using Google's (D) search engine; it only indexes the images. Google (D) therefore cannot be deemed to distribute copies of these images."

(3) Yes. A search engine's owner's appropriation of a copyrighted image for use as an indexed thumbnail picture is a protected "fair use" under the copyright law where the balance of the statutory fair use factors favors the search engine owner. Although Perfect 10 (P) would likely prevail in its prima facie case that Google's (D)

Continued on next page.

thumbnail images infringe its display rights, Perfect 10 (P) has the burden of showing a likelihood that it will prevail against Google's (D) affirmative fair use defense. The first fair use factor, 17 U.S.C. § 107(1), requires a court to consider "the purpose and character of the use, including whether such use is of a commercial nature or is for nonprofit educational purposes." A "transformative work" is one that alters the original work "with new expression, meaning, or message." Here, Google's (D) use of thumbnails is highly transformative. Google's (D) search engine provides social benefit by incorporating an original work into a new work that serves as an electronic reference tool, thereby providing an entirely new use for the original work. The district court concluded that because Google's (D) use of the thumbnails could supersede Perfect 10's (P) cell phone download use and because the use was commercial because Google's (D) thumbnails "lead users to sites that directly benefit Google's bottom line" through the AdSense program, this fair use factor weighed "slightly" in favor of Perfect 10 (P). The district court's conclusion as to this factor is erroneous because the superseding use was nonexistent insofar as the district court did not find that any downloads for mobile phone use had taken place, and because there was no evidence that AdSense websites containing infringing images significantly contributed to Google's (D) bottom line. Accordingly, the significantly transformative nature of Google's (D) search engine, particularly in light of its public benefit, outweighs Google's (D) superseding and commercial uses of the thumbnails in this case. A weighing of these considerations must promote flexibility and account for the rule that "the more transformative the new work, the less will be the significance of other factors, like commercialism, that may weigh against a finding of fair use." The second fair use factor is "the nature of the copyrighted work," 17 U.S.C. § 107(2). Perfect 10's (P) images are "creative in nature" and thus "closer to the core of intended copyright protection than are more fact-based works." However, because the photos appeared on the Internet before Google (D) used thumbnail versions in its search engine results, this factor weighs only slightly in favor of Perfect 10 (P). The third fair use factor, 17 U.S.C. § 107(3), asks whether the amount and substantiality of the portion used in relation to the copyrighted work as a whole are reasonable in relation to the purpose of the copying. Here, this factor is neutral and does not weigh in favor of either party because Google's (D) use of the entire photographic image was reasonable in light of the purpose of a search engine and since using less than the entire image would be less helpful to a computer user. The fourth fair use factor is "the effect of the use upon the potential market for or value of the copyrighted work." The district court here correctly held that Google's (D) use of thumbnails did not hurt Perfect 10's (P) market for full-size images. Perfect 10 (P) argues that the dis-

trict court erred because the likelihood of market harm may be presumed if the intended use of an image is for commercial gain. However, this presumption does not arise when a work is transformative because "market substitution is at least less certain, and market harm may not be so readily inferred." As already discussed, Google's (D) thumbnail images were highly transformative, and there was no evidence of market harm to Perfect 10's (P) full-size images. Accordingly, the district court did not err as to this ruling. The district court did err, however, in determining that Google's (D) thumbnails would harm the market for reduced-size images, since Perfect 10 (P) adduced no evidence that actual sales of such images had been made for cell phone use. Any potential harm to Perfect 10's (P) market remains hypothetical, and, therefore, this factor favors neither party. Weighing the fair use factors leads to the conclusion that Google's (D) use was a fair use, especially in light of the public utility served by its search engine and the transformative nature of its use. Perfect 10 (P) is unlikely to be able to overcome Google's (D) fair use defense. Accordingly, the preliminary injunction regarding Google's (D) use of thumbnail images is vacated. Reversed as to this issue.

▶ ANALYSIS

Although finding that Google (D) was not liable for its copyright infringement since its use was a fair use, the court in this case nevertheless ruled that Google (D) could be contributorily liable for copyright infringement since an actor may be contributorily liable for intentionally encouraging direct infringement if the actor knowingly takes steps that are substantially certain to result in such direct infringement. Here, the court found that Google (D) substantially assisted websites to distribute their infringing copies to a worldwide market and assisted a worldwide audience of users to access infringing materials. The court said it could not discount the effect of such a service on copyright owners, even though Google's (D) assistance is available to all websites, not just infringing ones. The court concluded that Google (D) could be held contributorily liable if it had knowledge that infringing Perfect 10 (P) images were available using its search engine, could take simple measures to prevent further damage to Perfect 10's (P) copyrighted works, and failed to take such steps. The court remanded so the district court could make factual findings necessary to resolve this issue.

■═■

Quicknotes

COPYRIGHT Refers to the exclusive rights granted to an artist pursuant to Article I, section 8, clause 8 of the

Continued on next page.

United States Constitution over the reproduction, display, performance, distribution, and adaptation of his work for a period prescribed by statute.

COPYRIGHT INFRINGEMENT A violation of one of the exclusive rights granted to an artist pursuant to Article I, section 8, clause 8 of the United States Constitution over the reproduction, display, performance, distribution, and adaptation of his work for a period prescribed by statute.

FAIR USE An affirmative defense to a claim of copyright infringement providing an exception from the copyright owner's exclusive rights in a work for the purposes of criticism, comment, news reporting, teaching, scholarship or research; the determination of whether a use is fair is made on a case-by-case basis and requires the court to consider: (1) the purpose and character of the use; (2) the nature of the work; (3) the amount and substantiality of the portion used; and (4) the effect of the use on the potential market for, or value of, the work.

PRELIMINARY INJUNCTION A judicial mandate issued to require or restrain a party from certain conduct; used to preserve a trial's subject matter or to prevent threatened injury.

Sheldon v. Metro-Goldwyn Pictures Corp.

Playwright (P) v. Movie studio (D)

309 U.S. 390 (1940).

NATURE OF CASE: Appeal of ruling apportioning profits derived from copyrighted play.

FACT SUMMARY: Playwright and copyright-infringing movie studio disputed the amount of movie profits that should be awarded to the playwright.

🏛 RULE OF LAW
There is no basis to award someone who has had his copyright infringed upon any amount of profits made by the infringer above that which cannot be attributed to the infringement itself.

FACTS: Sheldon (P) wrote and copyrighted the play "Dishonored Lady" based on a true story of Madeleine Smith, who was tried for the murder of her lover in Scotland in 1857. Metro-Goldwyn Pictures Corp. (M-G Pictures) (D) had entered into negotiations to buy the rights to the play in order to produce a movie, but the negotiations fell through, and M-G Pictures (D) produced a movie entitled "Letty Lynton," which was based on a novel about the same subject. Sheldon (P) charged infringement of his play and sought an injunction and an accounting of profit. The court of appeals ruled against M-G Pictures (D), concluding that it had infringed upon the copyright of Sheldon's (P) play. A further dispute between Sheldon (P) and M-G Pictures (D) arose over how much of the movie's profits should be awarded to Sheldon (P).

ISSUE: In the apportionment of an award of profits for copyright infringement, may the apportionment be pro-rated to give the author only the part of the profits attributable to the use of the infringed material?

HOLDING AND DECISION: (Hughes, C.J.) Yes. In the apportionment of an award of profits for copyright infringement, the apportionment may be pro-rated to give the author only the part of the profits attributable to the use of the infringed material. The purpose of awarding profits to Sheldon (P), whose work has been infringed upon, is just compensation for the violation by M-G Pictures (D). Such an award is not meant to impose a penalty on M-G Pictures (D) by giving Sheldon (P) profits "which are not attributable to the infringement," but to prevent M-G Pictures (D) from unjust enrichment. There is nothing in either the Copyright Act of 1909 or in subsequent case law that would allow a court to award profits for which there has been no showing of being due to the infringement itself.

▶ ANALYSIS

It would be unfair to let M-G Pictures (D) profit at the expense of Sheldon's (P) work. It would be equally unfair,

however, to let Sheldon (P) reap a profit from certain parts of the "Letty Lynton" movie, since those parts were not based on Sheldon's (P) play. The Court, therefore, sought to protect each of the two entities' "original" portions of their respective work.

Quicknotes

COPYRIGHT Refers to the exclusive rights granted to an artist pursuant to Article I, section 8, clause 8 of the United States Constitution over the reproduction, display, performance, distribution, and adaptation of his work for a period prescribed by statute.

COPYRIGHT INFRINGEMENT A violation of one of the exclusive rights granted to an artist pursuant to Article I, section 8, clause 8 of the United States Constitution over the reproduction, display, performance, distribution, and adaptation of his work for a period prescribed by statute.

Quick Reference Rules of Law

Qualitex Co. v. Jacobson Products Co., Inc.

Dry cleaning product manufacturer (P) v. Competitor (D)

514 U.S. 159 (1995).

NATURE OF CASE: Review of order reversing finding of a trademark violation.

FACT SUMMARY: Qualitex Co. (P) sought to register a trademark on a color.

🏛 RULE OF LAW
Color alone may be registered as a trademark.

FACTS: Qualitex Co. (P) manufactured and sold pads used by dry cleaners on their presses. The pads made by Qualitex Co. (P) were of a distinctive green-gold color. When Qualitex (P) discovered that Jacobson Products Co. (Jacobson) (D) was also selling pads of the same color, it brought an unfair competition action and also sought to register the color as a trademark. The district court held Jacobson (D) to be in violation of Qualitex's trademark. The Ninth Circuit Court of Appeals reversed, holding that color alone could not be registered as a trademark. The United States Supreme Court accepted review.

ISSUE: May color alone be registered as a trademark?

HOLDING AND DECISION: (Breyer, J.) Yes. Color alone may be registered as a trademark. The Lanham Act, which establishes federal trademark law, is quite liberal with respect to the universe of things that can be trademarked. Any symbol that carries a secondary meaning linking it with a particular product may be trademarked. There seems to be no reason why a color cannot fall within this definition. Jacobson's (D) arguments to the contrary are mostly based on pre-Lanham Act common law. Jacobson (D) also argues that since the number of colors is finite, color should not be trademarked. It is not necessary to establish a blanket prohibition for a rare problem. Reversed.

▶ ANALYSIS

Numerous things of tenuous tangibility have become trademarks: a bottle shape (Coca-Cola) and sound (NBC Broadcasting Co.). Given this, allowing color to be the subject of a trademark is not unusual.

Quicknotes

LANHAM ACT Name of the Trademark Act of 1946, which governs federal law regarding trademarks.

TRADEMARK Any word, name, symbol, device, or combination thereof, which is either currently utilized, or which a person has a bona fide intent to utilize, in commerce in order to distinguish his goods from those of another.

TRADEMARK INFRINGEMENT The unauthorized use of another's trademark in such a manner as to cause a likelihood of confusion as to the source of the product or service in connection with which it is utilized.

Zatarain's, Inc. v. Oak Grove Smokehouse, Inc.

Food manufacturer (P) v. Competitor (D)

698 F.2d 786 (5th Cir. 1983).

NATURE OF CASE: Appeal from a finding of lack of any trademark infringement.

FACT SUMMARY: Zatarain's (P) claimed that its trademark was a "suggestive" term and that Oak Grove Smokehouse, Inc. (Oak Grove) (D) should be liable for infringing it, but Oak Grove (D) claimed it was a "descriptive" term subject to a fair use exception.

 RULE OF LAW
Descriptive terms are not protected by trademark absent a showing of secondary meaning in the minds of the public.

FACTS: Zatarain's (P) manufactured and distributed food products. It registered the terms "Fish-Fri" and "Chick-Fri" as trademarks for its batter mixes used to fry foods. Oak Grove Smokehouse, Inc. (Oak Grove) (D) began marketing a "fish fry" and a "chicken fry" in packages similar to those used by Zatarain's (P). Zatarain's (P) sued for trademark infringement and unfair competition under the Lanham Act. The district court held that Zatarain's (P) trademark "Fish-Fri" was a descriptive term with an established secondary meaning, but held that the alleged infringers had a fair use defense to any asserted infringement of the term and that the registration of the term "Chick-Fri" should be canceled because it was a descriptive term that lacked any secondary meaning. Zatarain's (P) appealed, claiming that its trademark "Fish-Fri" was a suggestive term that was automatically protected upon registration and therefore not subject to the "fair use" defense.

ISSUE: Are descriptive terms protected by trademark absent a showing of secondary meaning in the minds of the consuming public?

HOLDING AND DECISION: (Goldberg, J.) No. Descriptive terms are not protected by trademark absent a showing of secondary meaning in the minds of the public. Applying the four prevailing tests of descriptiveness—i.e., the dictionary definition, the imagination test, usefulness of the term to competitors, and actual use of the term by other merchants—the district court did not err in finding that "Fish-Fri" was a descriptive term identifying a function of the product being sold. Proof of secondary meaning is an issue only with respect to descriptive marks, and the burden of proof rests at all times with the plaintiff to establish such a meaning. The district court found that Zatarain's (P) evidence established a secondary meaning for the term in the New Orleans area. However, Zatarain's (P) has no legal claim to an exclusive right in the original, descriptive sense of the term. Therefore Oak Grove (D) is still free to use the words "fish fry" in their ordinary, descriptive sense, so long as such use will not tend to confuse customers as to the source of the goods. The record contains ample evidence to support the district court's determination that Oak Grove's (D) use of the term was fair and in good faith. Affirmed.

ANALYSIS

The trademark "fair use" defense is different from the copyright law fair use doctrine. In trademark law, a junior user is not liable of infringement of a senior user's established trademark meaning if the mark is being used in its descriptive sense. Such a defense is only available to infringers of "descriptive" marks.

Quicknotes

FAIR USE An affirmative defense to a claim of copyright infringement providing an exception from the copyright owner's exclusive rights in a work for the purposes of criticism, comment, news reporting, teaching, scholarship, or research; the determination of whether a use is fair is made on a case-by-case basis and requires the court to consider: (1) the purpose and character of the use; (2) the nature of the work; (3) the amount and substantiality of the portion used; and (4) the effect of the use on the potential market for, of value of, the work.

SECONDARY MEANING Attribute of a word or mark that might not be distinctive at its initial use but upon substantial use becomes associated with a particular merchant as its source of origin.

TRADEMARK Any word, name, symbol, device, or combination thereof, which is either currently utilized, or which a person has a bona fide intent to utilize, in commerce in order to distinguish his goods from those of another.

TRADEMARK INFRINGEMENT The unauthorized use of another's trademark in such a manner as to cause a likelihood of confusion as to the source of the product or service in connection with which it is utilized.

The Murphy Door Bed Co., Inc. v. Interior Sleep Systems, Inc.

Bed manufacturer (P) v. Competitor (D)

874 F.2d 95 (2d Cir. 1989).

NATURE OF CASE: Appeal from an order enjoining the use of the Murphy name.

FACT SUMMARY: The Murphy Door Bed Co. (P), manufacturer of Murphy beds, claimed that its common law trademark had been infringed.

> 🏛 **RULE OF LAW**
> Where the public is said to have expropriated a term established by a product developer, the burden is on the defendant to prove the term has become generic.

FACTS: At the turn of the century, William Lawrence Murphy invented and manufactured a bed that when not in use could be concealed in a wall closet. He obtained a patent in 1918 and has used the words "Murphy bed" as a trademark for concealed beds since the Murphy Door Bed Company (MDBC) (P) was founded in 1925. The Patent and Trademark Office in 1981 denied MDBC's (P) application to register the Murphy bed trademark because the words "Murphy bed" had become generic and the phrase was merely descriptive of a characteristic of the goods. In 1984 the Trademark Trial and Appeal Board (TTAB) affirmed the denial of registration. Interior Sleep Systems, Inc. (Interior Sleep) (D) entered into a distributorship agreement with MDBC (P) in 1981 and, when it learned of the TTAB's denial of MDBC's application for trademark registration, it began using the term "Murphy bed" in the title of a new corporation that made such beds. When MDBC (P) sued, the district court found that the name Murphy was not generic because a secondary meaning had been attributed to it by the general public, and that the common law of trademark protected MDBC (P). The court found that Interior Sleep (D) had not met its burden to show abandonment of the Murphy trademark. Interior Sleep (D) appealed, claiming that since the Murphy mark was unregistered, the court erred in shifting the burden of proof to them.

ISSUE: Where the public is said to have expropriated a term established by a product developer, is the burden on the defendant to prove the term has become generic?

HOLDING AND DECISION: (Miner, J.) Yes. Where the public is said to have expropriated a term established by a product developer, the burden is on the defendant to prove the term has become generic. The district court was correct in placing the burden of proof of genericness upon Interior Sleep (D). But Interior Sleep (D) did indeed establish that the term "Murphy bed" is a generic term, having been appropriated by the public to designate generally a type of bed. The factors of the TTAB

finding, standard dictionary definitions, and evidence of numerous newspaper and magazine use of the phrase to describe generally a type of bed lead to that conclusion. MDBC's (P) efforts at policing its mark are of no consequence when the mark has entered the public domain beyond recall. Reversed.

▶ ANALYSIS

This case shows why companies fight so hard to prevent their trademarks from becoming generic through casual use. In another part of this case, the court held that Interior Sleep (D) had engaged in unfair competition by passing off beds of their own manufacture as beds of the MDBC (P). The court also found that Interior Sleep (D) had breached its contractual obligation to refrain from using the term after termination of the agreement.

◼️━◼️

Quicknotes

SECONDARY MEANING Attribute of a word or mark that might not be distinctive at its initial use but upon substantial use becomes associated with a particular merchant as its source of origin.

TRADEMARK Any word, name, symbol, device, or combination thereof, which is either currently utilized, or which a person has a bona fide intent to utilize, in commerce in order to distinguish his goods from those of another.

TRADEMARK INFRINGEMENT The unauthorized use of another's trademark in such a manner as to cause a likelihood of confusion as to the source of the product or service in connection with which it is utilized.

◼️━◼️

Two Pesos, Inc. v. Taco Cabana, Inc.

Fast food restaurant (D) v. Competitor (P)

505 U.S. 763 (1992).

NATURE OF CASE: Review of judgment awarding damages for trademark infringement.

FACT SUMMARY: Taco Cabana, Inc. (P) sought to assert trademark protection for its trade dress, despite such dress not having acquired a secondary meaning.

🏛 RULE OF LAW
Inherently distinctive trade dress may be subject to trademark protection even if it has not acquired a secondary meaning.

FACTS: Taco Cabana, Inc. (P) operated six restaurants in the San Antonio, Texas, area. The restaurants served Mexican food and sought to exude a festive, colorful atmosphere. Two Pesos, Inc. (D) began opening a chain of restaurants of its own, which strove for a similar atmosphere and boasted similar decor. Taco Cabana (P) brought a trademark infringement action under the Lanham Act, contending that it enjoyed a trademark on its "trade dress," which may be loosely defined as the totality of its ambiance. The district court held that trade dress could be a trademark if it was inherently distinctive or had acquired a secondary meaning. The jury found Taco Cabana's (P) trade dress to be inherently distinctive and awarded damages. The court of appeals affirmed. The United States Supreme Court granted review.

ISSUE: Is inherently distinctive trade dress subject to trademark protection even if it has not acquired a secondary meaning?

HOLDING AND DECISION: (White, J.) Yes. Inherently distinctive trade dress is subject to trademark protection even if it has not acquired a secondary meaning. A mark may be trademarked if it is distinctive, per the Lanham Act. A mark is distinct if it is either (1) inherently distinctive, or (2) has acquired a secondary meaning. Secondary meaning refers to that situation where an aspect of a product that is not necessarily distinctive thereof has, either through successful marketing or some other mechanism, become associated in the public mind with that product. As a consequence of these definitions, a mark cannot both be inherently distinctive and at the same time have secondary meaning. From the above it follows that, to the extent that trade dress is inherently distinctive, it need not have secondary meaning to be subject to trademark law. Here, the jury found Taco Cabana's (P) trade dress to be inherently distinctive, and this was sufficient to bring it within the Lanham Act. Affirmed.

▶ ANALYSIS

It is generally agreed that there are five categories into which marks may fall: (1) generic; (2) descriptive; (3) suggestive; (4) arbitrary; or (5) fanciful. The last three categories are inherently subject to trademark law; the first is not. Most issues in trademark law relate to the second category.

■▬■

Quicknotes

LANHAM ACT § 43 Protects qualifying unregistered trademarks.

SECONDARY MEANING Attribute of a word or mark that might not be distinctive at its initial use but upon substantial use becomes associated with a particular merchant as its source of origin.

TRADEMARK Any word, name, symbol, device, or combination thereof, which is either currently utilized, or which a person has a bona fide intent to utilize, in commerce in order to distinguish his goods from those of another.

TRADE DRESS The overall image of, or impression created by, a product that a court may enforce as a trademark if it determines that such image has acquired secondary meaning and that the public recognizes it as an indication of source.

TRADEMARK INFRINGEMENT The unauthorized use of another's trademark in such a manner as to cause a likelihood of confusion as to the source of the product or service in connection with which it is utilized.

■▬■

Wal-Mart Stores, Inc. v. Samara Brothers, Inc.

Retailer (D) v. Clothing manufacturer (P)

529 U.S. 205 (2000).

NATURE OF THE CASE: Appeal from affirmance from judgment for plaintiff in trade dress infringement.

FACT SUMMARY: Samara Brothers, Inc. (P) sued Wal-Mart Stores, Inc. (D) for, among other causes of action, infringement of an unregistered trade dress design under the Trademark Act of 1946.

> 🏛 **RULE OF LAW**
> An unregistered trade dress design under § 43(a) of the Lanham Act, absent a showing of a secondary meaning, is not distinctive and, therefore, not protected from infringement.

FACTS: Samara Brothers, Inc. (Samara) (P) is a designer and manufacturer of children's clothes, its primary product being spring and summer one-piece seersucker clothes. Various stores sell this line of clothes. Wal-Mart Stores (Wal-Mart) (D) is one of the largest and most well-known retailers in the United States. Wal-Mart (D) contracted with Judy-Philippine, Inc. (J-P), one of its suppliers, to manufacture a line of spring and summer children's clothes, sending J-P photographs of several of Samara's (P) garments upon which J-P was to base the clothes for Wal-Mart (D). J-P then copied, with minor modifications, 16 of Samara's (P) garments, many of which contained elements that were copyrighted. Wal-Mart (D) sold J-P's garments and earned over $1.5 million in gross profits from those sales. Samara (P) sent cease-and-desist letters to Wal-Mart (D), finally bringing suit for copyright infringement. A jury found for Samara (P) on all its claims, and the court of appeals affirmed. The United States Supreme Court granted certiorari.

ISSUE: In an action for trademark infringement of an unregistered trade dress is a product's design, in and of itself, distinctive and therefore protected under § 43(a) of the Lanham Act?

HOLDING AND DECISION: (Scalia, J) No. In an action for trademark-infringement of an unregistered trade dress, a product's design, in and of itself, is not distinctive and is, therefore, not protected under § 43(a) of the Lanham Act. The relevant portion of § 43(a) gives a producer "a cause of action for the use by any person of 'any word, term, name, symbol, or device, or any combination thereof... which ... is likely to cause confusion ... as to the origin, sponsorship, or approval of his or her goods ...'" 15 U.S.C. § 1125(a). Courts, in interpreting this section, have required a producer to demonstrate that a trade dress mark is distinctive. The producer can show distinctiveness in one of two ways: (1) that the mark's intrinsic nature identifies the mark as being from a particular source, or (2) that in the minds of the general public, the mark has attained distinctiveness. This court has held that in regard to one category of a trademark—color—there is no inherent distinctness, so color could only be protected if the producer showed that the color had a secondary meaning. Here, Samara's (P) product design can be equated to color and, therefore, a consumer is not predisposed to equate the product design feature with Samara (P). As such, in an infringement of an unregistered trade dress suit, under § 43(a) of the Lanham Act, a product's design is only distinctive and protected if the producer can demonstrate that a secondary meaning is attached to that product. Samara (P) never adequately demonstrated any distinctiveness attributable to its children's clothing line. Reversed and remanded.

▶ *ANALYSIS*

In this ruling, the Court desired to avoid lower courts having to evaluate differences with product design or product packaging, which are sometimes difficult to ascertain. In short, the Court wanted to avoid a ruling that would encourage a "slippery slope" analysis when deciding if certain products are inherently distinctive.

■══■

Quicknotes

LANHAM ACT, § 43(a) Federal trademark infringement statute.

SECONDARY MEANING Attribute of a word or mark that might not be distinctive at its initial use but upon substantial use becomes associated with a particular merchant as its source of origin.

TRADE DRESS The overall image of, or impression created by, a product that a court may enforce as a trademark if it determines that such image has acquired secondary meaning and that the public recognizes it as an indication of source.

TRADEMARK Any word, name, symbol, device, or combination thereof, which is either currently utilized, or which a person has a bona fide intent to utilize, in commerce in order to distinguish his goods from those of another.

■══■

TrafFix Devices, Inc. v. Marketing Displays, Inc.

Competitor (D) v. Road sign manufacturer (P)

532 U.S. 23 (2001).

NATURE OF THE CASE: Trade dress infringement.

FACT SUMMARY: Marketing Displays, Inc. (MDI) (P) sued TrafFix Devices, Inc. (D) for trade dress infringement of a dual-spring mechanism designed to allow temporary road signs to remain standing in high gusts of wind.

 RULE OF LAW

An expired utility patent, determined to serve solely functional purposes, is not entitled to trademark protection.

FACTS: Robert Sarkinsian, an inventor, designed a dual-spring mechanism to attach to temporary road signs (e.g., "Road Work Ahead") so they would remain upright in high gusts of wind. He secured two utility patents for the design. Marketing Displays, Inc. (MDI) (P) obtained the patents and had a successful business manufacturing and selling road signs that utilized the dual-spring design under the name "WindMaster." Once the patents expired, TrafFix Devices, Inc. (TrafFix) (D) began selling road signs that incorporated a similar dual-spring mechanism under the name "WindBuster." MDI (P) sued TrafFix (D) for trade dress infringement. The district court found for TrafFix (D) and the court of appeals reversed. The United States Supreme Court granted certiorari.

ISSUE: Is the holder of an expired utility patent that is determined to be solely functional in nature entitled to trademark protection?

HOLDING AND DECISION: (Kennedy, J.) No. The holder of an expired patent that is determined to be solely functional in nature is not entitled to trademark protection. Under trade dress law, a "design or packaging of a product may acquire a distinctiveness which serves to identify the product with its manufacturer or source; and a design or package which acquires this secondary meaning, assuming other requisites are met, is a trade dress which may not be used in a manner likely to cause confusion as to the origin, sponsorship, or approval of the goods." Trade dress protection, however, may not prohibit the copying of goods and products, unless an intellectual property right protects those items. Here, the patent had expired. Where a trade dress patent has expired, the person who seeks to re-establish the patent must demonstrate that the feature of the patent in question is not solely functional by showing "that it is merely an ornamental, incidental, or arbitrary aspect of the device." The dual-spring design's main purpose is to keep the sign standing upright in heavy winds.

This purpose was specifically stated in the patent application. Further, the design is essential to the use of those specific road signs. Therefore, the design is decidedly functional. Due to its functionality, competitors do not need to significantly alter or hide the dual-spring design. The court of appeals decision is reversed and remanded.

▌ ANALYSIS

The Supreme Court has stated that copying is not always prevented or discouraged in the interest of promoting competition. When competitors are allowed to copy certain products, it not only promotes competition, but can also lead to modifications that promote advances in technology or goods.

■■■

Quicknotes

TRADE DRESS The overall image of, or impression created by, a product that a court may enforce as a trademark if it determines that such image has acquired secondary meaning and that the public recognizes it as an indication of source.

TRADEMARK Any word, name, symbol, device, or combination thereof, which is either currently utilized, or which a person has a bona fide intent to utilize, in commerce in order to distinguish his goods from those of another.

PATENT A limited monopoly conferred on the invention or discovery of any new or useful machine or process that is novel and nonobvious.

■■■

Zazu Designs v. L'Oreal, S.A.

Hair salon (P) v. Hair care product manufacturer (D)

979 F.2d 499 (7th Cir. 1992).

NATURE OF CASE: Appeal from injunction and damages award for trademark violation.

FACT SUMMARY: L'Oreal, S.A. (D) was sued under the Lanham Act for using a mark for its hair products that was already in use.

🏛 RULE OF LAW
Only active use allows consumers to associate a mark with particular goods and notifies other firms that the mark is so associated.

FACTS: A licensee of L'Oreal, S.A. (D) in the United States developed a line of hair cosmetics in electric hair colors in 1985. When researching the availability of "ZAZU" as trademark, a state service mark registration using that word was found to belong to Zazu Hair Designs in Hinsdale, Illinois, (ZHD) (P). ZHD (P) had registered the ZAZU mark with Illinois in 1980 as a trade name for its beauty salon. L'Oreal (D) called to find out if ZHD (P) was selling its own products and was informed that it was not at that time but that it might later on. L'Oreal (D) paid the sole holder of a federal registration, an apparel manufacturer, for a covenant not to sue if L'Oreal (D) used the mark on cosmetics. L'Oreal (D) then began shipping hair cosmetics under the ZAZU name and also applied for federal registration. At that time, ZHD (P) was selling small quantities of shampoo in bottles labeled with the ZAZU name. ZHD (P) sued L'Oreal (D) for trademark infringement. After a bench trial, the district court held that ZHD's (P) sales gave it an exclusive right to use the ZAZU name nationally for hair products, enjoined L'Oreal (D) from using the mark, and awarded ZHD (P) damages for lost profits and punitive damages. L'Oreal (D) appealed.

ISSUE: Does only active use allow consumers to associate a mark with particular goods and notify other firms that the mark is so associated?

HOLDING AND DECISION: (Easterbrook, J.) Yes. Only active use allows consumers to associate a mark with particular goods and notifies other firms that the mark is so associated. ZHD's (P) sales of hair care products were insufficient as a matter of law to establish national trademark rights at the time L'Oreal (D) put its electric hair colors on the market. ZHD (P) applied for registration of ZAZU after L'Oreal (D) had applied to register the mark and had also put its product on the market nationwide. Intent to use a mark, like a naked registration, establishes no rights at all. Because the mark was not registered for use in conjunction with hair products, any knowledge L'Oreal (D) may have had of ZHD's (P) plans is irrelevant. The

district court erred in equating a use sufficient to support registration with a use sufficient to generate nationwide rights in the absence of registration. Reversed and remanded.

DISSENT: (Cudahy, C.J.) Even if ZHD (P) did fail to demonstrate more than a de minimis market penetration nationally, at the very least it successfully established exclusive rights within its primary area of operation. ZHD (P) has achieved market penetration and exclusive rights to the ZAZU mark, at the very least in the Chicago area. L'Oreal (D) did not act in good faith since it had prior knowledge of ZHD's (P) use of the mark.

▶ ANALYSIS

The Lanham Act defined a trademark and codified common law protection for trademarks. This case was decided before Congress made several important changes in trademark law in 1989. Prior to 1989, actual use in commerce prior to registration was a requirement of registration. The Trademark Law Revision Act of 1989 adopted an "intent to use" registration under § 1 of the Lanham Act.

■=■

Quicknotes

DAMAGES Monetary compensation that may be awarded by the court to a party who has sustained injury or loss to his or her person, property or rights due to another party's unlawful act, omission, or negligence.

INJUNCTION A remedy imposed by the court ordering a party to cease the conduct of a specific activity.

LANHAM ACT Name of the Trademark Act of 1946 which governs federal law regarding trademarks.

TRADEMARK Any word, name, symbol, device, or combination thereof, which is either currently utilized, or which a person has a bona fide intent to utilize, in commerce in order to distinguish his goods from those of another.

■=■

In re Nantucket, Inc.

[Parties not identified.]

C.C.P.A., 677 F.2d 95 (1982).

NATURE OF CASE: Appeal from decision of the Trademark Trial and Appeal Board affirming a refusal to register a mark.

FACT SUMMARY: The mark NANTUCKET for men's shirts was refused by the Patent and Trademark Office (PTO) Appeal Board on the grounds that it was "primarily geographically deceptively misdescriptive."

🏛 RULE OF LAW
For a mark to be geographically deceptively misdescriptive, there must be a reasonable basis for believing that purchasers are likely to be deceived.

FACTS: Nantucket, Inc. applied to the PTO to register the mark NANTUCKET for its men's shirts. Refusal to register was based on the Lanham Act, which provides that a mark is primarily geographical if it is the name of a place which has general renown to the public at large and which is a place from which goods and services are known to emanate as a result of commercial activity. The examiner concluded that the mark NANTUCKET was either primarily geographically descriptive or misdescriptive, depending on whether Nantucket's shirts did or did not come from Nantucket Island. Since the shirts did not come from there, the examiner held that the mark was primarily geographically deceptively misdescriptive. Nantucket appealed, claiming that as applied to shirts, NANTUCKET was arbitrary and descriptive because there was no association in the public mind of men's shirts with Nantucket Island.

ISSUE: For a mark to be geographically deceptively misdescriptive, must there be a reasonable basis for believing that purchasers are likely to be deceived?

HOLDING AND DECISION: (Markey, C.J.) Yes. For a mark to be geographically deceptively misdescriptive, there must be a reasonable basis for believing that purchasers are likely to be deceived. There is no evidence that the purchasing public would expect men's shirts to have their origin in Nantucket when seen in the market place with NANTUCKET on them. Hence buyers are not likely to be deceived, and registration cannot be refused on the ground that the mark is "primarily geographically deceptively misdescriptive." Reversed.

▶ ANALYSIS

This ruling clarified the PTO's mechanical test for registrability of geographic terms. If the mark is recognizable to a large segment of the population as the name of a geographical area, the mark must be denied registration under

the test. The court noted that one flaw in the Board's test was its factoring out the nature of the applicant's goods.

Quicknotes

LANHAM ACT Name of the Trademark Act of 1946, which governs federal law regarding trademarks.

TRADEMARK Any word, name, symbol, device, or combination thereof, which is either currently utilized, or which a person has a bona fide intent to utilize, in commerce in order to distinguish his goods from those of another.

Park 'N Fly, Inc. v. Dollar Park and Fly, Inc.

Parking lot operator (P) v. Competitor (D)

469 U.S. 189 (1985).

NATURE OF CASE: Review of order for permanent injunction of infringing service mark reversed on appeal.

FACT SUMMARY: An incontestable service mark was alleged to be merely descriptive and could not be used to enjoin the use of another infringing service mark.

RULE OF LAW
An incontestable mark cannot be challenged on the grounds that it is merely descriptive.

FACTS: Park 'N Fly, Inc. (P) operated long-term parking lots near airports in several states and had established a service mark consisting of the logo of an airplane and the words "Park 'N Fly" with the United States Patent and Trademark Office. Park 'N Fly (P) successfully sought an injunction against Dollar Park and Fly, Inc. (D), which provided long-term parking services in Oregon. Dollar (D) counterclaimed and sought cancellation of Park 'N Fly's (P) mark on the grounds that it was a generic term. Dollar (D) also argued that the mark was unenforceable because it was merely descriptive. After a bench trial, the district court found that the mark was not generic an also found sufficient evidence of likelihood of confusion. It permanently enjoined Dollar (D) from using the words "Park and Fly." The court of appeals reversed because it found that incontestability may not be used offensively to enjoin another's use. The court of appeals also found that the mark was descriptive and therefore Dollar (D) could not be enjoined from using the name "Park and Fly." The United States Supreme Court granted certiorari.

ISSUE: May an incontestable mark be challenged on the grounds that it is merely descriptive?

HOLDING AND DECISION: (O'Connor, J.) No. An incontestable mark cannot be challenged on the grounds that it is merely descriptive. The holder of a registered mark may rely on incontestability to enjoin infringement, and such an action may not be defended on the grounds that the mark is merely descriptive. Congress expressly provided in §§ 33(b) and 15 of the Lanham Act that an incontestable mark could be challenged on specified grounds, and the grounds identified by Congress do not include mere descriptiveness. Reversed and remanded.

DISSENT: (Stevens, J.) The mark "Park 'N Fly" is at best merely descriptive in the context of airport parking. Section 2 of the Lanham Act clearly prohibits the registration of such a mark unless the applicant proves that the mark has acquired a secondary meaning such that the mark has become distinctive of the applicant's goods in commerce. If no proof of secondary meaning is ever presented,

there is simply no rational basis for leaping to the conclusion that the passage of time has transformed an inherently defective mark into an incontestable mark.

ANALYSIS

Trademark holders have the right to exclude others from using the same specific trademark. They do not have any property rights such as the right to alienate. Registered trademarks are entitled to a presumption of validity.

Quicknotes

COUNTERCLAIM An independent cause of action brought by a defendant to a lawsuit in order to oppose or deduct from the plaintiff's claim.

INCONTESTABLE MARK The incontestable right of a registrant to use a trademark in commerce in connection with a particular good or service for which the mark has been in continuous use for five consecutive years subsequent to the date of registration and is still in use, if there is no final decision adverse to the registrant's claim of ownership or right to register, there is no pending proceeding involving the rights asserted and an affidavit is filed within one year after the expiration of the five-year period setting forth the goods or services stated in the registration or in connection with which the mark has been used for the five-year period, and the mark is not the generic name for the good or service.

LANHAM ACT § 14 Distinguishes marks that are the common descriptive name of an article from those merely descriptive.

SECONDARY MEANING Attribute of a word or mark that might not be distinctive at its initial use but upon substantial use becomes associated with a particular merchant as the source of origin.

Rescuecom Corp. v. Google, Inc.

Computer service company/trademark holder (P) v. Internet search company (D)

562 F.3d 123 (2d Cir. 2009).

NATURE OF CASE: Appeal from dismissal of trademark infringement action.

FACT SUMMARY: Rescuecom Corp. (P) contended that Google, Inc.'s (D) use of Rescuecom's trademark was a use in commerce and infringed its trademark through Google's (D) recommendation and sale of Rescuecom's (P) mark to Google's (D) advertisers, including Rescuecom's (P) competitors, so as to trigger the appearance of their advertisements and links in a manner likely to cause consumer confusion when a Google (D) user launched a search of the term "Rescuecom."

RULE OF LAW

A trademark owner states a cause of action for trademark infringement by alleging that the owner of an Internet search engine has recommended and sold the trademark to advertisers, including the trademark owner's competitors, so as to trigger the appearance of their advertisements and links in a manner likely to cause consumer confusion when a user launches a search using the trademark as a keyword.

FACTS: Rescuecom Corp. (P) is a national computer service franchising company that conducts a substantial amount of business over the Internet. "Rescuecom" is a registered federal trademark. Google, Inc. (D) operates an Internet search engine that helps users locate information on the Internet. If a user is looking for information about a provider's products and services, Google (D) will direct the user, who types the name of the provider into Google's (D) search engine, to the provider's website and to information about the provider. In addition, Google (D) may display context-based advertising along with the other search results if an advertiser, having determined that its ad is likely to be of interest to a searcher who enters the particular term, has purchased from Google (D) the placement of its ad on the screen of the searcher who entered that search term. Such ads contain a link to the advertiser's website, and if the user links to this website, the user may be offered not only information about the advertiser, but also the opportunity to purchase products or services therefrom. Google (D) uses at least two programs to offer such context-based links: AdWords and Keyword Suggestion Tool. AdWords is a Google (D) program through which advertisers purchase terms (or keywords). When entered as a search term, the keyword triggers the appearance of the advertiser's ad and link on the user's screen. Keyword Suggestion Tool is a different Google (D) program that recommends keywords to advertisers to be purchased for use in AdWords. Google (D) allegedly makes 97 percent of

its revenue from selling advertisements through its AdWords program, and therefore has an economic incentive to increase the number of advertisements and links that appear for every term entered into its search engine. Through its Keyword Suggestion Tool, Google (D) recommended the Rescuecom trademark to Rescuecom's (P) competitors as a search term to be purchased through AdWords, so that whenever a user launches a search for the term "Rescuecom," seeking to be connected to Rescuecom's (P) website, the competitors' advertisement and link will appear on the searcher's screen. Rescuecom (P) brought suit for trademark infringement, alleging that this practice enabled Rescuecom's (P) competitors to deceive and divert users searching for Rescuecom's (P) website by causing the searcher to believe mistakenly that a competitor's advertisement and website link was sponsored by, endorsed by, approved by, or affiliated with Rescuecom (P). The district court dismissed the action, finding that Google's (D) use of the Rescuecom trademark was not made in commerce, which is an essential element of a trademark infringement claim under the Lanham Act, because the competitors' advertisements triggered by Google's (D) programs did not exhibit Rescuecom's (P) trademark. The court rejected the argument that Google (D) "used" Rescuecom's (P) mark in recommending and selling it as a keyword to trigger competitor's advertisements because the court read the decision in *1-800 Contacts, Inc. v. WhenU.com, Inc.,* 414 F.3d 400 (2d Cir. 2005) (*1-800*) to compel the conclusion that this was an internal use and therefore could not be a "use in commerce" under the Lanham Act. The court of appeals granted review.

ISSUE: Does a trademark owner state a cause of action for trademark infringement by alleging that the owner of an Internet search engine has recommended and sold the trademark to advertisers, including the trademark owner's competitors, so as to trigger the appearance of their advertisements and links in a manner likely to cause consumer confusion when a user launches a search using the trademark as a keyword?

HOLDING AND DECISION: (Leval, J.) Yes. A trademark owner states a cause of action for trademark infringement by alleging that the owner of an Internet search engine has recommended and sold the trademark to advertisers, including the trademark owner's competitors, so as to trigger the appearance of their advertisements and links in a manner likely to cause consumer confusion

Continued on next page.

when a user launches a search using the trademark as a keyword. Here, contrary to the district court's determination, which relied on the court's interpretation of *1-800*, Google (D) used Rescuecom's (P) trademark in commerce. The case at bar is distinguishable from *1-800* in two important ways. First, in *1-800*, the defendant did not use, reproduce, or display the plaintiff's mark at all. Here, in contrast, Google (D) recommended and sold Rescuecom's (P) trademark to trigger the appearance of advertisements. Second, in *1-800*, under the defendant's program advertisers could not request or purchase keywords to trigger their ads. Even if an advertiser wanted to display its advertisement to a searcher using the plaintiff's trademark as a search term, the defendant's program did not offer this possibility. Here, in stark contrast, Google (D) encouraged advertisers to purchase Rescuecom's (P) trademark. Such use clearly is "in commerce." Google (D) responds to this conclusion by arguing that the inclusion of a trademark in an internal computer directory cannot constitute trademark use. While several courts in this Circuit have reached that conclusion, regardless of whether Google's (D) use of Rescuecom's (P) mark in its internal search algorithm could constitute an actionable trademark use, Google's (D) recommendation and sale of Rescuecom's (P) mark to its advertising customers are not internal uses. Mere use of a trademark in an internal software program does not insulate an alleged infringer from a charge of infringement. To hold otherwise would be to give free rein to search engine operators to use trademarks in ways designed to deceive and cause consumer confusion. Google (D) also contends that its use is like "product placement" in a store, where a store-brand generic product is placed next to a trademarked product to induce a customer who specifically sought out the trademarked product to consider the typically less expensive, generic brand as an alternative. Benign product placement, however, does not cause consumer confusion. If retail product placement was conducted in a deceptive manner intended to cause confusion so that a consumer seeking to purchase a famous brand would receive the off-brand, believing she had gotten the brand she was seeking, that practice would not escape liability merely because it could claim the mantle of "product placement." Google's (D) alleged practices are significantly different from benign product placement that does not violate the Lanham Act. To prevail on its claim, Rescuecom (P) will need to prove that Google's (D) use of the Rescuecom trademark in fact caused the likelihood of confusion or mistake Rescuecom (P) claims. However, at this stage of the proceedings, Rescuecom's (P) claim must be permitted to proceed, and should not have been dismissed. Vacated and remanded.

▶ ANALYSIS

The court in this case rejected the trademark use doctrine, and in an appendix to the case explains its position that the Lanham Act's language does not support it. The court indicates that the definition of "use in commerce" set forth in § 1127 was intended to apply to the Act's use of that term in defining favored conduct, which qualifies to receive the protection of the Act, rather than applying to the specification of conduct by an alleged infringer, which causes imposition of liability. Some leading commentators approve of such a position, not only finding that the Act's language does not support a trademark use requirement, but also observing that imposing such a requirement unduly limits appropriate common law development of trademark law. Others, in disagreement, support the trademark use doctrine, finding that, for various normative reasons, it should shield defendants from even potential liability for certain types of commercial uses of marks, especially in connection with online contextual advertising, and that the specter of contributory infringement liability is enough to regulate such uses. As with the commentators, the courts are split on this issue.

■■■

Quicknotes

TRADEMARK Any word, name, symbol, device, or combination thereof, which is either currently utilized, or which a person has a bona fide intent to utilize, in commerce in order to distinguish his goods from those of another.

TRADEMARK INFRINGEMENT The unauthorized use of another's trademark in such a manner as to cause a likelihood of confusion as to the source of the product or service in connection with which it is utilized.

■■■

AMF, Inc. v. Sleekcraft Boats

Boat manufacturer (P) v. Competitor (D)

599 F.2d 341 (9th Cir. 1979).

NATURE OF CASE: Appeal from denial of request for injunctive relief for trademark infringement.

FACT SUMMARY: AMF, Inc. (P) sought to enjoin Sleekcraft Boats (Sleekcraft) (D) from using its mark because it was sufficiently similar to AMF's (P) Slickcraft mark that confusion could be expected.

🏛 **RULE OF LAW**
In determining whether confusion between related goods is likely, several factors must be considered including strength and similarity of the marks, type and proximity of the goods, and marketing channels used.

FACTS: AMF, Inc. (P) manufactured Slickcraft boats and its mark was federally registered in 1969. Sleekcraft Boats (Sleekcraft) (D) also manufactured boats and its name was selected without knowledge of AMF's (P) use. AMF (P) claimed that the boat lines were competitive and sued for infringement of its trademark. Sleekcraft (D) claimed that its boats are not competitive with Slickcraft boats because they manufactured only high performance boats intended for racing enthusiasts. The district court held that AMF's (P) trademark was valid but not infringed because confusion was unlikely. AMF (P) appealed.

ISSUE: In determining whether confusion between related goods is likely, must several factors be considered?

HOLDING AND DECISION: (Anderson, J.) Yes. In determining whether confusion between related goods is likely, several factors must be considered. The strength of the mark, the proximity of the goods, the similarity of the marks, evidence of actual confusion, the marketing channels used, the type of goods, the defendant's intent in selecting the mark, and the likelihood of expansion of the product lines must all be considered. In this case, Slickcraft is a weak mark, albeit protectable. The boats are similar in use and function. As far as the marks are concerned, Sleekcraft (D) and Slickcraft are similar in sight, sound, and meaning. Although there is little evidence of actual confusion, the general class of boat purchasers exposed to the product does overlap. A limited mandatory injunction is warranted. Upon remand, the district court should consider the above interests in structuring appropriate relief. Remanded.

▶ *ANALYSIS*

When the goods produced by the alleged infringer compete for sales with those of the trademark owner, infringement will usually be found if the marks are suffi-ciently similar that confusion can be expected. If the goods are totally unrelated, there can be no infringement because confusion is unlikely. In this case, the two lines of boats were found to be non-competing, but they were extremely close in use and function.

Quicknotes

MANDATORY INJUNCTION A court order that (1) requires the defendant to do a particular thing; (2) prohibits defendant from refusing to do some thing or act to which the plaintiff is legally entitled; or (3) prevents the defendant from continuing the previous wrongful act, thus compelling him to undo it.

TRADEMARK INFRINGEMENT The unauthorized use of another's trademark in such a manner as to cause a likelihood of confusion as to the source of the product or service in connect with which it is utilized.

Louis Vuitton Malletier S.A. v. Haute Diggity Dog, LLC

Luxury goods manufacturer/trademark owner (P) v. Pet products manufacturer (D)

507 F.3d 252 (4th Cir. 2007).

NATURE OF CASE: Appeal from summary judgment for defendant in action for, inter alia, trademark dilution.

FACT SUMMARY: Louis Vuitton Malletier S.A. (LVM) (P), a luxury goods manufacturer, claimed that Haute Diggity Dog, LLC (D), a pet products manufacturer, among other things, diluted LVM's (P) trademarks by creating and selling a line of "Chewy Vuiton" dog chew toys that spoofed LVM's (P) handbags and trademarked designs.

> ## 🏛 RULE OF LAW
> (1) Trademark dilution by blurring does not occur under the Trademark Dilution Revision Act of 2006 where a famous and distinctive mark is parodied, but the mark is only mimicked and not actually used.
> (2) Trademark dilution by tarnishment does not occur under the Trademark Dilution Revision Act of 2006 where harm to a famous mark is only speculative and without record support.

FACTS: Louis Vuitton Malletier S.A. (LVM) (P) is a well-known manufacturer and seller of various luxury goods, including ladies handbags, that has adopted trademarks and trade dress that are well recognized and have become famous and distinct. LVM (P) has registered trademarks for "LOUIS VUITTON," (the "LOUIS VUITTON mark"); for a stylized monogram of "LV" (the "LV mark"); for a monogram canvas design consisting of a canvas with repetitions of the LV mark along with four-pointed stars, four-pointed stars inset in curved diamonds, and four-pointed flowers inset in circles (the "Monogram Canvas mark"). It also adopted a brightly colored version of the Monogram Canvas mark in which the LV mark and the designs were of various colors and the background was white (the "Multicolor design"). It also adopted another design consisting of a canvas with repetitions of the LV mark and smiling cherries on a brown background (the "Cherry design"). LVM's (P) products are very expensive, usually costing hundreds or thousands of dollars. Although LVM (P) also markets a limited selection of luxury pet accessories, it does not make dog toys. Haute Diggity Dog, LLC (Haute Diggity Dog) (D) manufactures and sells a line of pet chew toys and beds whose names parody elegant high-end brands of products. In particular, Haute Diggity Dog (D) created a line of "Chewy Vuiton" chew toys that resembled LVM's (P) handbags. The toys loosely resemble miniature handbags and undisputedly evoke LVM (P) handbags of similar shape, design, and color. In lieu of

the LOUIS VUITTON mark, the dog toy uses "Chewy Vuiton"; in lieu of the LV mark, it uses "CV"; and the other symbols and colors employed are imitations, but not exact ones, of those used in the LVM (P) Multicolor and Cherry designs. The chew toys were sold mainly in pet stores and cost around $20. LVM (P) brought suit against Haute Diggity Dog (D) for, inter alia, trademark dilution, claiming that Haute Diggity Dog's (D) advertising, sale, and distribution of the "Chewy Vuiton" dog toys diluted its LOUIS VUITTON, LV, and Monogram Canvas marks, which are famous and distinctive, in violation of the Trademark Dilution Revision Act of 2006 (TDRA) (there were other copyright and trademark claims). On cross-motions for summary judgment, the district court concluded that Haute Diggity Dog's (D) "Chewy Vuiton" dog toys were successful parodies of LVM's (P) trademarks, designs, and products, and on that basis, entered judgment in favor of Haute Diggity Dog (D) on all of LVM's (P) claims. The court of appeals granted review.

ISSUE:

(1) Does trademark dilution by blurring occur under the Trademark Dilution Revision Act of 2006 where a famous and distinctive mark is parodied, but the mark is only mimicked and not actually used?

(2) Does trademark dilution by tarnishment occur under the Trademark Dilution Revision Act of 2006 where harm to a famous mark is only speculative and without record support?

HOLDING AND DECISION: (Niemeyer, J.)

(1) No. Trademark dilution by blurring does not occur under the Trademark Dilution Revision Act of 2006 where a famous and distinctive mark is parodied, but the mark is only mimicked and not actually used. To state a dilution claim under the TDRA, a plaintiff must show: (1) that the plaintiff owns a famous mark that is distinctive; (2) that the defendant has commenced using a mark in commerce that allegedly is diluting the famous mark; (3) that a similarity between the defendant's mark and the famous mark gives rise to an association between the marks; and (4) that the association is likely to impair the distinctiveness of the famous mark or likely to harm the reputation of the famous mark. In the context of blurring, distinctiveness refers to the ability of the famous mark uniquely to identify a single source and thus maintain its selling power. Here, the only statutory factor at issue is the

Continued on next page.

fourth factor—whether the association between Haute Diggity Dog's (D) marks and LVM's (P) marks will impair the distinctiveness of LVM's (P) marks. LVM (P) suggests that any use by a third person of an imitation of its famous marks dilutes the famous marks as a matter of law. Such an interpretation, however, goes too far. The TDRA has six statutory factors that must be considered when determining if a junior mark has diluted a famous mark, but the district court did not consider these. The factors are: (i) The degree of similarity between the mark or trade name and the famous mark. (ii) The degree of inherent or acquired distinctiveness of the famous mark. (iii) The extent to which the owner of the famous mark is engaging in substantially exclusive use of the mark. (iv) The degree of recognition of the famous mark. (v) Whether the user of the mark or trade name intended to create an association with the famous mark. (vi) Any actual association between the mark or trade name and the famous mark. Although the district court erred by not considering these factors, when they are considered, the conclusion is the same as that reached by the district court. Under the TDRA, which provides that fair use is a complete defense, parody is not automatically a complete defense to a claim of dilution by blurring where the defendant uses the parody as its own designation of source, i.e., as a trademark. Nevertheless, a court is directed by the TDRA to consider all relevant factors, so that a court may take into account the existence of a parody that is used as a trademark as part of the circumstances to be considered. A defendant's use of a mark as a parody is relevant to the overall question of whether the defendant's use is likely to impair the famous mark's distinctiveness, as well as to several of the listed factors. Regarding the fifth and sixth factors, a parody intentionally creates an association with the famous mark in order to be a parody, but also intentionally communicates, if it is successful, that it is not the famous mark, but rather a satire of the famous mark. The first, second, and fourth factors are also directly implicated when the defendant's use of the mark is a parody. In fact, a successful parody may render the famous mark even more distinctive. Thus, while a defendant's use of a parody as a mark does not support a "fair use" defense, it may be considered in determining whether the plaintiff has proved its claim that the defendant's use of a parody mark is likely to impair the distinctiveness of the famous mark. It is undisputed that LVM's (P) marks are distinctive, famous, and strong—even iconic. Accordingly, because these famous marks are particularly strong and distinctive, it becomes more likely that a parody will not impair their distinctiveness. That is the case here; because Haute Diggity Dog's (D) "Chewy Vuiton" marks are a successful parody, they will not blur the distinctiveness of the famous marks as a unique identifier of their source. While this might not be true if the parody is so similar to the famous mark that it likely could be construed as actual use of the famous mark itself, here Haute Diggity Dog (D) mimicked the famous marks; it did not come so close to them as to destroy the success of its parody and, more importantly, to diminish the LVM (P) marks' capacity to identify a single source. The imitations by Haute Diggity Dog (D) are intentionally imperfect so that it is clear that they are a parody. Haute Diggity Dog (D) intentionally associated its marks, but only partially and imperfectly, so as to convey the simultaneous message that it was not in fact a source of LVM (P) products. Rather, as a parody, it separated itself from the LVM (P) marks in order to make fun of them. When all these factors are considered, it is clear that the distinctiveness of LVM's (P) marks will not likely be impaired by Haute Diggity Dog's (D) marketing and sale of its "Chewy Vuiton" products. Affirmed as to this issue.

(2) No. Trademark dilution by tarnishment does not occur under the Trademark Dilution Revision Act of 2006 where harm to a famous mark is only speculative and without record support. To establish dilution by tarnishment, LVM (P) must prove that Haute Diggity Dog's (D) use of the "Chewy Vuiton" mark on dog toys actually harmed the reputation of LVM's (P) marks. The only argument LVM (P) makes in this regard is that a dog could choke on a "Chewy Vuiton" toy, but presents no evidence that a dog has ever choked on one of these toys or that there is a likelihood that a dog ever will. Therefore, LVM (P) failed to demonstrate a claim for dilution by tarnishment. Affirmed as to this issue.

▶ *ANALYSIS*

One of the effects of the Trademark Dilution Revision Act of 2006 was to overturn the Supreme Court decision in *Moseley v. V Secret Catalogue, Inc.*, 537 U.S. 418 (2003), which had held a plaintiff needed to prove actual dilution under the Federal Trademark Dilution Act (FTDA). The TDRA revised the FTDA so that a plaintiff only needs to show the defendant's mark is likely to cause dilution, thus facilitating claims brought by owners of famous marks for dilution. However, the TDRA also limited famous marks to those that are "widely recognized by the general consuming public of the United States" and abolished the concept of niche fame, thus reducing the number of dilution claims that could be brought successfully.

■===■

Quicknotes

DILUTION The diminishment of the capability of a trademark to identify and distinguish the particular good or service with which it is associated.

■===■

People for the Ethical Treatment of Animals v. Doughney

Animal rights group (P) v. Individual's website (D)

263 F.3d 359 (4th Cir. 2001).

NATURE OF CASE: Appeal of an anticyber-squatting trademark infringement decision.

FACT SUMMARY: Doughney (D) created a web page entitled, "People Eating Tasty Animals," which was a parody of the website run by the People for the Ethical Treatment of Animals (P).

> ## 🏛 RULE OF LAW
> To establish an Anticybersquatting Consumer Protection Act (ACPA) violation, it must be proved there was a bad faith intent to profit from using the parodied domain name and that the domain name is identical or confusingly similar to, or dilutive of, the distinctive and famous mark.

FACTS: People for the Ethical Treatment of Animals (PETA) is an advocacy group opposed to eating meat, wearing fur, and conducting research on animals. PETA has an Internet website of "peta.com." Doughney (D) registered an Internet domain with the name "peta.org" and set up a page entitled "People Eating Tasty Animals," which he intended to use as a parody of PETA (P) and its goals and beliefs. PETA (P) sued Doughney (D) over the registration of that domain name.

ISSUE: To establish an ACPA violation, must it be proved there was a bad faith intent to profit from using the parodied domain name and that the domain name is identical or confusingly similar to, or dilutive of, the distinctive and famous mark?

HOLDING AND DECISION: (Gregory, J.) Yes. To establish an ACPA violation, it must be proved there was a bad faith intent to profit from using the parodied domain name and that the domain name is identical or confusingly similar to, or dilutive of, the distinctive and famous mark. To establish a violation under the ACPA, PETA (P) must prove that: (1) Doughney (D) had a bad faith intent to profit from the use of "peta.org" and (2) that this domain name "is identical or confusingly similar to, or dilutive of," the distinctive and more famous PETA (P) trademark. The lower court had found that PETA (P) met both of the above requirements. Doughney (D) now makes several arguments and concludes that he is entitled to protection under the ACPA's safe harbor provision, allowing protection of a website if the person believes or has reasonable grounds to believe that use of the domain name was fair or lawful. Doughney's (D) arguments refuting PETA's (P) suit include: (1) that the ACPA, effective in 1999, cannot be applied to events of 1995 and 1996 because it was not meant to be retroactive; in fact the ACPA explicitly states that it applies to "domain names registered before, on, or after the date of enactment." (2) Doughney (D) states that he did not seek any financial gain from the use of PETA's (P) trademark; there is no dispute that Doughney (D) made numerous statements, both on the website and to the press, suggesting that PETA (P) pay him to shut down the site. (3) Doughney (D) claims that he did not act in bad faith, a claim that this court finds unavailing because of the fact that Doughney (D), when registering his domain name, made false statements and knew that he was registering a name identical to PETA (P). Doughney (D) also had registered other domain names similar or identical to the trademarks or names of other organizations and famous people. Finally, the court finds that Doughney (D) "clearly intended to confuse Internet users into accessing his website." Doughney (D) did not establish that he had "reasonable grounds to believe" that his use of PETA's (P) trademark was lawful; merely "thinking" it to be lawful does not make that belief reasonable. For the above stated reasons, Doughney (D) is not entitled to relief under the safe harbor provision of the ACPA. Affirmed.

▶ ANALYSIS

Parody can be protected against claims of infringement. It is not, however, an absolute protection against an infringement charge. The fact that Doughney (D) suggested that PETA (P) settle with him undercut his good faith argument. And the fact that Doughney (D) lied when he registered his website undercuts his argument that he reasonably believed he had a lawful right to parody PETA (P).

■═■

Quicknotes

BAD FAITH Conduct that is intentionally misleading or deceptive.

TRADEMARK Any word, name, symbol, device, or combination thereof, which is either currently utilized, or which a person has a bona fide intent to utilize, in commerce in order to distinguish his goods from those of another.

TRADEMARK INFRINGEMENT The unauthorized use of another's trademark in such a manner as to cause a likelihood of confusion as to the source of the product or service in connection with which it is utilized.

■═■

Lamparello v. Falwell

Gripe website operator (P) v. Nationally known commentator/trademark owner (D)

420 F.3d 309 (4th Cir. 2005).

NATURE OF CASE: Appeal from grant of summary judgment to defendant; grant of injunction against plaintiff; and order to transfer a domain name in an action seeking a declaratory judgment of noninfringement.

FACT SUMMARY: Lamparello (P) contended that his gripe website, www.fallwell.com, aimed at criticizing the views of Reverend Jerry Falwell (Reverend Falwell) (D), a nationally known and outspoken minister, did not infringe Reverend Falwell's (D) trademarks; did not constitute false designation of origin; and did not constitute illegal cybersquatting.

🏛 RULE OF LAW
(1) A gripe website, the domain name of which contains an almost identical spelling of a trademark owned by the target of the site's criticism, does not infringe the owner's trademark or cause false designation of origin where there is no likelihood of confusion that the site is sponsored by the trademark owner.
(2) The use of a trademark in a domain name for a gripe site criticizing the markholder does not constitute cybersquatting under the Anticybersquatting Consumer Protection Act of 1999 where the use is not for profit and the site's operator does not engage in selling domain names.

FACTS: Reverend Jerry Falwell (Reverend Falwell) (D) is a nationally known and outspoken minister who actively comments on politics and public affairs. He holds the common law trademarks "Jerry Falwell" and "Falwell," and the registered trademark "Listen America with Jerry Falwell." Jerry Falwell Ministries can be found online at "www.falwell.com," a website that receives 9,000 hits a day. After hearing Reverend Falwell's (D) views on homosexuality, Lamparello (P) registered the domain name www.fallwell.com and created a website at that domain name to respond to what he believed were "untruths about gay people." The homepage prominently indicated that the website was not affiliated with Reverend Falwell (D) or his ministry and provided a link to Reverend Falwell's (D) site for those who wished to visit that site. Lamparello's (P) site received about 200 hits per day, and no goods or services were sold on it. Reverend Falwell (D) sent Lamparello (P) cease and desist letters to stop using www.fallwell.com or any variation of Reverend Falwell's (D) name as a domain name. Ultimately, Lamparello (P) filed an action against Reverend Falwell (D) seeking a declaratory judgment of noninfringement. Reverend Falwell (D) counterclaimed, alleging trademark infringement under 15 U.S.C. § 1114 (2000), false designation of origin under 15 U.S.C.

§ 1125(a), unfair competition under 15 U.S.C. § 1126 and state common law and cybersquatting under 15 U.S.C. § 1125(d). The district court granted summary judgment to Reverend Falwell (D), enjoined Lamparello (P) from using Reverend Falwell's (D) mark at www.fallwell.com, and required Lamparello (P) to transfer the domain name to Reverend Falwell (D). The court of appeals granted review.

ISSUE:
(1) Does a gripe website, the domain name of which contains an almost identical spelling of a trademark owned by the target of the site's criticism, infringe the owner's trademark or cause false designation of origin where there is no likelihood of confusion that the site is sponsored by the trademark owner?
(2) Does the use of a trademark in a domain name for a gripe site criticizing the markholder constitute cybersquatting under the Anticybersquatting Consumer Protection Act of 1999 where the use is not for profit and the site's operator does not engage in selling domain names?

HOLDING AND DECISION: (Motz, J.)
(1) No. A gripe website, the domain name of which contains an almost identical spelling of a trademark owned by the target of the site's criticism, does not infringe the owner's trademark or cause false designation of origin where there is no likelihood of confusion that the site is sponsored by the trademark owner. While trademark law protects product identification, it cannot be used to control language, lest much useful social and commercial discourse would be all but impossible if speakers were under threat of an infringement lawsuit every time they made reference to a person, company or product by using its trademark. On one hand, it is arguable that the Lanham Act reaches only "commercial speech" so that trademark law does not become a tool for unconstitutional censorship. Some courts have endorsed this view, and it is clear from Congress's more recent enactments in the trademark area that it intended for trademark laws not to impinge the First Amendment rights of critics and commentators. On the other hand, the trademark infringement and false designation of origin provisions of the Lanham Act (Sections 32 and 43(a), respectively) do not employ the term "noncommercial." They state that they pertain only to the use of a mark "in connection with the sale, offering for sale, distribution, or advertising of any goods or services," or "in connection with any goods or services." However,

Continued on next page.

courts have been reluctant to define those terms narrowly. In any event, it is not necessary to reach the issue of whether the Lanham Act reaches only "commercial speech," since here it is clear there is no likelihood of confusion—the hallmark of trademark infringement and false designation claims. A review of the likelihood of confusion factors leads to the conclusion that those viewing the content of Lamparello's (P) website probably would not confuse Reverend Falwell (D) with the source of that material. Additionally, Reverend Falwell's (D) contention that he must prevail under the "initial interest confusion" doctrine must be rejected. This relatively new and seldom-use doctrine provides that "the Lanham Act forbids a competitor from luring potential customers away from a producer by initially passing off its goods as those of the producer's, even if confusion as to the source of the goods is dispelled by the time any sales are consummated." Under this doctrine, the court would compare his Reverend Falwell's (D) mark with Lamparello's (P) website domain name without considering the content of Lamparello's (P) website. Reverend Falwell (D) argues that some people who misspell his name may go to www.fallwell.com assuming it is his site, thus giving Lamparello (P) an unearned audience—albeit one that quickly disappears when it realizes it has not reached Reverend Falwell's (D) site. This argument fails for two reasons. First, this court has never adopted the "initial interest confusion" doctrine, but instead has required a determination as to whether a likelihood of confusion exists by "examining the allegedly infringing use in the context in which it is seen by the ordinary consumer." In the context of domain names, this means that the allegedly infringing domain name must be evaluated in conjunction with the content of the website identified by the domain name. Second, even if the doctrine were to be applied here, it would not be helpful to Reverend Falwell (D) because it requires that the use of another's mark be for financial gain. That element clearly is absent here, given that Lamparello (P) is not competing for a share of Reverend Falwell's (D) market; use of another firm's mark to capture the markholder's customers and profits simply does not exist when the alleged infringer establishes a gripe site that criticizes the markholder. To hold otherwise would enable the markholder to insulate himself from criticism—or at least minimize his access to it. Such use of the Lanham Act as a shield from criticism has been rejected. Accordingly, the district court erred in granting summary judgment to Reverend Falwell (D) on his infringement, false designation, and unfair competition claims. Reversed as to this issue.

(2) No. The use of a trademark in a domain name for a gripe site criticizing the markholder does not constitute cybersquatting under the Anticybersquatting Consumer Protection Act of 1999 where the use is not for profit and the site's operator does not engage in selling domain names. To prevail on a claim under the Anti-cybersquatting Consumer Protection Act of 1999 (ACPA), a markholder must show that the defendant (1) "had a bad faith intent to profit from using the domain name," and (2) the domain name "is identical or confusingly similar to, or dilutive of, the distinctive and famous mark." The ACPA was primarily intended to prevent the registration of multiple marks in the hope of selling them to their legitimate owner or to the highest bidder, not to prevent criticism of a markholder or such noncommercial uses. Here, Lamparello (P) did not have a bad faith intent to profit from using the www.fallwell.com domain name, which he clearly employed simply to criticize Reverend Falwell's (D) views. Additionally, Lamparello (P) did not engage in the kind of conduct at which the ACPA was primarily aimed: he did not create a likelihood of confusion as to the source, sponsorship, affiliation, or endorsement of the site, and he did not attempt—or even indicate a willingness—to transfer, sell, or otherwise assign the domain name to Reverend Falwell (D) or any third party for financial gain. He also registered just one domain name, not multiple names. Therefore, consistent with the holdings of other Circuits in similar cases, Lamparello (P) did not engage in cybersquatting under the ACPA. Reversed and remanded for entry of summary judgment for Lamparello (P).

▶ *ANALYSIS*

This opinion, among other things, manifests the court's skepticism about the "initial interest confusion" doctrine. This is in keeping with traditional precepts of trademark law, which has always protected against only a substantial likelihood of confusion by the reasonable consumer, and not against "temporary confusion" or confusion caused wholly by consumer carelessness. By rejecting the "initial interest confusion" doctrine, the court seems to have rendered a decision that establishes trademark law principles that go beyond the specific issue of domain names and the Internet, and that can be applied in other contexts as well.

■━■

Quicknotes

SUMMARY JUDGMENT Judgment rendered by a court in response to a motion made by one of the parties, claiming that the lack of a question of material fact in respect to an issue warrants disposition of the issue without consideration by the jury.

■━■

Tiffany Inc. v. eBay Inc.

Trademark holder (P) v. Alleged infringer (D)

600 F.3d 93 (2d Cir. 2010).

NATURE OF CASE: Appeal from finding of no infringement in trademark case.

FACT SUMMARY: Tiffany (NJ) Inc. (P) and Tiffany and Company (P) (Tiffany) sold high-end jewelry in retail stores, catalogues, and online but not through second-hand vendors or third-party online retailers. eBay Inc. (D) sells goods online by connecting third-party sellers and buyers and without ever taking possession of the goods. Tiffany (P) accused eBay (D) of knowingly permitting the sale of counterfeit Tiffany goods in violation of Tiffany's (P) trademark.

RULE OF LAW

Service provider liability for contributory trademark infringement requires a showing of intentional inducement to infringe or "knows or should have known" of the direct infringement and a continued providing of the service to the infringer.

FACTS: eBay (D) is an Internet marketplace that permits registered sellers to sell various items to registered buyers without eBay ever taking possession of the item. eBay, an extremely successful company, makes its money by charging sellers to list goods and charging a percentage of the final sale price. eBay also makes money through its ownership of Pay-Pal, which charges a percentage and small flat fee for eBay users to process purchases. Tiffany (P) is a world-famous jeweler. It sells its merchandise exclusively through its own retail stores, catalogue, and website. It does not sell overstock, discontinued, or discount merchandise. Tiffany (P) learned of counterfeit Tiffany sales on eBay (D) and alerted eBay (D) to the problem. eBay initiated a variety of anticounterfeit sales measures, including a fraud engine, a notice-and-takedown system so rights holders could complete a Notice of Claimed Infringement Form and request the takedown of a particular seller's allegedly counterfeit goods, and cancellation of seller accounts of repeat offenders. Tiffany (P) also put a buyers' notice on the eBay (D) site informing buyers of the potential danger in purchasing Tiffany products on the second-hand market. Tiffany (P) filed suit against eBay (D), claiming inter alia, eBay's (D) conduct constituted direct and contributory trademark infringement, trademark dilution, and false advertising. The district court found for eBay (D) on all counts. Tiffany (P) appealed.

ISSUE: Does service provider liability for contributory trademark infringement require a showing of intentional inducement to infringe or "knows or should have known" of the direct infringement and a continued providing of the service to the infringer?

HOLDING AND DECISION: (Sack, J.) Yes. Service provider liability for contributory trademark infringement requires a showing of intentional inducement to infringe or "knows or should have known" of the direct infringement and a continued providing of the service to the infringer. The district court correctly found eBay's (D) use of Tiffany's (P) mark to be nominative fair use and did not suggest Tiffany (P) endorsed or partnered with eBay (D). Tiffany's (P) argument that eBay (D) knew or should have known of the counterfeit sales and thus directly infringed upon its mark for failing to identify and remove the illegitimate goods fails. It would unduly limit the resale of legitimate second-hand Tiffany goods to impose liability on eBay (D) for an inability to guarantee the genuineness of all purported Tiffany products. Next, Tiffany (P) argues eBay's conduct constitutes contributory trademark infringement, which is a more difficult argument. This is a judicially created doctrine most recently addressed by the United States Supreme Court in *Inwood Laboratories, Inc. v. Ives Laboratories, Inc.*, 456 U.S. 844 (1982). *Inwood*, applies on its face to manufacturers and distributors of goods but has been extended to providers of services. This Court's precedent in related decisions does not provide great insight and this is the first case in which *Inwood* is applied to an online marketplace. *Inwood* assesses liability for contributory infringement on service providers if the provider: (1) intentionally induces the infringement; or (2) knows or has reason to know of infringement and continues to supply its service to the offending party. Tiffany (P) argues the second factor applies to eBay (D). Tiffany (P) does not challenge the district court's finding that eBay (D) was not liable for those sales it terminated upon receipt of notice from Tiffany (P) about allegedly offending products. Tiffany (P) does challenge the district court's finding eBay (D) had insufficient knowledge about infringement of other, nonterminated listings because its generalized knowledge of counterfeit products on its site did not translate into sufficient knowledge under *Inwood*. It is a high burden to prove "knowledge" of contributory infringement. Tiffany (P) argues here that generalized knowledge and specific knowledge of particular sellers is the same under *Inwood* and creates liability. This court does not read *Inwood* to be so broad and does not find *Inwood* established the parameters of "knows or has reason to know" when it only applied the inducement prong of the test. Another United States Supreme Court case held *Inwood* had a narrow standard and interpreted *Inwood*'s second prong to require knowledge of identified individuals. *Sony Corp. of America*

Continued on next page.

v. Universal City Studios, Inc. 464 U.S. 417 (1984). eBay (D) had no such knowledge here. Tiffany (P) argues "willful blindness" cannot be permitted to overcome liability. If eBay (D) deliberately shielded itself from knowledge of offending sales, it could become liable under the *Inwood* second prong. That is not the case, however, as eBay (D) had only general knowledge and did not ignore the issue. Finally, Tiffany's (P) dilution claims fail because eBay (D) did not use the Tiffany mark to associate it with its own products but to identify Tiffany products on its site. [False advertising analysis is omitted from the casebook excerpt.] Affirmed as to trademark infringement and dilution; remand as to false advertising.

▌ANALYSIS

Consumer advocates worried a victory for Tiffany (P) would require online merchants to prohibit even lawful uses of trademarks on their sites because of the fear of liability for contributory trademark infringement. eBay's (D) existing safeguards and rapid response to notifications of counterfeit products gave it a significant advantage in this case, but not many online retailers are so responsive. Trademark infringement is rampant online and rights holders must be vigilant about policing the use of their marks. This case did not offer the hoped-for protection for trademark holders.

■═■

Quicknotes

INFRINGEMENT Conduct in violation of statute or that interferes with another's rights pursuant to law.

■═■

Johnson & Johnson * Merck Consumer Pharmaceuticals Co. v. SmithKline Beecham Corp.

Pharmaceutical manufacturer (P) v. Competitor (D)

960 F.2d 294 (2d. Cir. 1992).

NATURE OF CASE: Appeal from denial of injunctive relief and dismissal of claim for false advertising.

FACT SUMMARY: Merck (P) alleged that Smithkline's (D) television commercials were false and misleading because they knowingly exploited a public misperception.

🏛 RULE OF LAW
An advertisement is false and misleading only if a significant part of the audience holds the false belief and injury is suffered.

FACTS: Smithkline Beecham Corp. (Smithkline) (D) produced the antacid TUMS. It instituted a television advertising campaign that compared the ingredients contained in TUMS to competing products. Merck (P), the maker of MYLANTA, alleged that the advertisement falsely represented that occasional ingestion of TUMS resulted in nutritional benefit and that the magnesium and aluminum contained in MYLANTA was unsafe for human consumption. It sought to enjoin the ads. The trial court dismissed all claims because Merck (P) had failed to demonstrate that the ads were either false or misleading. Merck (P) appealed.

ISSUE: Is an advertisement false and misleading if most of the audience is not misled and no injury is suffered?

HOLDING AND DECISION: (Walker, J.) No. An advertisement is false and misleading only if a significant part of the audience holds the false belief and injury is suffered. Without injury there can be no claim. Consumer surveys determine what message the target audience actually received. The trial court reviewed the results of consumer surveys and found that the ads did not communicate that the aluminum in MYLANTA was harmful or unsafe. The trial court's evaluation of the survey questions was not clearly erroneous. Affirmed.

▶ ANALYSIS

False or misleading statements about the advertiser's own products were prohibited under § 43 (a) of the Lanham Act. In 1988 the Trademark Law Reform Act amended the law to include disparagement of another's product. False advertising covers both representations made to sophisticated business customers, as well as to individual consumers.

Quicknotes

INJUNCTIVE RELIEF A court order issued as a remedy, requiring a person to do, or prohibiting that person from doing, a specific act.

LANHAM ACT, § 43 (a) Federal trademark infringement statute.

Major League Baseball Properties, Inc. v. Sed Non Olet Denarius, Ltd.

Baseball team (P) v. Restaurant (D)

817 F. Supp. 1103 (S.D.N.Y. 1993).

NATURE OF CASE: Motion to enjoin use of registered trademarks in action alleging infringement, and wrongful appropriation, and unfair competition.

FACT SUMMARY: Major League Baseball Properties, Inc. (P) and the Los Angeles Dodgers (P) claimed that Sed Non Olet Denarius, Ltd. (SNOD) (D) was infringing on their trademarks and unfairly competing with them by opening restaurants in Brooklyn under the name "The Brooklyn Dodger Sports Bar and Restaurant."

🏛 RULE OF LAW
Abandonment under the Lanham Act requires both nonuse and intent not to resume use.

FACTS: Sed Non Olet Denarius, Ltd. (SNOD) (D) began doing business as a restaurant under the name "The Brooklyn Dodger Sports Bar and Restaurant" in 1988. Major League Baseball Properties, Inc. (Properties) (P) and the Los Angeles Dodgers (Los Angeles) (P) in their complaint alleged an infringement of their trademarks, a wrongful appropriation of their trademarks, unfair competition and the intentional use of a counterfeit mark. SNOD (D) counterclaimed for the cancellation of various trademark registrations for "Brooklyn Dodgers" filed by Los Angeles (P) after SNOD's (D) application to register the "Brooklyn Dodgers" servicemark in 1988.

ISSUE: Does abandonment under the Lanham Act require both nonuse and intent not to resume use?

HOLDING AND DECISION: (Motley, J.) Yes. Abandonment under the Lanham Act requires both nonuse and intent not to resume use. The evidence presented at trial established that between 1958, when the Dodgers baseball team left Brooklyn for Los Angeles, and 1981 Los Angeles (P) made no commercial trademark use whatsoever of any "Brooklyn Dodgers" mark. The "Brooklyn Dodgers" name had acquired secondary meaning in New York in the early part of this century, prior to 1958. In this case, in order to maintain use of the mark, Los Angeles (P) would have had to continue to use "Brooklyn Dodgers" as the name of its baseball team. Under the law, warehousing is not permitted. Los Angeles (P) attempted to "warehouse" this trademark by using the name "Brooklyn Dodgers" strictly in conjunction with items of historical interest after 1958. Los Angeles's (P) failure to use the "Brooklyn Dodgers" trademark between 1958 and 1981 constitutes abandonment of the trademark. Once prima facie abandonment has been proven, the trademark registrants, Los Angeles (P), must prove an intent to resume use of the trademark to prevail.

Los Angeles (P) has in no way demonstrated an intent to resume commercial use of the "Brooklyn Dodgers" mark within two years after leaving Brooklyn in 1958 or at any time in the ensuing quarter century. Los Angeles's (P) recent resumed limited use of the trademark on clothing and novelty items does not preclude SNOD's (D) use of the mark in their restaurant business in Brooklyn, where the idea of trading on any "good will" is almost laughable since the departure of the Dodgers in 1958 was accompanied by monumental hard feelings throughout the borough of Brooklyn. Motion denied.

▶ ANALYSIS

The Lanham Act was amended in 1994. As of January 1, 1996, the presumptive abandonment period is three years, not two years. The trademark rights are aimed primarily at avoiding confusion in the minds of the public.

■▬■

Quicknotes

ABANDONMENT The surrender of rights in a trademark with the intent to abandon the mark and to permanently relinquish its use; course of conduct of a trademark owner that causes the mark to become generic in association with goods or services or to diminish in its significance.

TRADEMARK Any word, name, symbol, device, or combination thereof, which is either currently utilized, or which a person has a bona fide intent to utilize, in commerce in order to distinguish his goods from those of another.

TRADEMARK INFRINGEMENT The unauthorized use of anther's trademark in such a manner as to cause a likelihood of confusion as to the source of the product or service in connect with which it is utilized.

15 U.S.C. § 1127 A mark is abandoned when its use has been discontinued without intent to resume.

■▬■

Dawn Donut Company, Inc. v. Hart's Food Stores, Inc.

Doughnut mix wholesaler (P) v. Local shop (D)

267 F.2d 358 (2d Cir. 1959).

NATURE OF CASE: Appeal of denial of injunction prohibiting product name use.

FACT SUMMARY: Dawn Donut Company, Inc. (P), which distributed doughnut mix under the name "Dawn" in an area of New York separate from Hart Food's (D) use of the name, sought to enjoin such use.

⚖ RULE OF LAW
The holder of a registered trademark may not enjoin another's use thereof in a different market.

FACTS: Dawn Donut Company, Inc. (Dawn Donut Co.) (P) sold doughnut mix at the wholesale level in several states, including parts of New York. The buyers of the mixes were allowed to call themselves "Dawn Donut Shops." Dawn Donut Co. (P) registered the name "Dawn" in connection with doughnuts. Subsequent to this, Hart's Food Stores, Inc. (Hart's) (D) began selling "Dawn Donuts" in six New York counties adjacent to Rochester. Dawn Donut Co. (P) did not distribute mix in this area. Dawn Donut Co. (P) brought an action seeking to enjoin Hart's (D) use of the name. The district court dismissed the action, and Dawn Donut Co. (P) appealed.

ISSUE: May the holder of a registered trademark enjoin another's use thereof in a different market?

HOLDING AND DECISION: (Lumbard, J.) No. The holder of a registered trademark may not enjoin another's use thereof in a different market. The Lanham Act, 15 U.S.C. § 1114, sets out the standard for awarding a registrant relief against the unauthorized use of his mark by another. It provides that the registrant may enjoin only that concurrent use which creates a likelihood of confusion in the perception of the public as to the origin of the products in connection with the use of the products. Where the product markets overlap, the junior user's use of the mark may not be enjoined. Here, the district court found that the two markets involved did not overlap, and this finding was not clearly erroneous. The court was therefore correct in holding that an injunction should not issue. The action was properly dismissed, although if Dawn (P) ever expands into the area serviced by Hart's (D), it may then seek the injunction denied here. Affirmed.

▶ ANALYSIS

At one time, Dawn Donut Co. (P) did operate in the area serviced by Hart's (D), but had ceased doing so before Hart's (D) commenced its operations. This, however, did not constitute abandonment. Under 15 U.S.C. § 1127, only abandonment at the retail level entirely can constitute abandonment. This left Dawn Donut Co. (P) free to reenter the area occupied by Hart's (D).

━━━

Quicknotes

ABANDONMENT The surrender of rights in a trademark with the intent to abandon the mark and to permanently relinquish its use; course of conduct of a trademark owner that causes the mark to become generic in association with goods or services or to diminish in its significance.

ENJOIN The ordering of a party to cease the conduct of a specific activity.

TRADEMARK Any word, name, symbol, device, or combination thereof, which is either currently utilized, or which a person has a bona fide intent to utilize, in commerce in order to distinguish his goods from those of another.

15 U.S.C. § 1127 A mark is abandoned when its use has been discontinued without intent to resume.

━━━

KP Permanent Make-up, Inc. v. Lasting Impression I, Inc.

Alleged infringers (P) v. Trademark owners (D)

543 U.S. 111 (2004).

NATURE OF CASE: Appeal from summary judgment granted to counterclaim-defendant in declaratory judgment action.

FACT SUMMARY: Two permanent make-up sellers employed the phrase "micro color" in marketing materials. KP Permanent Make-Up, Inc. (KP) (P) claimed it first used the phrase while Lasting Impression I, Inc. (Lasting) (D) had an incontestable trademark for the phrase. KP (P) sued Lasting (D) in a declaratory judgment action and Lasting (D) counterclaimed for trademark infringement. KP (P) moved for summary judgment on the counterclaim.

🏛 RULE OF LAW
The plaintiff in a trademark infringement action has the burden of proof to show that a fair-use defendant's use of mark is likely to cause consumer confusion.

FACTS: KP Permanent Make-Up, Inc. (KP) (P), a seller of permanent makeup, uses the phrase "micro color" to market and sell its products. Lasting Impression I, Inc. (Lasting) (D) also sells permanent make-up and also uses the phrase "micro color" to market and sell its products. KP (P) claimed it first used "micro color." Subsequent to that first use date, Lasting (D) applied for and obtained trademark registration of the phrase "micro colors." That registration then became incontestable. KP (P), after the date of incontestability, produced an advertising brochure employing the phrase "micro color." Lasting (D) made demand upon KP (P) to cease use of "micro color." KP (P) filed a declaratory judgment action against Lasting (D) asking the court to declare no infringement existed. Lasting (D) counterclaimed for trademark infringement. KP (P) filed a motion for summary judgment on the counterclaim based on the "fair use" defense. The trial court granted KP's (P) motion and Lasting (D) appealed. The appellate court determined the trial court should have considered the likelihood of confusion and reversed the judgment. KP (P) petitioned for a writ of certiorari, which the United States Supreme Court granted on the issue of which party had the burden of proof to demonstrate likelihood of confusion.

ISSUE: Does the plaintiff in a trademark infringement action have the burden of proof to show that a fair-use defendant's use of mark is likely to cause consumer confusion?

HOLDING AND DECISION: (Souter, J.) Yes. The plaintiff in a trademark infringement action has the burden of proof to show that a fair-use defendant's use of mark is likely to cause consumer confusion. The fair-use defendant does not have to demonstrate the opposition proposition, which is that confusion is unlikely. Some confusion is likely to arise just because the mark is descriptive and that is a risk the trademark registrar undertook. If the confusion leads to an objectively unfair use, the courts may then consider it infringement. KP (P) does not have to bear the burden of proof in demonstrating that confusion is unlikely because it is the trademark infringement defendant. Vacated and remanded.

▶ ANALYSIS

As the Supreme Court noted, the mere existence of a risk of confusion does not negate a fair use defense and a plaintiff cannot rely on that alone to overcome the defense or meet its burden of proof to show likelihood of confusion. A defendant claiming fair use as its defense must affirmatively prove the elements of fair use separate from the plaintiff's demonstration of likelihood of confusion.

■▬■

Quicknotes

FAIR USE An affirmative defense to a claim of copyright infringement providing an exception from the copyright owner's exclusive rights in a work for the purposes of criticism, comment, news reporting, teaching, scholarship or research.

■▬■

Mattel, Inc. v. MCA Records

Doll maker (P) v. Music company (D)

296 F.3d 894 (9th Cir. 2002).

NATURE OF THE CASE: Appeal of trademark violation parody use decision.

FACT SUMMARY: The music group Aqua, on an MCA Records-produced (D) album, recorded a song called *Barbie Girl*. Mattel, Inc. (P), the manufacturer of the Barbie doll, sued for trademark infringement.

🏛 RULE OF LAW
The parody of a well-known product, where such a product has assumed a role in society outside the protections offered under trademark law, is allowed under the First Amendment as protected noncommercial free speech.

FACTS: The Danish band Aqua, who is signed to the record label MCA Records, Inc. (MCA) (D), produced a song entitled *Barbie Girl* on their *Aquarium* album. The song made it onto some Top 40 music charts. The song consists of one band member impersonating the doll Barbie in a high-pitched voice, while another band member pretends to be Ken, who asks Barbie to "go party." Barbie, the doll, has long been a best seller in the United States and has become an American cultural icon. Mattel, Inc. (P), the maker of the doll Barbie, brought suit for trademark infringement. The lower court found for MCA (D), and Mattel (P) now appeals that ruling—that *Barbie Girl* is a parody of Barbie and, therefore, is a nominative fair use of the product. The lower court also ruled that MCA's (D) use of the term "Barbie" is not likely to confuse consumers as to Mattel's (P) affiliation with *Barbie Girl* or dilute the Barbie trademark.

ISSUE: Is the parody of a well-known product, where such product has assumed a role in society outside the protection offered under trademark law, allowed under the First Amendment as protected noncommercial free speech?

HOLDING AND DECISION: (Kozinski, J.) Yes. The parody of a well-known product, where such product has assumed a role in society outside the protection offered under trademark law, is allowed under the First Amendment as protected noncommercial free speech. Trademarks identify a manufacturer or sponsor of a good or service. Some trademarks, for example, Rolls Royce or Band-Aid, become so well known that they transcend their original identifying purpose and become a part of society's collective vocabulary (asking for a Band-Aid when one has a cut, for instance). At that point, where the product has transcended its original purpose, the trademark assumes "a role outside the bounds of trademark law." A likelihood-of-confusion test must then be applied, balancing the trademark owner's rights with the public's expressive value interests. This test ensures that trade-

mark rights do not encroach upon First Amendment free speech rights. There is no doubt that the lyrics of *Barbie Girl* refer to Mattel's (P) Barbie and Ken dolls, making fun of the values that the band believes the Barbie doll represents. Significantly, the song does not use Barbie, the doll, to make fun of another subject matter, but makes fun of Barbie herself. The title, *Barbie Girl*, does not explicitly mislead consumers as to its source; it in no way suggests that it was produced by Mattel (P). It is, therefore, outside the bounds protected by Mattel's (P) trademark. Mattel (P) further argues that, under the Federal Trademark Dilution Act (FTDA), *Barbie Girl* dilutes Barbie in two ways: (1) it tarnishes the doll's image because of the song's inappropriateness for young girls, and (2) it diminishes Mattel's (P) ability to identify and distinguish its product. The FTDA is designed to protect the distinctiveness of a trademark. Under the FTDA, dilution is prevented if the use of a famous product somehow dilutes the distinctive quality of that famous trademark. Such use, however, is allowable if it falls under one of three exceptions—comparative ads, news reports and commentary, or noncommercial use. It is undisputed by MCA (D) that *Barbie Girl* brings to mind Barbie the doll and that consumers may think of both the song and the doll when they hear the term "Barbie" or perhaps even only of the song. Clearly, the only viable exception that *Barbie Girl* may fall under is the "noncommercial use" exception. The Court's test for noncommercial use is if the speech has a purpose beyond a commercial transaction. Here, *Barbie Girl* is not "purely commercial speech." While MCA (D) does use Barbie the doll to sell the song, the song also parodies Barbie and humorously comments on the values that Aqua sees Barbie as representing. *Barbie Girl* has a meaning and function beyond a strictly commercial use only and is, therefore, protected noncommercial speech under the FTDA. Affirmed.

▶ ANALYSIS

In trademark law, courts have long made an exception for parody. Not only is parody protected under the First Amendment, the exception is also a "common sense" recognition to how society functions and entertains itself—parody occurs regularly, and to not allow it as an exception would limit how people communicate with one another.

■▬■

Quicknotes

FAIR USE An affirmative defense to a claim of copyright infringement providing an exception from the copyright

Continued on next page.

owner's exclusive rights in a work for the purposes of criticism, comment, news reporting, teaching, scholarship or research; the determination of whether a use is fair is made on a case-by-case basis and requires the court to consider: (1) the purpose and character of the use; (2) the nature of the work; (3) the amount and substantiality of the portion used; and (4) the effect of the use on the potential market for, or value of, the work.

TRADEMARK Any word, name, symbol, device or combination thereof, which is either currently utilized, or which a person has a bona fide intent to utilize, in commerce in order to distinguish his goods from those of another.

Lindy Pen Company, Inc. v. Bic Pen Corporation

Pen manufacturer (P) v. Competitor (D)

982 F.2d 1400 (9th Cir. 1993).

NATURE OF CASE: Appeal from refusal to order an accounting in a trademark infringement case.

FACT SUMMARY: Lindy Pen Company, Inc. (P) sued Bic Pen Corporation (D) alleging trademark infringement, unfair competition, breach of contract, and trademark dilution, and an accounting was ordered by the Ninth Circuit.

> ## 🏛 RULE OF LAW
> In order to deter trademark infringement, an accounting of profits will be ordered in those cases where infringement yields financial rewards.

FACTS: Lindy Pen Company, Inc. (Lindy) (P) alleged that Bic Pen Corporation (Bic) (D) infringed its trademark by using the word "Auditor's" on its pen barrels. The district court entered judgment in favor of Bic (D), and the circuit court upheld the ruling because Bic (D) did not infringe in the major retail markets, but remanded the case to determine whether there was a likelihood of confusion in telephone order sales. The district court determined that any confusion in the telephone order market could be cured upon receipt of the goods. The circuit court disagreed, however, and found that post-sale inspection could not cure the confusion. It ordered an accounting to award damages. On remand, the district court held that an accounting of profits was inappropriate because Bic's (D) infringement was innocent. Lindy (P) appealed.

ISSUE: In order to deter trademark infringement, will an accounting of profits be ordered in those cases where infringement yields financial rewards?

HOLDING AND DECISION: (Roll, J.) Yes. In order to deter trademark infringement, an accounting of profits will be ordered in those cases where infringement yields financial rewards. The district court determined that Lindy's (P) mark was weak and there was no evidence of actual confusion since Bic's (D) infringement was unintentional. To award profits in this situation would amount to a punishment in violation of the Lanham Act, which clearly stipulates that a remedy shall constitute compensation, and not a penalty. The district court was correct in finding that Lindy (P) failed to sustain its burden of proving reasonably forecast profits. An accounting is intended to award profits only on sales that are attributable to the infringing conduct. Lindy (P) failed to come forward with any evidence of sales of the Bic (D) "Auditor's Fine Point" in the infringing market. Affirmed.

certainty. Once gross profits are demonstrated, they are presumed to be the result of the infringing activity. Since Lindy (P) failed to produce a reasonable estimate of Bic's (D) sales in the telephone submarket, the question of actual damages failed due to a lack of proof at the damages proceeding.

Quicknotes

TRADEMARK INFRINGEMENT The unauthorized use of another's trademark in such a manner as to cause a likelihood of confusion as to the source of the product or service in connection with which it is utilized.

⟩ ANALYSIS

The court held that Lindy (P) had only to establish Bic's (D) gross profits from the infringing activity with reasonable

Big O Tire Dealers, Inc. v. The Goodyear Tire & Rubber Company

Tire dealer (P) v. Tire manufacturer (D)

561 F.2d 1365 (10th Cir. 1977).

NATURE OF CASE: Appeal from an order awarding damages and an injunction in a trademark infringement case.

FACT SUMMARY: Reverse confusion was claimed not to be actionable if Goodyear Tire & Rubber Company's (D) second use of Big O Tire Dealers, Inc.'s (P) trademark merely created likelihood of confusion concerning the source of Big O Tire Dealers' (P) "Big Foot" tires.

🏛 RULE OF LAW
The second use of a trademark is actionable if it merely creates a likelihood of confusion concerning the source of the first user's product.

FACTS: Big O Tire Dealers, Inc. (P) asserted claims of unfair competition against Goodyear Tire & Rubber Company (Goodyear) (D) based upon false designation of origin and common law trademark infringement. The jury found that Goodyear (D) was liable only for trademark infringement and trademark disparagement and awarded general compensatory and punitive damages. The district court permanently enjoined Goodyear (D) from infringing on Big O Tire Dealers' (P) "Big Foot" trademark. Goodyear (D) appealed, arguing that its second use of the "Bigfoot" trademark was not actionable if it merely created a likelihood of confusion concerning the source of the first user's product.

ISSUE: Is the second use of a trademark actionable if it merely creates a likelihood of confusion concerning the source of the first user's product?

HOLDING AND DECISION: (Lewis, C.J.) Yes. The second use of a trademark is actionable if it merely creates a likelihood of confusion concerning the source of the first user's product. The Colorado courts, if given the opportunity, would extend their common law trademark infringement actions to include reverse confusion situations. The jury could have reasonably inferred a likelihood of confusion from witnesses' testimony of actual confusion. Affirmed.

▌ ANALYSIS

The court also ruled that Goodyear (D) had to pay money damages for the cost of corrective advertising to undo the damage done when it had used the trademark name. That Goodyear (D) did not intend to trade on the good will of Big O (P) or to palm off its products was irrelevant in this case. The court found that Colorado's policy was to widen the scope of its policy of protecting trade names and preventing public confusion.

Quicknotes

DAMAGES Monetary compensation that may be awarded by the court to a party who has sustained injury or loss to his or her person, property or rights due to another party's unlawful act, omission, or negligence.

INJUNCTION A remedy imposed by the court ordering a party to cease the conduct of a specific activity.

TRADEMARK INFRINGEMENT The unauthorized use of another's trademark in such a manner as to cause a likelihood of confusion as to the source of the product or service in connection with which it is utilized.

CHAPTER 6

State Intellectual Property Law and Federal Preemption

Quick Reference Rules of Law

International News Service v. Associated Press

Press service (D) v. Competitor (P)

248 U.S. 215 (1918).

NATURE OF CASE: Appeal from injunction in action for unfair competition.

FACT SUMMARY: Associated Press (P) brought suit against International News Service (D), a competitor in the business of distributing news to newspapers throughout the United States, for pirating Associated Press's (P) news.

🏛 RULE OF LAW
One who has gathered general information or news for the purpose of publication has an interest that is entitled to protection from interference.

FACTS: Associated Press (P) and the International News Service (INS) (D) are competitors in the gathering and the distribution of news and its publication for profit in newspapers throughout the United States. Associated Press (P) brought suit to restrain the pirating of its news by INS (D). Allegedly, INS (D) bribed employees of newspapers to furnish Associated Press (P) news to itself before publication, for transmission by telegraph and telephone to INS's (D) clients for publication by them; by inducing Associated Press members to violate its bylaws and permit INS (D) to obtain news before publications and by copying news from bulletin boards and from early editions of Associated Press's (P) newspapers and by selling this, either bodily or after rewriting it, to INS (D) customers. The district court granted a preliminary injunction as to the first and second practices. The circuit court of appeals sustained the injunction order. Writ of certiorari was granted.

ISSUE: Does one who has gathered general information or news at pain and expense for the purpose of subsequent publication through the press have such an interest in its publication that it may be protected from interference?

HOLDING AND DECISION: (Pitney, J.) Yes. One who has gathered general information or news for the purpose of publication has an interest that is entitled to protection. The question of unfair competition in business as it relates to the gathering and production of news must turn upon the rights of the parties as between themselves. Regarding the news, therefore, as the material out of which both parties are seeking to make profits at the same time and in the same field, such news must be regarded as quasi-property between the two parties. News has an exchange value to one who can misappropriate it. Here, the acquisition and the transmission of news required elaborate organization and a large expenditure of money, skill, and effort. Because INS (D) sold Associated Press's (P) goods as

its own, it is guilty of unfair competition by virtue of misappropriation. The preliminary injunction should not be modified. Affirmed.

CONCURRENCE: (Holmes, J.) Within the limits recognized by the majority, INS (D) should be enjoined from publishing news obtained from Associated Press (P) for hours after publication by Associated Press (P) unless it gives express credit to Associated Press (P).

DISSENT: (Brandeis, J.) The Court should decline to determine limitations that should be set upon any property right in news or of the circumstances under which news gathered by a private agency should be deemed affected with a public interest.

▶ ANALYSIS

The underlying premise of this opinion is the fact that news is not copyrightable because the news element is not the creation of the writer. Basing its opinion, therefore, on the basis of unfair competition, the majority proceeded on a misappropriation theory while Justice Holmes approached it as a misrepresentation, i.e., a reverse "palming off."

■▬■

Quicknotes

INJUNCTION A remedy imposed by the court ordering a party to cease the conduct of a specific activity.

MISAPPROPRIATION The unlawful use of another's property or funds.

UNFAIR COMPETITION Any dishonest or fraudulent rivalry in trade and commerce, particularly imitation and counterfeiting.

■▬■

ProCD, Inc. v. Zeidenberg

Seller (P) v. Buyer (D)

86 F.3d 1447 (7th Cir. 1996).

NATURE OF CASE: Breach of contract suit.

FACT SUMMARY: ProCD, Inc. (P) brought suit against Zeidenberg (D) for violation of a shrink-wrapped license included inside its CD-ROM database.

🏛 RULE OF LAW
Shrink-wrap licenses are enforceable unless their terms are objectionable on grounds applicable to contracts in general.

FACTS: ProCD, Inc. (P) compiled information from more than 3,000 telephone directories into a computer database. The database cost over $10 million to compile and was expensive to keep current. ProCD (P) included a license in every CD-ROM box stating that the software came with specified restrictions. The license limits the use of application program and listing for noncommercial purposes. Zeidenberg (D) bought a consumer package of ProCD's (P) CD-ROM box in 1994 and formed Silken Mountain Web Services to resell the information in Select-Phone's database. Zeidenberg (D) offered the information via the Internet at a price less than ProCD (P) charged its commercial customers. ProCD (P) filed suit seeking an injunction against further dissemination in violation of the licenses included in the box. The district court held that the licenses were ineffective. ProCD (P) appealed.

ISSUE: Are shrink-wrap licenses enforceable unless their terms are objectionable on grounds applicable to contracts in general?

HOLDING AND DECISION: (Easterbrook, J.) Yes. Shrink-wrap licenses are enforceable unless their terms are objectionable on grounds applicable to contracts in general. The district court concluded that neither the UCC, nor Wisconsin's version of the UCC, authorized the payment of money prior to the disclosure of the terms of a contract. UCC section 2-204 states that "a contract for sale of goods may be made in any manner sufficient to show agreement, including conduct by both parties which recognizes the existence of such a contract." The vendor invites acceptance of the offer by conduct and may restrict the manner in which acceptance may be made. Here ProCD (P) proposed a contract that the buyer would accept by using the software after reading the license. Zeidenberg (D) accepted. Section 2-606 also supports this conclusion. A buyer accepts goods if he fails to make an effective rejection after an opportunity to inspect. Zeidenberg (D) accepted the goods, had an opportunity to inspect and did not reject them. Reversed and remanded.

▶ ANALYSIS

Decisions in the courts about shrink-wrapped licenses have varied with the enforceability of such license being upheld in many recent cases.

■■■

Quicknotes

BREACH OF CONTRACT Unlawful failure by a party to perform its obligations pursuant to contract.

■■■

Specht v. Netscape Communications Corp.

Internet browser users (P) v. Browser provider (D)

306 F.3d 17 (2d Cir. 2002).

NATURE OF THE CASE: Appeal from the denial of a motion made by Netscape Communications (D) to stay court proceedings and compel arbitration.

FACT SUMMARY: Internet users (P) sued Netscape Communications (D) over the ambiguous terms in an online contract to download various Internet programs.

🏛 RULE OF LAW
Where a computer user is invited to download "free" products, when the terms of the contract are not reasonably conspicuous to the user, the user cannot be bound by the terms of said contract.

FACTS: Netscape Communications Corp. (Netscape) (D), an Internet browser provider, offers software programs that include Communicator and SmartDownload. Specht (P) and other plaintiffs claimed that when these software programs were downloaded, they collectively allow unlawful "eavesdropping" of the customers' use of the those programs and other websites. Netscape (D) argued that Specht (P) had consented to the terms of the licenses, which allowed Netscape (D) to "eavesdrop" and, more importantly here, compelled this dispute to be settled by arbitration, since an arbitration clause was agreed to by Specht (P) in the license agreement. When downloading the programs, Specht (P) had to "click" on several agreements in order to perform the actual downloads.

ISSUE: If an Internet browser webpage does not adequately alert users to the existence of the license terms of software and does not require users to manifestly and unambiguously assent to the those terms as a condition of downloading the software, is a user bound by the terms of said license contract?

HOLDING AND DECISION: (Sotomayor, J.) No. If an Internet browser webpage does not adequately alert users to the existence of the license terms of software and does not require users to manifestly and unambiguously assent to those terms as a condition of downloading the software, a user is not bound by the terms of said license contract. The Communicator license agreement that Specht (P) viewed did not mention SmartDownload or the other plug-in programs. And had a user scrolled down to the download button, something Specht (P) did not do, SmartDownload's license agreement was not immediately displayed. Instead, the user was taken to another link, which, had it been "clicked," led to yet another webpage that contained the arbitration clause agreement. The existence of SmartDownload's full license agreement was not, then, readily available to Specht (P). Whether under the Uniform Commercial Code (UCC) or under common law, a contract requires "a manifestation of agreement between the parties." Netscape (D) argues that Specht (P) was on "inquiry notice" as to the terms of the agreement, and had Specht (P) used reasonable prudence, the license terms would have been apparent. There is, however, an exception when the written terms do not appear in the contract and the terms are then not made apparent to the signer; if so, a contract is not formed since there would be no "manifest agreement" by both parties. The court is not persuaded by Netscape's (D) argument that a prudent offeree would have been aware of the license terms. A reasonably prudent offeree in plaintiffs' position would not have known or learned, prior to acting on the invitation to download, of the reference to SmartDownload's license terms hidden below the "Download" button on the next screen. As such, the district court's decision that the plaintiffs are not bound by the arbitration clause in the terms of this contract is affirmed.

▌ ANALYSIS

The court seems to recognize that in the "pop-up" world of the Internet, forming a contract must involve a more explicit wording of the terms than used in the circumstances here. The court alludes to the fact that contract law has changed due to the new technology of the Internet. Simply because someone "clicks" an assent to a contract does not necessarily mean that a person has manifestly agreed to the terms of that contract.

■═■

Quicknotes

ARBITRATION An agreement to have a dispute heard and decided by a neutral third party, rather than through legal proceedings.

STAY An order by a court requiring a party to refrain from a specific activity until the happening of an event or upon further action by the court.

■═■

ProCD, Inc. v. Zeidenberg

Seller (P) v. Buyer (D)

86 F.3d 1447 (7th Cir. 1996).

NATURE OF CASE: Breach of contract suit.

FACT SUMMARY: ProCD, Inc. (P) brought suit against Zeidenberg (D) for violation of a shrink-wrapped license included inside its CD-ROM database.

🏛 RULE OF LAW
Shrink-wrap licenses are enforceable unless their terms are objectionable on grounds applicable to contracts in general.

FACTS: ProCD, Inc. (P) compiled information from more than 3,000 telephone directories into a computer database. The database cost over $10 million to compile and was expensive to keep current. ProCD (P) included a license in every CD-ROM box stating that the software came with specified restrictions. The license limits the use of application program and listing for non-commercial purposes. Zeidenberg (D) bought a consumer package of ProCD's (P) CD-ROM box in 1994 and formed Silken Mountain Web Services to resell the information in Select-Phone's database. Zeidenberg (D) offered the information via the Internet at a price less than ProCD (P) charged its commercial customers. ProCD (P) filed suit seeking an injunction against further dissemination in violation of the licenses included in the box. The district court held that the licenses were ineffective. ProCD (P) appealed.

ISSUE: Even if Wisconsin treats shrink-wrap licenses as contracts, does section 301 of the Copyright Act prevent their enforcement?

HOLDING AND DECISION: (Easterbrook, J.) Yes. The district court held that if the licenses were to be treated as contracts, Copyright Act section 301 would preclude their enforcement. Section 301 preempts state legal and equitable rights equivalent to any of the exclusive rights under section 106 in works of authorship that are fixed in a tangible medium of expression and fall within the subject matter of copyright as specified in sections 102 and 103. ProCD's (P) software fell within the subject matter of copyright. However, the breach of contract alleged here is not equivalent to an infringement claim. Reversed and remanded.

▶ ANALYSIS

The court notes that its decision does not exempt any form of contract as being outside the scope of the preemption clause. Rather, it states that some contracts may nevertheless fall within the scope of section 301 if the contract

would "interfere with the attainment of national objectives." This was not such a case.

Quicknotes

BREACH OF CONTRACT Unlawful failure by a party to perform its obligations pursuant to contract.

COPYRIGHT Refers to the exclusive rights granted to an artist pursuant to Article I, section 8, clause 8 of the United States Constitution over the reproduction, display, performance, distribution, and adaptation of his work for a period prescribed by statute.

Nadel v. Play-by-Play Toys & Novelties, Inc.

Toy idea person (P) v. Toy manufacturer (D)

208 F.3d 368 (2d Cir. 2000)

NATURE OF CASE: Appeal of dismissal of plaintiff's suit.

FACT SUMMARY: Nadel (P), a toy idea person, brought suit against Play-by-Play Toys & Novelities, Inc. (D), a toy manufacturer, for taking its idea for a toy without paying compensation.

🏛 RULE OF LAW
A showing of genuine novelty or invention can sustain claims for breach of contract, quasi-contract, and unfair competition.

FACTS: Nadel (P), a toy idea person, proposed a toy in the form of an upright, sound-emitting, spinning plush toy monkey to Play-by-Play Toys & Novelties, Inc. (Play-by-Play Toys) (D), a toy manufacturer, alleging that, after rejecting his idea, the toy company used his idea in one of their own toy products without paying compensation to Nadel (P). The federal district court granted summary judgment in favor of Play-by-Play Toys and dismissed Nadel's (P) suit. Nadel (P) appealed the dismissal.

ISSUE: Can a showing of genuine novelty or invention sustain claims for breach of contract, quasi-contract, and unfair competition?

HOLDING AND DECISION: (Sotomayor, J.) Yes. A showing of genuine novelty or invention can sustain claims for breach of contract, quasi-contract, and unfair competition. The record contained a genuine issue of material fact as to whether Nadel's (P) toy idea was sufficiently novel or original at the time of its disclosure to Play-by-Play (D) where the proposed toy, in the form of a monkey, was an upright, sound-emitting, spinning plush toy that may have constituted "novelty to the buyer" even if unoriginal or non-novel in a general sense. A court may only conclude that, as a matter of law, an idea lacks both the originality necessary to support a misappropriation claim and the novelty to the buyer necessary to support a contract claim if the idea is so lacking in novelty that it obviously bespeaks widespread and public knowledge of the idea. That was not the case here. The lower court failed to decide whether Nadel's (P) idea exhibited genuine novelty or invention or whether it was merely a clever or useful adaptation of existing knowledge. The determination of novelty in a given case depends upon several factors, including the idea's specificity, its commonality, its uniqueness, and its commercial availability. These factors were not examined by the district court. Reversed and remanded.

▶ ANALYSIS

The court noted that the "novelty to the buyer" standard is not limited to cases involving an express post-disclosure contract for payment based on an idea's use. A seller may, as Nadel (P) did here, bring an action against a buyer who allegedly used the seller's ideas without payment, claiming both misappropriation of property and breach of an express or implied-in-fact contract.

Quicknotes

BREACH OF CONTRACT Unlawful failure by a party to perform its obligations pursuant to contract.

QUASI-CONTRACT An implied contract created by law to prevent unjust enrichment.

UNFAIR COMPETITION Any dishonest or fraudulent rivalry in trade and commerce, particularly imitation and counterfeiting.

Desny v. Wilder

Writer (P) v. Movie director (D)

Cal. Sup. Ct., 46 Cal. 2d 715, 299 P.2d 257 (1956).

NATURE OF CASE: Appeal from summary judgment for defendant in an action to recover the reasonable value of a literary composition.

FACT SUMMARY: Desny (P), who had telephoned the famous director Billy Wilder's (D) office and read a synopsis of a story to Wilder's (D) secretary and was told he would be paid if his ideas were used, sued when his ideas were allegedly later used by Wilder (D) without payment.

> **RULE OF LAW**
> Even though an idea may be widely known, it may be protected by an express contract providing that it will be paid for regardless of its lack of novelty.

FACTS: Desny (P) attempted to call director Billy Wilder (D) at Paramount Studios and told his secretary the plot for a screenplay based on a real life tragedy involving a man trapped underground for two weeks. He was told by the secretary that he would be paid for his idea if it was used. The next year a photoplay was produced and exhibited by Wilder (D) that closely resembled Desny's (P) synopsis and the historical material concerning the subject's life and death. When Desny (P) sued to recover the reasonable value of his idea for the photoplay, summary judgment was granted to Wilder (D). Desny (P) appealed.

ISSUE: May an idea that is widely known be protected by an express contract regardless of its lack of novelty?

HOLDING AND DECISION: (Schauer, J.) Yes. Even though an idea may be widely known, it may be protected by an express contract regardless of its lack of novelty. To prevail in an action to recover compensation for an abstract idea, the purveyor of the idea must have obtained an express promise to pay or circumstances and the conduct of the offeree acting with knowledge of the circumstances must show a promise of the type known as implied or implied in fact. It does not appear that a contract to pay for conveyance of the abstract photoplay idea had been made in this case, or that the basis for inferring such a contract from subsequent related acts of Wilder (D) had been established. However, Wilder's (D) script used in producing his photoplay closely resembles Desny's (P) synopsis. Wilder (D) had no right except by purchase on the terms Desny (P) had offered to acquire and use the synopsis prepared by him. Summary judgment was erroneously granted and should be reversed. Affirmed in part, reversed in part and remanded to determine whether Wilder (D) actually accepted and used Desny's (P) synopsis or whether he conducted his own re-

search into the historical event that was the subject of the synopsis.

CONCURRENCE: (Carter, J.) In the ordinary situation when a so-called "idea man" has an opportunity to see or talk with the prospective purchaser or someone in his employ, it is at that time known to both parties that the one is there to sell and the other to buy.

> ## ANALYSIS

Note that Desny's (P) alleged agreement with Wilder (D) was never reduced to writing. However, this may make no difference regarding the enforcement of the agreement, so long as Desny's (P) ideas are considered protectable. A similar situation arose in *Blaustein v. Burton*, 88 Cal. Rptr. 319 (Cal. Ct. App. 1970), when Blaustein suggested in a "pitch" that Richard Burton and Elizabeth Taylor should appear as the husband and wife in a cinematic "Taming of the Shrew." Again, the court denied summary judgment, concluding that a trier of fact could find such a pitch enforceable as an implied contract.

Quicknotes

EXPRESS CONTRACT A contract the terms of which are specifically stated; may be oral or written.

SUMMARY JUDGMENT Judgment rendered by a court in response to a motion by one of the parties, claiming that the lack of a question of material fact in respect to an issue warrants disposition of the issue without consideration by the jury.

Midler v. Ford Motor Co.

Motor Company Singer (P) v. Car company (D)

849 F.2d 460 (9th Cir. 1988).

NATURE OF CASE: Appeal from summary judgment for defendants in right of publicity (appropriation of identity) action.

FACT SUMMARY: Young & Rubicam, Ford Motor Co.'s (Ford) (D) ad agency, could not get Bette Midler (P) to re-create her 1970s hit "Do You Want to Dance" for its television commercial for Ford (D), so it hired a former Midler (P) backup singer to impersonate her voice.

🏛 RULE OF LAW
Deliberate imitation of a celebrity's distinctive and widely known voice for commercial purposes constitutes tortious misappropriation under California law.

FACTS: Young & Rubicam, Ford Motor Co.'s (Ford) (D) ad agency, developed a series of television commercials designed to appeal to "yuppies" by evoking memories of college days through use of popular song hits of the 1970s. One such commercial was to feature the song "Do You Want to Dance," originally performed by Bette Midler (P). Midler (P) was a nationally known singer/actress/comedienne whose albums had gone platinum and gold and had been nominated for an Academy Award. Ford (D) approved the concept after viewing the proposed commercial with an actual recording of Midler (P), but Midler (P), through her agent, refused to rerecord the song for the commercial. Consequently, Young & Rubicam hired a former back-up singer for Midler (P) to act as a "sound-alike." The singer was instructed to "sound as much as possible like the Bette Midler record," a task she accomplished so well that "a number of people" told Midler (P) after the commercial aired that she "sounded exactly" like the original. Neither Midler's (P) name nor picture was used in the commercial. Midler (P) sued for misappropriation of her right of publicity in her voice, and although the district court held that Ford (D) and Rubicam had acted like "common thieves," it granted Ford's (D) motion for summary judgment because it believed Midler (P) had no legal basis for her claim.

ISSUE: Does deliberate imitation of a celebrity's distinctive and widely known voice for commercial purposes constitute tortious misappropriation under California law?

HOLDING AND DECISION: (Noonan, J.) Yes. When a distinctive voice of a professional singer is widely known and is deliberately imitated in order to sell a product, the sellers have appropriated what is not theirs and have committed a tort in California. California recognizes an injury from the appropriation of the attributes of one's identity, including the voice, which is one of the most palpable ways

identity is manifested. A singer manifests herself in her song; to impersonate her voice is to pirate her identity. The value of this attribute is what the market would have paid for Midler (P) to have sung the commercial in person. Midler (P) has made a showing, sufficient to defeat summary judgment, that Ford (D) for its own profit to sell their product did appropriate her identity. Reversed and remanded for trial.

▶ ANALYSIS

The court here somewhat deftly sidesteps the issue of federal preemption of California's tort under the Copyright Act, which provides in the Notes of the Judiciary Committee to § 114(b) that: "Mere imitation of a recorded performance would not constitute a copyright infringement even where one performer sets out to simulate another's performance as exactly as possible." However, there had been an unreported decision foreshadowing the Midler holding in *Apple Corps Limited v. Leber*, 229 U.S.P.Q. 1015 (Cal. Unrep. 1986), in which the Los Angeles Superior Court had held that a multimedia production of Beatles imitators who performed about thirty Beatles numbers "so accurately imitated the Beatles in concert that the audience . . . suspended their disbelief and fell prey to the illusion that they were actually viewing the Beatles in performance."

Quicknotes

CAL. CIVIL CODE § 3344 Awards damages to a person injured by another who uses the person's name, photograph, voice, or likeness in any manner.

MISAPPROPRIATION The unlawful use of another's property or funds.

SUMMARY JUDGMENT Judgment rendered by a court in response to a motion by one of the parties, claiming that the lack of a question of material fact in respect to an issue warrants disposition of the issue without consideration by the jury.

White v. Samsung Electronics America, Inc.

Celebrity (P) v. Electronics manufacturer (D)

989 F.2d 1512 (9th Cir. 1993).

NATURE OF CASE: Appeal from dismissal of action seeking damages for commercial misappropriation.

FACT SUMMARY: Vanna White (P), a well-known television personality, contended that an advertisement by Samsung Electronics America, Inc. (D) had usurped her right of publicity, even though her likeness had not been incorporated in the advertisement.

🏛 RULE OF LAW
A person's right of publicity may be usurped even if the offending use did not incorporate that person's likeness.

FACTS: Samsung Electronics America, Inc. (Samsung) (D) ran an advertisement that clearly indicated that Vanna White (P) of the television game show "Wheel of Fortune" had been the basis for the images. However, White's (P) likeness was not used in the advertisement. White (P) sued, alleging violations of state statutory and common law right to publicity and the federal Lanham Act. The district court dismissed, and White (D) appealed.

ISSUE: May a person's right to publicity be usurped even if the offending use did not incorporate that person's likeness?

HOLDING AND DECISION: (Goodwin, J.) Yes. A person's right to publicity may be usurped even if the offending use did not incorporate that person's likeness.

DISSENT: (Kozinski, J.) Reducing too much intellectual property to private property is harmful. Creativity is impossible without a rich public domain. The majority opinion is a classic case of overprotection and erects a property right of remarkable and dangerous breadth: "Under the majority's opinion, it's now a tort for advertisers to remind the public of a celebrity. Not to use a celebrity's name, voice, signature or likeness; not to imply the celebrity endorses a product; but simply to evoke the celebrity's image in the public's mind. This Orwellian notion withdraws far more from the public domain than prudence and common sense allow. It conflicts with the Copyright Act and the Copyright Clause. It raises serious First Amendment problems." Samsung (D) didn't use White's (P) name, likeness, voice or signature—no one seeing the ad would have thought it was supposed to be White (P). Therefore, under California's right of publicity precedent, the district court was correct in ruling that White's (P) rights were not violated. Reminding the public of someone's copyrighted property does not, as the majority indicates, "eviscerate" the copyright holder's rights. "All creators draw in part on the work of those who came before, referring to it, building on it, poking fun at it; we call this creativity, not piracy." Instead of preventing the "evisceration" of White's (P) existing rights, the majority is instead creating a new and much broader property right. Now, a celebrity has the additional, exclusive right to anything that reminds the viewer of her or him. Here, the majority is giving White (P) an exclusive right in what she does for a living. This is not an appropriate balancing of the public's interest with the copyright holder's rights, because it does not contain the essential limitations of intellectual property law. It does not leave anything in the public domain. It robs the public of parodies of celebrities and undermines the essence of the copyright system. Intellectual property law assures authors the right to their original expression, but encourages others to build freely on the ideas that underlie it. This result is neither unfair nor unfortunate: It is the means by which intellectual property law advances the progress of science and art. We give authors certain exclusive rights, but in exchange we get a richer public domain. The majority ignores this wise teaching, and all of us are the poorer for it. By refusing to recognize a parody exception to the right of publicity, the majority directly contradicts the federal Copyright Act's fair use provisions. That is because it is impossible to parody a movie or televisions show without at the same time evoking the identities of the actors, who should not have a veto over fair use parodies of the shows in which they appear. The majority's holding also conflicts with the federal copyright system, under which the dormant Copyright Clause requires that state intellectual property laws can stand only so long as they don't prejudice the interest of other states. However, the right of publicity is not limited geographically, so that one state's right of publicity can restrict conduct everywhere, thereby interfering with other states' legitimate interests. Finally, the majority opinion conflicts with the First Amendment. Not allowing any means of reminding people of someone is a speech restriction unparalleled in First Amendment law.

▶ ANALYSIS

A similar and better-known case was *Midler v. Ford Motor Co.*, 849 F.2d. 460 (9th Cir. 1988). There, Ford had unsuccessfully attempted to hire entertainer Bette Midler to release the rights to her version of the song "Do You Want to Dance" to be used in an advertisement. Ford then hired a "sound-alike" of Midler to record the song, which Ford incorporated into an advertisement. Midler successfully argued that her right of publicity had been violated.

◼▬◼

Quicknotes

CAL. CIVIL CODE § 3344 Awards damages to a person injured by another who uses the person's name, photograph, voice, or likeness in any manner.

MISAPPROPRIATION The unlawful use of another's property or funds.

■■■

Comedy III Productions, Inc. v. Gary Saderup, Inc.

Owner of rights (P) v. Artist (D)

Cal. Sup. Ct., 25 Cal. 4th 387, 21 P.3d 797 (2001).

NATURE OF CASE: Appeal of damages award for violation of right-of-publicity statute.

FACT SUMMARY: Owner of rights to former comedy act sued producer of lithographs and silkscreened T-shirts depicting such comedy act, alleging the lithographs and T-shirts violated a right-of-publicity statute.

🏛 RULE OF LAW
In balancing between the First Amendment and the right of publicity, the test is whether the work adds significant creative elements as to be transformed into something more than a mere celebrity likeness or imitation.

FACTS: Comedy III Productions (P) owned the rights to The Three Stooges materials. Gary Saderup (D), without compensating Comedy III Productions (P), produced and sold lithographs and silkscreened T-shirts depicting The Three Stooges. The Three Stooges are deceased. Comedy III Productions (P) sued Gary Saderup (D) under a California "right of publicity" statute that authorizes recovery of damages against any person who uses a deceased personality's name or likeness on products, goods, or services, without permission. The trial court awarded damages, and the court of appeals affirmed. Gary Saderup (D) appealed, and the state's highest court granted review.

ISSUE: In balancing between the First Amendment and the right of publicity, is the test whether the work adds significant creative elements as to be transformed into something more than a mere celebrity likeness or imitation?

HOLDING AND DECISION: (Mosk, J.) Yes. In balancing between the First Amendment and the right of publicity, the test is whether the work adds significantly creative elements as to be transformed into something more than a mere celebrity likeness or imitation. The celebrities depicted, The Three Stooges, "possess a kind of mythic status in our culture." Through their talent and labor, they joined the relatively small group of actors who constructed identifiable, recurrent comic personalities that they brought to the many parts they were scripted to play. Gary Saderup's (D) production and sale of lithographs and silkscreened T-shirts of these characters failed to contain any significant transformative elements, and the inquiry into whether a work is transformative is necessarily at the heart of any judicial attempt to square the right of publicity with the First Amendment. When, as here, artistic expression takes the form of a literal depiction or imitation of a celebrity for commercial gain, directly trespassing on the right of publicity without adding significant expression beyond that trespass, the state law interest in protecting the fruits of artistic labor outweighs the expressive interests of the imitative artist. In this case, Gary Saderup's (D) undeniable skill was manifestly subordinate to his overall goal of merely creating literal, conventional depictions of The Three Stooges so as to exploit their fame for profit. Affirmed.

▶ ANALYSIS

The court pointed out that another way of stating the inquiry is whether the celebrity likeness is one of the "raw materials" from which an original work is synthesized, or whether the depiction or imitation of the celebrity is the very sum and substance of the work in question.

■▬■

Quicknotes

RIGHT OF PUBLICITY The right of a person to control the commercial exploitation of his name or likeness.

■▬■

eBay, Inc. v. Bidder's Edge, Inc.

Internet trading site (P) v. Competitor (D)

100 F. Supp. 2d 1058 (N.D. Cal. 2000).

NATURE OF THE CASE: Motion for preliminary injunction.

FACT SUMMARY: eBay, Inc. (P) sought a preliminary injunction enjoining Bidder's Edge, Inc. (D) for trespass against eBay's (P) online trading site.

🏛 RULE OF LAW
A preliminary injunction may be granted if it is to prevent an increase in the complained-of activity when the increase presents a likelihood of harm.

FACTS: eBay, Inc. (P), an Internet person-to-person trading site offers people the ability to sell a variety of items, to the highest bidder, on its website. eBay (P) users must register and agree to a User Agreement, which includes a prohibition of the use of software "robots" or "spiders" on eBay (P). A software "robot" or "spider" is a computer program that performs wide searches, copying and retrieving information from other websites across the Internet. These programs can search sites by executing thousands of instructions each minute, which can slow those sites to the point where they become overwhelmed and can "crash." Such crashes or malfunctions can result in the loss of data and interrupt that website's services. Bidder's Edge, Inc. (D) is an online "auction aggregation" site that offers buyers the ability to search the World Wide Web by utilizing the "robot/spider" search capacity, allowing the buyers to search several auction websites at one time rather than individually. eBay (P) and Bidder's Edge (D) negotiated to agree to terms that would allow Bidder's Edge (D) to access eBay (P), but when the negotiations broke down eBay (P) attempted to block Bidder's Edge (D) by using software that can interrupt the "robot/spider" searches. A lawsuit was filed and eBay (P) moved for preliminary injunctive relief to prevent Bidder's Edge (D) from accessing eBay's (P) website.

ISSUE: Can a preliminary injunction be issued to prevent an increase in the complained-of activity, where such an increase prevents the likelihood of irreparable harm?

HOLDING AND DECISION: (Whyte, J.) Yes. A preliminary injunction can be issued to prevent an increase in the complained-of activity, where such an increase prevents the likelihood of irreparable harm. eBay (P) alleged that Bidder's Edge (D) "robot/spider" searches caused economic loss and potential harm from the damage that would be caused by a possible "crash" of the eBay (P) website. Potential monetary damages are usually not "a proper foundation for a preliminary injunction" and eBay (P) does not seem to have made a showing that monetary

damages could support relief. If Bidder's Edge (D) activities were allowed to continue and similar "robot/spider" engines also joined in searching eBay (P) at the same time, eBay (P) could suffer great harm if the website crashed. For eBay (P) to prevail on a trespass claim, it must establish that: (1) Bidder's Edge (D) intentionally and without authorization interfered with eBay's (P) possessory interest; and (2) this unauthorized use proximately caused damage to eBay (P). First, eBay (P) explicitly and repeatedly told Bidder's Edge (D) that the latter's use of the website was unauthorized. The unauthorized use did cause damage to eBay (P), even if eBay (P) cannot demonstrate that Bidder's Edge (D) use of the site did slow it down. eBay's (P) website is personal property, and a person does not have to cause physical or material damage to that property for that person to be considered a trespasser. So even if eBay (P) cannot demonstrate that Bidder's Edge (D) slowed the website to the point that eBay's (P) ability to serve other customers was hindered, eBay (P) has still met the requirements necessary to demonstrate trespass. Preliminary injunctive relief is, therefore, the proper remedy.

▶ ANALYSIS

The court sought to prevent the loss of profits and loss of customer goodwill, which since such losses are difficult to calculate or monetarily compensate, is appropriate injunctive relief.

■━■

Quicknotes

ENJOIN The ordering of a party to cease the conduct of a specific activity.

PRELIMINARY INJUNCTION An order issued by the court at the commencement of an action, requiring a party to refrain from conducting a specified activity that is the subject of the controversy, until the matter is determined.

TRESPASS Unlawful interference with, or damage to, the real or personal property of another.

■━■

Kewanee Oil Co. v. Bicron Corp.

Trade secret holder (P) v. Alleged misappropriator (D)

416 U.S. 470 (1974).

NATURE OF CASE: Review of reversal of grant of an injunction in a trade secrets action.

FACT SUMMARY: Kewanee Oil Co. (P) successfully sought an injunction against Bicron Corp. (D) under state trade secret law but was reversed on appeal.

🏛 RULE OF LAW
State trade secret protection is not preempted by federal patent law.

FACTS: Kewanee Oil Co. (P) brought a diversity action seeking injunctive relief and damages for the misappropriation of trade secrets. The district court applied Ohio state law and granted a permanent injunction against the disclosure of twenty of the claimed forty trade secrets until such time as the trade secrets had been released to the public. The Court of Appeals for the Sixth Circuit held that state trade secret protection was preempted by operation of the federal patent law and reversed. The United States Supreme Court granted certiorari.

ISSUE: Is state trade secret protection preempted by federal patent law?

HOLDING AND DECISION: (Burger, C.J.) No. State trade secret protection is not preempted by federal patent law. In regulating the area of patents and copyrights, states may not conflict with the operation of laws in this area passed by Congress. However, trade secret law protects items that would not be proper subjects for patent protection. Since Congress has left the area of nonpatentable subject matter unattended, no reason exists why the state should not be free to act. Reversed.

DISSENT: (Douglas, J.) Today's holding conflicts with the Court's earlier rulings that state law may not prohibit others from copying articles unprotected by a patent because every article not covered by a valid patent is in the public domain.

▶ ANALYSIS

This ruling reflects the Court's interest in maintaining the patent law's goal of promoting invention. This case did not overrule earlier rulings curtailing state laws preventing copying. Trade secret laws generally permit reverse engineering of products in the public domain.

Quicknotes

PREEMPTION Doctrine stating that certain matters are of a national character so that federal laws preempt or take precedence over state or local laws.

Bonito Boats, Inc. v. Thunder Craft Boats, Inc.

Boat designer (P) v. Boat manufacturer (D)

489 U.S. 141 (1989).

NATURE OF CASE: Review of order voiding state law prohibiting duplication of boat hulls.

FACT SUMMARY: Thunder Craft Boats, Inc. (D) contended that Florida's law prohibiting the duplication of unpatented boat hulls violated federal patent laws.

🏛 RULE OF LAW
A state may not prohibit the duplication of unpatented or unpatentable articles.

FACTS: Florida enacted a law prohibiting the duplication of molded boat hulls. Bonito Boats, Inc. (Bonito) (P), which had designed a certain type of boat hull mold and had commercially exploited it, brought an action against Thunder Craft Boats, Inc. (Thunder Craft) (D). Bonito (P) alleged that Thunder Craft (D) had copied the design of its hull. The design was not patented.

ISSUE: May a state prohibit the duplication of unpatented or unpatentable articles?

HOLDING AND DECISION: (O'Connor, J.) No. A state may not prohibit the duplication of unpatented or unpatentable articles. Federal patent law reflects a very careful balance between healthy competition and rewarding innovation. A person who meets the requirements of novelty, usefulness, and nonobviousness will be rewarded with a temporary monopoly; all other utilitarian articles may be exploited by the public. Federal patent-law laws, in order to determine what is protected, must also determine what is not protected. The balance struck in patent laws requires that all nonpatented, publicly known designs be freely traded. If states were free to grant de facto monopolies to unpatented or unpatentable articles, the balance struck in federal patent laws would be upset. Here, the Florida law is a good illustration. Bonito (P) did not apply for a patent. Consequently, federal patent law would permit any competitor to use its design. The Florida law prevents this. Consequently, the Florida law acts to upset the fine balance created in patent law. Since the law is inconsistent with federal law, it must fail.

▶ ANALYSIS

This case should not be taken to mean that there is no place for state laws in the law of intellectual property. State unfair competition laws have coexisted with federal law in this area for quite some time, with little evidence of incompatibility. In the instant case, the Court indicated it had no inclination to strike down state trade secret or unfair competition laws.

Quicknotes

NOVELTY Requirement for patentability that an invention possess some element that is not found in any prior invention.

UNFAIR COMPETITION Any dishonest or fraudulent rivalry in trade and commerce, particularly imitation and counterfeiting.

■━■

Glossary

Common Latin Words and Phrases Encountered in the Law

A FORTIORI: Because one fact exists or has been proven, therefore a second fact that is related to the first fact must also exist.

A PRIORI: From the cause to the effect. A term of logic used to denote that when one generally accepted truth is shown to be a cause, another particular effect must necessarily follow.

AB INITIO: From the beginning; a condition which has existed throughout, as in a marriage which was void ab initio.

ACTUS REUS: The wrongful act; in criminal law, such action sufficient to trigger criminal liability.

AD VALOREM: According to value; an ad valorem tax is imposed upon an item located within the taxing jurisdiction calculated by the value of such item.

AMICUS CURIAE: Friend of the court. Its most common usage takes the form of an amicus curiae brief, filed by a person who is not a party to an action but is nonetheless allowed to offer an argument supporting his legal interests.

ARGUENDO: In arguing. A statement, possibly hypothetical, made for the purpose of argument, is one made arguendo.

BILL QUIA TIMET: A bill to quiet title (establish ownership) to real property.

BONA FIDE: True, honest, or genuine. May refer to a person's legal position based on good faith or lacking notice of fraud (such as a bona fide purchaser for value) or to the authenticity of a particular document (such as a bona fide last will and testament).

CAUSA MORTIS: With approaching death in mind. A gift causa mortis is a gift given by a party who feels certain that death is imminent.

CAVEAT EMPTOR: Let the buyer beware. This maxim is reflected in the rule of law that a buyer purchases at his own risk because it is his responsibility to examine, judge, test, and otherwise inspect what he is buying.

CERTIORARI: A writ of review. Petitions for review of a case by the United States Supreme Court are most often done by means of a writ of certiorari.

CONTRA: On the other hand. Opposite. Contrary to.

CORAM NOBIS: Before us; writs of error directed to the court that originally rendered the judgment.

CORAM VOBIS: Before you; writs of error directed by an appellate court to a lower court to correct a factual error.

CORPUS DELICTI: The body of the crime; the requisite elements of a crime amounting to objective proof that a crime has been committed.

CUM TESTAMENTO ANNEXO, ADMINISTRATOR (ADMINISTRATOR C.T.A.): With will annexed; an administrator c.t.a. settles an estate pursuant to a will in which he is not appointed.

DE BONIS NON, ADMINISTRATOR (ADMINISTRATOR D.B.N.): Of goods not administered; an administrator d.b.n. settles a partially settled estate.

DE FACTO: In fact; in reality; actually. Existing in fact but not officially approved or engendered.

DE JURE: By right; lawful. Describes a condition that is legitimate "as a matter of law," in contrast to the term "de facto," which connotes something existing in fact but not legally sanctioned or authorized. For example, de facto segregation refers to segregation brought about by housing patterns, etc., whereas de jure segregation refers to segregation created by law.

DE MINIMIS: Of minimal importance; insignificant; a trifle; not worth bothering about.

DE NOVO: Anew; a second time; afresh. A trial de novo is a new trial held at the appellate level as if the case originated there and the trial at a lower level had not taken place.

DICTA: Generally used as an abbreviated form of obiter dicta, a term describing those portions of a judicial opinion incidental or not necessary to resolution of the specific question before the court. Such nonessential statements and remarks are not considered to be binding precedent.

DUCES TECUM: Refers to a particular type of writ or subpoena requesting a party or organization to produce certain documents in their possession.

EN BANC: Full bench. Where a court sits with all justices present rather than the usual quorum.

EX PARTE: For one side or one party only. An ex parte proceeding is one undertaken for the benefit of only one party, without notice to, or an appearance by, an adverse party.

EX POST FACTO: After the fact. An ex post facto law is a law that retroactively changes the consequences of a prior act.

EX REL.: Abbreviated form of the term "ex relatione," meaning upon relation or information. When the state brings an action in which it has no interest against an individual at the instigation of one who has a private interest in the matter.

FORUM NON CONVENIENS: Inconvenient forum. Although a court may have jurisdiction over the case, the action should be tried in a more conveniently located court, one to which parties and witnesses may more easily travel, for example.

GUARDIAN AD LITEM: A guardian of an infant as to litigation, appointed to represent the infant and pursue his/her rights.

HABEAS CORPUS: You have the body. The modern writ of habeas corpus is a writ directing that a person (body) being detained (such as a prisoner) be brought before the court so that the legality of his detention can be judicially ascertained.

IN CAMERA: In private, in chambers. When a hearing is held before a judge in his chambers or when all spectators are excluded from the courtroom.

IN FORMA PAUPERIS: In the manner of a pauper. A party who proceeds in forma pauperis because of his poverty is one who is allowed to bring suit without liability for costs.

INFRA: Below, under. A word referring the reader to a later part of a book. (The opposite of supra.)

IN LOCO PARENTIS: In the place of a parent.

IN PARI DELICTO: Equally wrong; a court of equity will not grant requested relief to an applicant who is in pari delicto, or as much at fault in the transactions giving rise to the controversy as is the opponent of the applicant.

IN PARI MATERIA: On like subject matter or upon the same matter. Statutes relating to the same person or things are said to be in pari materia. It is a general rule of statutory construction that such statutes should be construed together, i.e., looked at as if they together constituted one law.

IN PERSONAM: Against the person. Jurisdiction over the person of an individual.

IN RE: In the matter of. Used to designate a proceeding involving an estate or other property.

IN REM: A term that signifies an action against the res, or thing. An action in rem is basically one that is taken directly against property, as distinguished from an action in personam, i.e., against the person.

INTER ALIA: Among other things. Used to show that the whole of a statement, pleading, list, statute, etc., has not been set forth in its entirety.

INTER PARTES: Between the parties. May refer to contracts, conveyances or other transactions having legal significance.

INTER VIVOS: Between the living. An inter vivos gift is a gift made by a living grantor, as distinguished from bequests contained in a will, which pass upon the death of the testator.

IPSO FACTO: By the mere fact itself.

JUS: Law or the entire body of law.

LEX LOCI: The law of the place; the notion that the rights of parties to a legal proceeding are governed by the law of the place where those rights arose.

MALUM IN SE: Evil or wrong in and of itself; inherently wrong. This term describes an act that is wrong by its very nature, as opposed to one which would not be wrong but for the fact that there is a specific legal prohibition against it (malum prohibitum).

MALUM PROHIBITUM: Wrong because prohibited, but not inherently evil. Used to describe something that is wrong because it is expressly forbidden by law but that is not in and of itself evil, e.g., speeding.

MANDAMUS: We command. A writ directing an official to take a certain action.

MENS REA: A guilty mind; a criminal intent. A term used to signify the mental state that accompanies a crime or other prohibited act. Some crimes require only a general mens rea (general intent to do the prohibited act), but others, like assault with intent to murder, require the existence of a specific mens rea.

MODUS OPERANDI: Method of operating; generally refers to the manner or style of a criminal in committing crimes, admissible in appropriate cases as evidence of the identity of a defendant.

NEXUS: A connection to.

NISI PRIUS: A court of first impression. A nisi prius court is one where issues of fact are tried before a judge or jury.

N.O.V. (NON OBSTANTE VEREDICTO): Notwithstanding the verdict. A judgment n.o.v. is a judgment given in favor of one party despite the fact that a verdict was returned in favor of the other party, the justification being that the verdict either had no reasonable support in fact or was contrary to law.

NUNC PRO TUNC: Now for then. This phrase refers to actions that may be taken and will then have full retroactive effect.

PENDENTE LITE: Pending the suit; pending litigation under way.

PER CAPITA: By head; beneficiaries of an estate, if they take in equal shares, take per capita.

PER CURIAM: By the court; signifies an opinion ostensibly written "by the whole court" and with no identified author.

PER SE: By itself, in itself; inherently.

PER STIRPES: By representation. Used primarily in the law of wills to describe the method of distribution where a person, generally because of death, is unable to take that which is left to him by the will of another, and therefore his heirs divide such property between them rather than take under the will individually.

PRIMA FACIE: On its face, at first sight. A prima facie case is one that is sufficient on its face, meaning that the evidence supporting it is adequate to establish the case until contradicted or overcome by other evidence.

PRO TANTO: For so much; as far as it goes. Often used in eminent domain cases when a property owner receives partial payment for his land without prejudice to his right to bring suit for the full amount he claims his land to be worth.

QUANTUM MERUIT: As much as he deserves. Refers to recovery based on the doctrine of unjust enrichment in those cases in which a party has rendered valuable services or furnished materials that were accepted and enjoyed by another under circumstances that would reasonably notify the recipient that the rendering party expected to be paid. In essence, the law implies a contract to pay the reasonable value of the services or materials furnished.

QUASI: Almost like; as if; nearly. This term is essentially used to signify that one subject or thing is almost analogous to another but that material differences between them do exist. For example, a quasi-criminal proceeding is one that is not strictly criminal but shares enough of the same characteristics to require some of the same safeguards (e.g., procedural due process must be followed in a parole hearing).

QUID PRO QUO: Something for something. In contract law, the consideration, something of value, passed between the parties to render the contract binding.

RES GESTAE: Things done; in evidence law, this principle justifies the admission of a statement that would otherwise be hearsay when it is made so closely to the event in question as to be said to be a part of it, or with such spontaneity as not to have the possibility of falsehood.

RES IPSA LOQUITUR: The thing speaks for itself. This doctrine gives rise to a rebuttable presumption of negligence when the instrumentality causing the injury was within the exclusive control of the defendant, and the injury was one that does not normally occur unless a person has been negligent.

RES JUDICATA: A matter adjudged. Doctrine which provides that once a court of competent jurisdiction has rendered a final judgment or decree on the merits, that judgment or decree is conclusive upon the parties to the case and prevents them from engaging in any other litigation on the points and issues determined therein.

RESPONDEAT SUPERIOR: Let the master reply. This doctrine holds the master liable for the wrongful acts of his servant (or the principal for his agent) in those cases in which the servant (or agent) was acting within the scope of his authority at the time of the injury.

STARE DECISIS: To stand by or adhere to that which has been decided. The common law doctrine of stare decisis attempts to give security and certainty to the law by following the policy that once a principle of law as applicable to a certain set of facts has been set forth in a decision, it forms a precedent which will subsequently be followed, even though a different decision might be made were it the first time the question had arisen. Of course, stare decisis is not an inviolable principle and is departed from in instances where there is good cause (e.g., considerations of public policy led the Supreme Court to disregard prior decisions sanctioning segregation).

SUPRA: Above. A word referring a reader to an earlier part of a book.

ULTRA VIRES: Beyond the power. This phrase is most commonly used to refer to actions taken by a corporation that are beyond the power or legal authority of the corporation.

Addendum of French Derivatives

IN PAIS: Not pursuant to legal proceedings.

CHATTEL: Tangible personal property.

CY PRES: Doctrine permitting courts to apply trust funds to purposes not expressed in the trust but necessary to carry out the settlor's intent.

PER AUTRE VIE: For another's life; during another's life. In property law, an estate may be granted that will terminate upon the death of someone other than the grantee.

PROFIT A PRENDRE: A license to remove minerals or other produce from land.

VOIR DIRE: Process of questioning jurors as to their predispositions about the case or parties to a proceeding in order to identify those jurors displaying bias or prejudice.

Casenote® Legal Briefs